Classical Guitarists

Classical Guitarists

Conversations

by
Jim Tosone

McFarland & Company, Inc., Publishers
Jefferson, North Carolina, and London

Library of Congress Cataloguing-in-Publication Data

Classical guitarists : conversations / by Jim Tosone
    p.   cm.
    ISBN 0-7864-0813-8 (softcover : 50# alkaline paper)
    1. Guitarists — Interviews. I. Tosone, Jim, 1953–
ML399.C53   2000
787.87'092'2 — dc21
[B]   00-64616

British Library cataloguing data are available

©2000 James V. Tosone. All rights reserved

No part of this book may be reproduced or transmitted in any form or by any means, electronic or mechanical, including photocopying or recording, or by any information storage and retrieval system, without permission in writing from the publisher.

On the cover: John Williams *(photograph by Julian Nieman)*

Manufactured in the United States of America

McFarland & Company, Inc., Publishers
   Box 611, Jefferson, North Carolina 28640
      www.mcfarlandpub.com

For Lynne and Austen

Contents

Preface	1
Introduction	3
1 — Sharon Isbin: Breaking New Ground	9
(including an interview with composer Aaron Jay Kernis)	
2 — Eliot Fisk: An American in Europe	34
3 — Richard Rodney Bennett: Composing for the Guitar	64
(including interviews with guitarists Julian Bream and David Leisner)	
4 — David Tanenbaum: The Classical Guitar in Today's World	81
5 — David Starobin: Making Modern Music	110
(including an interview with composer George Crumb)	
6 — Harold Shaw: The Art of Artist Management	133
7 — John Williams: The Guitarist	149
Appendix: Creating a Core Collection of Guitar Recordings	179
Glossary	183
Index	187

Preface

This book is not about the classical guitar. It is about the world-renowned classical guitarists who bring the instrument to life.

What does it take to reach the top of their world? Certainly, classical guitarists must be creative, to convey the intentions of a composer while expressing those intentions in their own unique style. But they must also be analytical, to understand the complex structure of the music they play and to solve the technical problems of playing that music on a challenging instrument. And they must be successful entrepreneurs because, despite the assistance of artist managers and publicity agents, the guitarists alone must chart and navigate the course of their careers. Most importantly, classical guitarists must love what they do—because in this specialized music market the words "rich and famous" are relative terms.

I wrote this book to try and capture the essence of these extraordinary individuals in their own words. Much of what they think and feel has never been captured in print—and certainly not in one volume. Taken together, these interviews provide a unique perspective on the similarities and differences among these distinguished artists. Here they reveal their passions and pursuits, and in so doing give us a deeper understanding of the classical guitar and of classical music.

The performers in this book are a select group of classical guitarists at the peak of their artistic prowess. In their own way, each has made important contributions to the classical guitar, from commissioning new repertoire and establishing significant academic programs to broadening the audience for the instrument. To give additional perspective on the performers, this book also includes interviews with the most important artist manager in the history of the classical guitar and some of the classical guitar's key composers in the latter part of the twentieth century.

In the spirit of the in-depth, memorable interviews that have distinguished such publications as the *Paris Review* and *Playboy*, the interviews in this book are probing and wide-ranging. The long-form interview compels the interviewees to go beyond prepared soundbites, and to speak openly and thoughtfully about their accomplishments, opportunities and lessons learned. It obliges them to talk not just about what they've done, but how they've done it and why.

With two exceptions, the interviews were conducted in various apartments, hotels and restaurants in New York City. Each performer's interview is accompanied by my reviews of some of their most important recordings and New York City concerts from the corresponding time period, along with a discography of their recordings.

This book would not have been possible without the help of many people. The interviewees were most gracious and gave generously of their time. Guitarist and teacher Nicholas Goluses provided me with invaluable advice and guidance on the early articles I wrote for *Guitar Review* and *Soundboard* magazines. Guitarist David Tanenbaum has been a great source of information and suggestions for my music articles. Mark DiPalma and Sal Cosentino at *Guitar Review* have been a pleasure to work with and very helpful to me in the writing I've done for that publication. Rose Augustine — editor and publisher of *Guitar Review*, head of the Augustine Foundation, patron saint of the classical guitar — deserves special recognition, not only for her support of this project, but for giving me my first opportunity to be published regularly. Amanda George, transcriber *extraordinaire*, accurately turned tens of thousands of spoken words into text. And finally my wife, Lynne Cusack Tosone — a gifted writer and editor — shared ideas, made editorial suggestions and provided encouragement that helped make this book a reality.

Introduction

> *The concert stage is empty except for an ordinary piano stool and a footstool just under five inches high. About three minutes after the scheduled starting time, a plump, mild-looking septuagenarian dressed in white tie and tails ambles on, carrying a beautiful wooden guitar.*
>
> *He settles himself comfortably on the piano stool, places his left foot on the smaller stool and looks out at the audience with an expression of benign indulgence. The murmur of conversations subsides, and when total silence has lasted perhaps twenty seconds, his well-muscled fingers begin to move across the strings. From that moment on, listeners experience a unique and unforgettable enchantment. For this is Andrés Segovia, the greatest classical guitarist in the world.*
>
> — Noel Busch, *Reader's Digest*, October 1972

The image of Segovia and his guitar on stage at the world's most esteemed concert halls symbolizes the pinnacle of a journey that began with the first steps taken by guitar-playing minstrels in the Middle Ages. In today's post–Segovian world, raising the guitar to even greater heights is the challenge faced by the modern day minstrels profiled in this book.

Appreciating the challenges and accomplishments of these contemporary performers requires at least a basic understanding of their musical ancestors and of the evolution of the guitar. (A deeper appreciation can be gained from the books *The Classical Guitar: Its Evolution, Players and Personalities Since 1800* by Maurice J. Summerfield, *The Early Guitar* by James Tyler and *The Guitar from the Renaissance to the Present Day* by Harvey Turnbull.)

The evolution of the guitar has been lengthy and complex, propelled by changes in the music world and the world at large, by the nature of the pieces being composed for the guitar and by the advances in the knowledge and techniques of guitar construction. Nonetheless, it is possible to highlight the major historical landmarks in the evolution of the guitar.

Our knowledge of the guitar in the Middle Ages is sketchy and speculative—based mostly on pictures, sculptures and textual references—because there are no surviving instruments and music from this period. Minstrels in the Late Middle Ages (1200–1450) played the guitarra morisca or the guitarra latina. The evidence indicates that these instruments trace their lineage back to the Roman, Greek and Persian tanburs (long-necked lutes with pear-shaped bodies).

During the Renaissance (1450–1600), the vihuela and the four-course guitar came into prominence. The vihuela is a guitar-like instrument, slightly larger with six pairs of strings, that was popular in Spain at the time. The four-course guitar has four pairs of strings, and is smaller and higher-pitched than a modern guitar. It was popular in Spain, Italy, England and particularly France. The defining characteristics of guitars from this period forward are their figure-eight shapes, flat backs and relatively long necks. Also popular during this period was a distant cousin of the guitar, the lute. Like the vihuela, the Renaissance lute was generally a six-course instrument, but with a short neck and a half-pear shaped body.

The Late Renaissance (1550–1600) and the Baroque era (1600–1750) saw the evolution of the four-course guitar into the five-course guitar, with the additional course strung below the others.

In the Classical era (1770–1830), the five-course guitar evolved into the six-course guitar, with the additional course being at a lower pitch than the other five. By the end of this period, the courses were replaced by single strings, which—in this aspect—brought the guitar in line with its modern form. It was also during this period that the design of the guitar changed (thinner top, back and sides—made possible by stronger interior bracing), which improved its tone and sound projection.

Toward the end of the Romantic/Post-Romantic period (1830–1910), luthiers like Antonio de Torres continued the development of the physical instrument (by standardizing the string length, making the fingerboard wider and making the body larger), which further increased the guitar's tonal and dynamic capabilities.

During the Twentieth Century musical period (1910–present), guitars with seven, eight and ten strings have been built—although the six-string guitar remains dominant. In the mid-twentieth century, luthier Albert Augustine worked with Andrés Segovia and the Du Pont Chemical Company to pioneer the development of the nylon guitar string—which provided increased sustain, improved intonation and greater longevity than the previously used gut strings. The end of the twentieth century has been characterized by continued refinement and innovation in guitar construction — such as the raised fretboard developed by luthier Thomas Humphrey, which makes playing easier in the higher positions on the fretboard.

The evolution of the instrument went hand in hand with the music being composed for it. It is important to note that up until the twentieth century, almost all of the composers of music for the guitar, vihuela and lute were also players — many of them virtuosos.

The earliest surviving guitar music was written during the Renaissance for the four-course guitar. Relatively little of this music is played today, an exception being the fantasias and pavanes (courtly dances) of the instrument's most prominent composer, Adrian Le Roy (1520–1598). This is due to the limited contrapuntal and melodic capabilities of the instrument, and the fact that it is higher pitched and has less sustain than the modern guitar. As such, the music does not translate well to today's instrument.

So Renaissance music played on the modern guitar is almost exclusively transcriptions of works written for the vihuela or lute. Prominent composers for the vihuela include Luys Milán (1500–1561), Luys de Narváez and Alonso Mudarra (1510–1580). Their contrapuntal-style works consist of fantasias, pavanes, and songs for voice and vihuela. Prominent composers for the lute during this period were Francesco da Milano (1497–1543) in Italy and John Dowland (1563–1626) in England, both of whom composed many fantasias.

The development of the five-course guitar during the Baroque era made possible the kind of contrapuntal music that translates well to the modern guitar. Francesco Corbetta (1615–1681) helped bring the five-course guitar to prominence through his solo works and his duets for voice and guitar. Corbetta was also a teacher, whose students included Louis XIV and Charles II. Gaspar Sanz (mid-seventeenth century through early-eighteenth century) composed many pieces based on the dance forms used in seventeenth-century Baroque music. In addition, he published an instructional method for Spanish guitar, which was the most comprehensive treatise of its time. Robert de Visée (second-half of the seventeenth century through the early eighteenth century) composed suites and other pieces for the guitar. He was a chamber musician in the court of Louis XIV, as well as his guitar teacher. Other sources of Baroque music for the modern guitar include the harpsichord sonatas of Domenico Scarlatti, the lute works of Sylvius Leopold Weiss and the works that Bach wrote for lute, keyboard, solo violin and solo 'cello.

The evolution of the guitar during the Classical era into an instrument with six single strings would seem to lay the foundation for the golden age of guitar music. But the guitar struggled for recognition and respect throughout the Classical and Romantic/Post-Romantic periods. As audiences and concert halls got larger, as other instruments got louder and orchestras got bigger, the guitar had difficulty competing.

The greatest composers of these periods — including Mozart, Beethoven and Brahms — never wrote for the guitar. Music for the guitar during this time continued to come from composer-guitarists. Fernando Sor (1778–1839) composed operas, symphonies, string quartets and ballets, in addition to his works for solo and duo guitars. Sor also published a guitar method and a set of studies. His 65-plus compositions for the guitar are an important part of the repertoire. Mauro Giuliani (1781–1829) composed many works for the guitar, most notably his technically demanding *Grand Overture* and *Les Rossinianes*. Dionysio Aguado (1784–1849) wrote studies, rondos, dances and fantasias. His guitar method was popular in the nineteenth century. Aguado was ahead of his time in recommending that guitarists use a fingernail-flesh combination (as opposed to fingertip flesh only) on the right hand to get a well-defined sound when plucking the strings. As the guitar evolved to six single strings, these three performers laid the foundation for modern guitar technique through their approaches to right- and left-hand fingerings and positions.

The bridge to the twentieth century was composer-guitarist Francisco Tárrega (1852–1909). His compositions for the guitar and his more than 100 transcriptions of works by Mendelssohn, Beethoven, Chopin and Spanish nationalist composers Albéniz and Granados helped lay the groundwork for the resurgence of guitar in the twentieth century. Tárrega was also a teacher, whose pupils included Miguel Llobet and Emilio Pujol. In the 1920s, Pujol pioneered the research, transcription and performance of vihuela music on the modern guitar. Tárrega also further advanced guitar technique, including the use of the footstool, the freeing of the little finger of the right hand from resting on the soundboard and the use of the reststroke to expand the guitar's tonal palette.

The guitar in the Twentieth Century period has several aspects that distinguish it from previous eras. One is the variety of musical styles, which includes expressionism, serialism and post-modernism. Another is the separation of composing and performing into distinct occupational specialties. Due to the efforts of the performers, many prominent Twentieth Century composers — including Benjamin Britten, Elliott Carter, Hans Werner Henze, Joaquín Rodrigo, Toru Takemitsu and William Walton — have written for the classical guitar. Prominent performers include Agustín Barrios (1885–1944), one of the last major composer-performers. Barrios was a virtuoso who composed more than 100 works, many of which are played extensively today. He played an important role in popularizing the classical guitar in Latin and South America and is believed to be first classical guitarist to make a phonograph record.

No history of the classical guitar would be complete without a discussion of Andrés Segovia (1893–1987). He is the only modern guitarist to achieve recognition with the general public, in part a result of his nearly eighty years of promoting the guitar through extensive touring, master classes and recordings. Segovia is generally acknowledged as having guided the guitar from near oblivion to a respected concert instrument worthy of serious attention by the century's leading composers. He expanded the guitar's repertoire through his transcriptions of works by lutenists and vihuelists, as well as his transcriptions of Bach's compositions. Segovia was able to get composers like Manuel Ponce, Joaquín Rodrigo, Mario Castelnuovo-Tedesco, Alexander Tansman, Federico Moreno Torroba, Joaquín Turina and Heitor Villa-Lobos to write for the guitar. Although self-taught, Segovia's contributions to the instrument are one of the reasons why guitar study is now offered at the world's most prestigious music conservatories. He also taught younger guitarists — including John Williams and Eliot Fisk — and encouraged them to continue the work he had begun.

After Segovia, Julian Bream (b. 1933) is the best known and most influential guitarist of the twentieth century. He built upon the foundation laid by Segovia and struggled to get himself and the guitar the recognition they deserved. When Bream studied music at the Royal Academy of Music, he had to study the guitar privately, since it was not taught as part of the academic program. He played concerts in Great Britain in the 1950s, when such concerts were rare. He took up the lute and formed the Julian Bream Consort in the 1950s, sparking a revival of that instrument. Bream's work in getting contemporary composers, particularly from Great Britain, to write for the guitar was an important factor in its acceptance. In many ways, Bream — who has retired from touring but still performs and records — is a bridge between the guitarists of the early part of the twentieth century and the guitarists featured in this book.

What lies in store for the guitar now that the "Segovia hush" is only a memory? Modern day musical events continue to get larger and louder, making many people less able or less willing to truly hear the soft-edged sound of an unamplified guitar. It is evident that the classical guitar does not have the volume of a Steinway concert grand or the projection and singing sustain of a Stradivarius. But it is also true that the subtleties in tone and color possible on the classical guitar, resulting from both hands being in direct contact with the strings, are unmatched by any other instrument.

Ironically, the innate qualities of the classical guitar may turn out to be an asset, as people look for quiet beauty to provide balance in their lives.

While rock albums of the 1960s proudly proclaimed, "This album is meant to be played LOUD," recent lute recordings have been encouraging listeners to capture the original musical experience by playing them softly.

The advent of digital recording has also been a blessing for the classical guitar, as the tape hiss of cassettes and the "pops and crackles" of phonograph records have given way to the electronic equivalent of the Segovia hush. And the digital revolution in the form of the Internet has made information about and recordings by classical guitarists available to an extent unimaginable prior to the end of the twentieth century.

So there is reason to be hopeful about the future of the classical guitar — a future that will be shaped by the heads, hearts and hands of the performers in this book.

References

Goluses, Nicholas. *The History and Literature of the Guitar.* unpublished, 1990.
Grout, Donald Jay. *A History of Western Music (3rd ed.).* New York: Norton, 1980.
Grunfeld, Frederic. *The Art and Times of the Guitar.* London: Macmillan, 1969.
Kozin, Allan et al. *The Guitar — The History, the Music, the Players.* New York: William Morrow & Co., 1984.
Sadie, Stanley (editor). *New Grove Dictionary of Music and Musicians.* London: Macmillan Publishers Limited, 1980.
Summerfield, Maurice J. *The Classical Guitar: Its Evolution, Players and Personalities Since 1800 (3rd ed.).* United Kingdom: Ashley Mark, 1992.
Tyler, James. *The Early Guitar.* London: Oxford University Press, 1980.
Wade, Graham. *Segovia: A Celebration of the Man and His Music.* London: Allison & Busby, 1983.
Wade, Graham. *Traditions of the Classical Guitar.* London: John Calder, 1980.

1

Sharon Isbin: Breaking New Ground

January/February 1997

Sharon Isbin was born August 7, 1956 in Minneapolis, Minnesota. She began her studies in Italy with Aldo Minella and continued them with Jeffrey Van, Oscar Ghiglia, Andrés Segovia and keyboardist–Bach scholar Rosalyn Tureck. A 1999 Grammy Award nominee for her recording Journey to the Amazon, *Isbin won first prize in the Toronto international guitar competition (1975), was the first guitarist to win the Munich competition (1976) and was a winner of Madrid's Queen Sofia Competition (1979). She served as the artistic director of and featured performer at Carnegie Hall's 1985* Guitarstream International Festival, *as well as the 1988* Guitarjam *radio series. Isbin is the director (and founder) of the Juilliard School Guitar Department and director of the Aspen Music Festival Guitar Department. She is also the author of the* Classical Guitar Answer Book.

Our interview took place in Sharon Isbin's Central Park West apartment. On that Sunday afternoon, a dose of mild weather gave New York City a break from its battle with the winter of 1997. Inside, Isbin was talking about another kind of battle: the challenge of learning a major new guitar work just weeks before the premiere. Nearby on its guitar stand, a Thomas Humphrey Millenium — her weapon of choice — stood ready.

IT TAKES TWO

Jim Tosone: You recently premiered Double Concerto for Violin and Guitar by Aaron Jay Kernis. How did that piece come about?

Sharon Isbin: I approached Aaron because [violinist] Nadja Salerno-Sonnenberg and I have worked together a lot and we wanted a project for the two of us. Aaron is one of today's finest composers. He has a distinct and creative voice, with tremendous variety to his work. And he has an affection for the guitar. The concerto he wrote for us is the best piece I've ever heard for violin, guitar and orchestra. It's jazz-inspired, extremely virtuosic and a lot of fun. It's also a demanding piece rhythmically, with some tricky syncopation — particularly in the percussion.

JT: The premiere was originally scheduled for April of 1996, but was postponed until February of 1997. What happened?

SI: We were scheduled to premiere Double Concerto in April '96, but Aaron didn't finish it in time. So in March of that year we decided to postpone. The premieres were rescheduled for February '97 with the St. Paul Chamber Orchestra and April '97 with the New York Chamber Symphony at Alice Tully Hall. I'll be recording it in November for London/Decca with [violinist] Cho-Liang Lin and the St. Paul Chamber Orchestra, for release in 1998.

JT: What took place during the month before the February premiere?

SI: I came down with walking pneumonia returning from Glasgow, Scotland, and was sick all of December. I started touring again in January, so I had to learn the entire concerto in two and a half weeks. I wasn't sure I could do it in such a short period of time. Major revisions to the guitar part were needed so chords were playable and left-hand shifts were possible. I was up until 5:30 A.M. most days and back up again at 8:30 A.M., working at least ten hours a day on the piece. It was the greatest challenge I've faced in my career. In St. Paul we began rehearsals two days before the premiere. When you start the actual rehearsals a whole new world of sound opens up and you have only a couple of days to adapt to it. I often hide a tape recorder in a bag and secretly tape the rehearsals, so I can learn from the tapes overnight. When you're doing a world premiere, it's a frenzied time.

JT: And the premiere itself?

SI: It was spectacular. Nadja's playing was magnificent. We were totally breathless by the end of the performance and felt like we were going to fly off the stage.

JT: How would you assess Kernis' knowledge of and comfort with the guitar, considering that he's written for the guitar before?

SI: Well, Double Concerto presented a special challenge because Aaron had not only to deal with the balance between the guitar and the orchestra, but with another solo instrument. As for the guitar part, some things came easily to him while others — like where chords change rapidly in succession — required some work together. Since Aaron wanted to be careful in writing for the guitar, he would consult me frequently about specific passages, looking for the best way to express on the guitar what he was trying to create musically. I think it's important for the performer to have an ongoing dialogue with a composer. I've always made myself available to work with whoever is writing a piece for me, so we can find together the representation of the sound, the timbre, the style, that the composer is looking for. In the end, Aaron achieved a wonderful balance between the solo instruments and the orchestra. The guitar part has both beautiful lyricism and finger-busting virtuosity. It's a magnificent piece.

From the East

JT: In October of 1996, you premiered Yi^2, a guitar concerto written for you by Tan Dun. He has a fascinating background.

SI: Yes. Tan came from Mainland China, where he was a violinist in the Peking Opera orchestra. During the Cultural Revolution he was banished to the countryside to work on a rice farm. That probably would've been his fate but for a freak accident. A boat carrying all the members of the Peking Opera orchestra sank and they were killed. The government had to call back many of the musicians they had sent away. So Tan returned to Beijing. He had already been exploring composition while in China, and during the time he was in the countryside, he was exposed to the folk music and the instruments of ancient China. Within a short time, he found his way to New York, where he did graduate work in composition at NYU. Now, he is one of the most celebrated composers in Asia and Europe. In Germany he was voted best opera composer in 1995 for his opera *Marco Polo*. The United States is just now beginning to discover him.

JT: And the premiere of Yi^2?

SI: The premiere took place with the National Orchestra of France at the Donaueschingen Festival in Germany. It's the biggest contemporary music festival in Europe. The concerto opened the festival on its seventy-fifth anniversary. It was broadcast live in Germany, France and thirty other countries, as well as taped for German television. The program sold out, so they had to open up another hall with TV cameras so people could see the performance. The premiere turned out beautifully. Tan improvised a vocal part in traditional Chinese ritual form while using stones as a percussion instrument. In November, we did a performance with Tan conducting the BBC Scottish Symphony. Recently, I was asked to tour China with the Orchestre National de France to perform Yi^2 in 1998. And I'll be doing the first recording.

JT: What about the piece itself?

SI: It has folkloric elements. Tan has always been drawn to the idea of using modern instruments to evoke ancient ones. So the concerto requires the guitar to imitate the pipa, or ancient Chinese lute. The pipa is played with a plectrum and uses a lot of tremolo effects. I had to find ways to do what he had in mind using special kinds of tremolo on the guitar. His idea was not only to relate back to this ancient Chinese instrument but to the guitar's early flamenco origins. It is a beautiful melding of two cultures in a way that is very innovative. In the first two measures, I have to stomp my feet, whack the guitar, use rasgueado and glissandi, and coordinate this with clapping that the conductor is doing. It creates a unique world of sound. You've never heard anything like it before. The piece is about thirty-three minutes, with a beautiful long cadenza that is very evocative of Chinese music.

JT: Did you do anything special to prepare the piece?

SI: I listened to a lot of pipa music. Listening to players like Wu Man gave me a sense of the language and style. There's an enormous amount possible with a pipa, both single notes and chordal effects.

ON REFLECTION

JT: Will your work commissioning concertos continue?

SI: Yes. Christopher Rouse, a Pulitzer Prize–winning composer whose flute concerto is one of the most beautiful pieces I've ever heard, will be writing a concerto for me. The premiere is scheduled for the 1999-2000 season. I have a few other concertos in mind, but I can't talk about them just yet.

JT: When you commissioned your first concerto, were you thinking in terms of a series, or did it just evolve over time?

SI: It evolved. The first was from Ami Maayani in 1977. Others followed, leading to Joseph Schwantner's *From Afar* in '88, Lukas Foss' *American Landscapes* in '89, and John Corigliano's *Troubadours* in '93. The Kernis was the eighth concerto that I commissioned.

JT: Are the concertos "catching on?"

SI: I'm still the only one playing them, but I've been doing lots of performances, so in that sense they're catching on. I've done over twenty-five performances of the Corigliano and quite a number of the Foss and the Schwantner. One of the things I've been lazy about is providing the publisher with the final proofs of the edited guitar parts so they can be made available. As soon as I finish one project, I'm on to another. I get very far behind and am constantly being hounded by the publishers [laughs]. But they are available for others to perform — with the exception of the Kernis and Dun, which are still in their exclusivity periods.

JT: Has your conception of these concertos changed, either musically or in terms of technique, from your first performance to, say, your twenty-fifth?

SI: *Troubadours* has undergone the most change. John always had this idea that while I was playing I would stroll within the orchestra and interact with various players. I'd play the opening phrases, which are ghostlike evocations of the thirteenth-century troubadour world in Provençal, France, while still backstage. Having the sound come in a soft voice from behind the curtain would evoke an ethereal, otherworldly sense. Then I would come out and walk amongst the orchestra while playing this long, fast guitar run — the longest run I've seen in the classical guitar literature! At the end of the piece, there is a recapitulation of the theme in a minor key, this being a metaphor for the end of the troubadour era, when many were persecuted, killed or forced to flee their homeland. During this part, John wanted me to walk offstage while playing and finish the piece from behind the curtain.

We decided not to try all this for the premiere. We had enough to deal with. But afterward John kept begging me, saying, "You can do it. You can do it." So I began to experiment with how I could play and walk at the same time — no small challenge for a classical guitarist! Sound projection was not a problem; since I use a wireless sound reinforcement system, it doesn't matter where I am in the hall. But a classical guitar is not designed for use with a neck strap. So I got in touch with someone who developed a special strap that would affix to the guitar with suction cups. Then I started practicing in my living room, pacing back and forth while playing this long run, until I could play it on automatic pilot. I finally felt I could do it and, in the thirteenth or fourteenth performance, I tried it. It worked and added a wonderful new dimension to the performance.

JT: There are two versions of *From Afar*, one for a symphony orchestra and one for chamber orchestra.

SI: Right. The premiere was in 1988 with the St. Louis Symphony, Leonard Slatkin conducting. When the record option became available, I explained to Joseph Schwantner that the recording would be with the St. Paul Chamber Orchestra. That meant he would have to reorchestrate it. Frankly, it's hard to tell the difference between the two versions. The full-orchestra version is available on the Leonard Slatkin retrospective collection *The Slatkin Years*, which came out last year.

JT: Regarding the Foss concerto, John Schneider in *Soundboard* called your performance "thrilling" and "simply magnificent." Of the concerto, he said that it's "entertaining but a bit gimmicky to win lasting admiration."

SI: Well that's his opinion. Many people really love the piece. The fact that the last movement has bluegrass elements and a musical joke at the end may not be serious enough for those steeped in a more austere contemporary music tradition. But it's done with all the sophistication, integrity and skill that is characteristic of Foss. Quoting from American themes is not a new

Sharon Isbin and composer John Corigliano following the world premiere of *Troubadours*, St. Paul, Minnesota, October 1993 (Kathy Isbin).

idea. Copland, who was Foss' teacher, was a master at that. I don't find the concerto gimmicky at all. I find it creative and fun.

JT: There are a couple of interesting aspects to the second movement, which is based on the theme *Wayfaring Stranger*.

SI: Right. Originally, when Lukas and I talked about this particular movement, he wondered if there was a way I could hook myself up to a time delay device, so a line I played would be repeated "x" number of seconds later. I checked out the technology available at that time and told Lukas I didn't recommend it. He said, "Don't worry about it, I'll write the delay it into the music." The result is a lot more engaging than it would have been using technology. The other interesting thing is that there are places where

Sharon Isbin and composer Lukas Foss reviewing the score of *American Landscapes* (Laura Koplewitz).

I have to — by tapping on different spots on the guitar — create low, middle, and high pitches. These form the contour of the *Wayfaring Stranger* theme. At the same time, I have to pluck the theme itself in canonic imitation, sometimes with the left hand, sometimes with the right. At one point, I thought I'd have to use my nose [laughs].

JT: What do you think about when performing a concerto?

SI: In one particular concerto, something very special. The summer of 1996 was a tragic one for me in that my brother, who I was very close to, died of AIDS. The night before he died, I learned that the piece he chose to be played at his memorial service was my recording of the slow movement from the *Concierto de Aranjuez*. I was astonished because two days later I was scheduled to perform only that movement in a special concert with the Baltimore Symphony in Washington, D.C. It was as if that could be my personal gift and tribute to him. Now, whenever I perform the work, I think of him.

JSB

JT: I'd like to talk about your studies with [Bach scholar] Rosalyn Tureck. One of the things she said was, "Because of Segovia, I now find myself involved with the lute music of Johann Sebastian Bach. It is due to Segovia's development of the field for classical guitar that I have associated my work with this instrument and have accepted a very talented guitarist as my student." That guitarist, of course, being you. How did you and Rosalyn get together?

SI: I called her in 1977 to see if I could have some lessons with her. She was intrigued because she was aware that lute music had been a strong influence on the harpsichord music of Bach. So for her it was a fascinating journey as well. Ironically, she was never able to tolerate Segovia's Bach playing. When I showed her Segovia's transcription of the Bach Chaconne, she was horrified. Within the first line there are terrible problems of voice leading, where he has jumped around octaves and abandoned various bass notes of the Passacaglia. The fingering is often uncontrapuntal and works against the voicing. And the off-beat slurs compound the problem. So it was a challenge to break down that whole tradition of approaching Bach's music without a structural viewpoint.

JT: Tureck developed a technique entirely different from conventional keyboard playing for Bach. Did you do the same for the guitar?

SI: That's what we did together. On keyboard, to achieve a contrapuntal delineation of the lines in Bach's music, Rosalyn would often use suspension of sound by holding one finger and playing with another under it. That meant recrafting the whole approach to keyboard technique. For the guitar, instead of a single-line approach, with slurs thrown in wherever you feel like it, we had to take into account the structure before we could even begin to think about fingering. It sometimes meant that cross-string fingerings would be called for; other times it meant eliminating certain slurs. That's just the surface of what is involved.

JT: Can you give a general framework for playing Bach?

SI: It's always best to learn from a model. I would certainly recommend listening to Rosalyn Tureck's performances on the keyboard of Bach because it gives you a sense of the articulation, the dynamics, the phrasing and the structure. Then listen to my Bach Lute Suite recordings that we edited together. This doesn't mean that you have to follow every fingering or embellishment. It gives you an example of one system that works. With that knowledge, you can make your own arrangements.

BEST SELLERS

JT: Your CDs for Virgin Records—*Complete Lute Suites, Road to the Sun* and *Nightshade Rounds*—were made in the same studio in Minneapolis, with the same producer and engineer. What did you learn from those recording experiences?

Sharon Isbin (left) and Bach scholar Rosalyn Tureck (courtesy of *Guitar Review*).

SI: You learn a lot through experience about mike placement. I think it's important to avoid the right-hand "naily" sounds you often get on guitar. What we eventually found worked particularly well — while recording *Nightshade Rounds* — was to have one pair of mikes placed close with a lot of the high-end equalized out to avoid an overly bright sound, and a second pair placed further away to get the ambient sound and the fuller spectrum. Together, that produced the warmest sound.

JT: We talked before about the visual aspect of performing *Troubadours*. There's also a visual aspect to your CDs. On *American Landscapes* there's a picture of you dressed in black against a black background. It's very striking, almost dance-like. Are you involved in the visual aspects of your CDs?

SI: The first five EMI/Virgin CDs were done by one photographer who I came to know quite by accident on a magazine photo shoot. He worked in the fashion industry and had never photographed a classical musician before. He brought a totally fresh perspective. His concept grew out of the music. He determined the design and the clothing, not unlike costuming an actress for a play.

JT: I understand that John Duarte, whose *English Suite* you recorded part of on your *Nightshade Rounds* CD, has written a new suite for you.

SI: It's a lovely work called *Appalachian Suite*. I expect to premiere it next year and eventually record it. It's based on Appalachian music from the United States. Most Appalachian music came originally from England, developing its own unique character over time. When I was researching source material for *Appalachian Suite*, I think I listened to over three hundred tunes.

JT: Any other recordings on the horizon?

SI: I'll be doing an album with a Brazilian percussionist, Thiago de Mello, which will include a number of his compositions. He hails from the Brazilian rain forest and his work often reflects a wonderful integration of his Indian origins and a contemporary vision. The instruments he uses come from the rain forest and evoke much of that spirit.

JT: You've also published a book, *The Acoustic Guitar Answer Book*. What was the idea behind it?

SI: I had been writing a column for four years for *Acoustic Guitar* magazine, a sort of "Dear Abby" of guitar. The publisher and editor decided from the beginning to collate these articles into a book when the right time came. The editor determined the table of contents and the ordering. I just had to do the final editing. It covers fifty topics, such as how to buy a guitar, memorize a piece, prepare for a concert and avoid finger squeaks.

ALL OF YOUR BUSINESS

JT: Do you get any pressure from the record company about piece selection when you're putting together a CD?

SI: I've been really lucky in that I've been given *carte blanche*. In the case of *Love Songs and Lullabies*, they had in mind a crossover album of lullabies with voice. I suggested we make it love songs and lullabies so I could create something that would have contrasts of tempi and mood. I asked Thiago de Mello to join me on the Latin numbers. That created the crossover feeling they wanted. As far as how they market my recordings, that's their problem [laughs].

JT: You once said that if you don't take an interest in your career from a business standpoint, you can't make it happen from an artistic one. What things have you done from a business standpoint that help you make it happen artistically?

SI: One of the first things I did was to present a major debut in New York in 1979. I did that after having won a number of competitions, so there was something marketable about me. Then, it was important to get major management. I've been with Columbia Artists Management since 1980. Also, once you're doing a lot of concerts you need a good press agent. The third aspect of developing a career is recording. You have to have something to say on disc. That's an even greater challenge today because all the standard stuff has been done many times over.

JT: And that's where transcription and new works come in?

SI: Right. It requires the ability to interest and to work with composers. I began commissioning when I was seventeen. The first commission I gave was for a concerto by an Israeli composer, Ami Maayani. I had heard a work of his for harp and thought of the guitar immediately. But when I approached him, he said, "I don't know anything about the guitar. I'm not interested." I realized I had to try harder. Eventually I played for him, and he said, "Well, maybe." A year later, his concerto arrived. That was the beginning of my commissioning career and it hasn't stopped since.

JT: A number of years back you were on CBS *Sunday Morning with Charles Kuralt*. Was there much subsequent impact or publicity?

SI: Being on television generates a lot of CD sales and interest by presenters in booking you. That segment was interesting because it gave a sense of the process, by showing how one piece went from rehearsal to performance.

JT: You also performed with Garrison Keillor on his radio program, *A Prairie Home Companion*. I assume there's a hometown Minnesota connection there?

SI: As they say in Minnesota, "you bet." I started to appear on Garrison's show even before it went national and continued after it went into syndication. Usually, I would just play a couple of tunes. Once, they had me in a sketch about a French school. It was my fling with being an actress [laughs]. Interestingly, I got a note from Garrison a few years back saying that he writes his monologues while listening to my Bach Lute Suite recording.

JT: The definition of classical music has expanded to encompass the crossover element you mentioned before. You've performed and recorded what could be called jazz-fusion with [guitarists] Laurindo Almeida and Larry Coryell and you've done Gershwin with [guitarist] Carlos Barbosa-Lima. How does your classical training help in performing that kind of music and how has performing that kind of music helped your performances of more traditional classical music?

SI: Laurindo, one of the finest exponents of Brazilian music, taught me about the rhythmic intricacies of playing Latin American music. Because both he and Larry improvised, it made me a lot looser in terms of performance flexibility and tuning in to the spontaneous process of improvising musicians. But I didn't attempt to compete with their improvisational skills. We created arrangements that fit our three different styles.

JT: Can classical music be self-sustaining and, if so, how?

SI: That's a complex question. Classical music is not designed for the masses the way pop music is, so the expectations have to be different. One can't pander to a strictly commercial taste because you lose the refinement that has always been a part of classical music. It's important that new works of quality be given the opportunity to be recorded. Ironically, those new works are selling the best now because they have nothing else to compete with. There's usually only one recording of each of them, as opposed to 300 of the Beethoven symphonies. Recording companies must never lose the commitment to quality in their zeal to sell. One can have a mixture of projects, some which appeal to a wide spectrum of people, and others that have a smaller appeal but have great value culturally and creatively.

SCHOOL DAYS

JT: Let's talk about that bastion of culture and creativity, Juilliard, where you head the guitar department. How many students do you now have in the guitar program?

SI: It ranges from five to eight graduate students. The program gives them many chamber music opportunities and there's a concert each year at Alice Tully Hall where they all perform. The guitar program has been embraced by the other departments. Because there was such a demand for guitarists to be part of chamber music ensembles, they even created a class, which [flutist] Carol Wincenc teaches, called Chamber Music for Winds, Harp and Guitar. The guitar program has been very successful and a number of the students have gone on to establish themselves as premier guitarists in their own countries.

JT: For instance?

SI: Luis Quintero from Venezuela, Mats Bergström from Sweden, Antigoni Goni from Greece and Kevin Gallagher from the United States. Both Antigoni and Kevin won first prizes in the GFA [Guitar Foundation of America] competition. Most of my students have made their New York debuts as winners of the Artists International Competition. Antigoni is now responsible for the pre-college division of guitar at Juilliard, which was created last year so students in elementary, junior high or high school have a place in New York where they can work with a really outstanding teacher. By the way, a number of people have approached me about a doctoral program for guitar. It hasn't happened yet, but it might.

JT: Is there something in either the guitar or the general program that helps students deal with the business aspects of music?

SI: They can attend visiting forums and classes taught by faculty who address this topic. As importantly, they are surrounded by people who are working within the profession, so they see firsthand how careers are built.

JT: What do you like and dislike about the academic scene at Juilliard?

SI: Gee, I've never thought of it as strictly academic. The spirit there is a musical rather than bookish. It's a place that values applied music and is dedicated to producing the best performers possible.

JT: Do you enjoy the non-musical aspects of being a department head?

SI: I'm the only guitar faculty so I only have meetings with myself [laughs]. It's a cushy position in that, other than filling out grades, giving lessons and master classes when I'm in town, making sure that the concerts are organized properly and guiding students, there's nothing else. No preparation and no involvements that take up time.

JT: Do you anticipate that you might have additional instructors?

SI: Actually, Juilliard prides itself on maintaining a specific student count. Their design is not to expand. I don't envision any expansion other than potentially a doctorate program.

STATUS REPORT

JT: You've been performing for over twenty-five years. What's been most gratifying?

SI: Getting major composers who otherwise had no affiliation with the guitar to write for it. Starting the guitar department at Juilliard and restarting the guitar program at the Aspen Music Festival. Working with Rosalyn Tureck to give the guitar a context for baroque performance. Bringing the guitar to a lot of people who weren't necessarily familiar with classical music and classical guitar, through the festivals I've created at Carnegie Hall and the Ordway Music Theatre. And creating the national radio series *Guitarjam*. The festivals and radio series help establish a new audience that will be supportive of the instrument in years to come.

JT: Do you have any anecdotal evidence that people who've been exposed to the guitar through outreach-type programs are then drawn into the core classical guitar repertoire?

SI: A lot of orchestras and major symphonies have never had a guitar on their program before. So one of the advantages of playing on their programs is that there are hundreds of people in the audience who never have heard classical guitar, either solo or with orchestra. I've played nineteen different guitar concertos in my career. People come up to me at receptions afterwards and say, "I never knew the guitar could do that" and "I'm so excited, I have to go out and buy some guitar recordings." It's a revelation to them, many who come from a generation where the guitar wasn't part of their youth experience.

JT: What will you be doing in the months ahead?

SI: I'll be doing over seventy concerts in the U.S. alone in the upcoming season, including the National Symphony in Washington, D.C. and a recital with mezzo-soprano Denyce Graves [the actual performer was Susanne Mentzer] in New York at the 92nd Street Y's Tisch Center in April 1998. And I'm looking forward to doing the Guitar Summit tour this year with [jazz guitarist] Herb Ellis, [blues guitarist] Rory Block and Michael Hedges on acoustic finger-style [guitar]. There will be a West Coast tour in October '97, and a Midwest and East Coast in February-March '98.

JT: Speaking of traveling, I heard that you've been into outer space.

SI: In a way. I always wanted to be either a rocket scientist or an astronaut when I was a kid and would spend many hours building and launching model rockets. My father would say, "Look, until you put in an hour on your guitar, you can't go out and launch your rockets." That's how my parents got me to practice. Last year, I received a phone call from an astronaut who was going up in the Atlantis space shuttle. He was taking a copy of the *American Landscape* CD and a SoloEtte travel guitar to give to the Russian cosmonauts on the space station Mir. So, in a sense, I finally made it into space.

Aaron Jay Kernis on the Concerto for Violin, Guitar and Orchestra
January-February 1997

Aaron Jay Kernis was born on January 15, 1960 in Philadelphia, Pennsylvania. When he was thirteen years old, he started to teach himself composition. Kernis went on to study formally with Theodore Antoniou, Joseph Franklin, John Adams, Elias Tanenbaum, Charles Wuorinen, Morton Subotnick, Bernard Rands and Jacob Druckman. His works include vocal, chamber and symphonic music. Some of Kernis' notable compositions include Symphony in Waves, Colored Fields *and* Still Movement with Hymn. *He has also written two works for David Tanenbaum—* Partita *for solo guitar and* 100 Greatest Dance Hits *for guitar and string quartet. Kernis' most recent composition for guitar is the* Double Concerto for Violin and Guitar, *written for Nadja Salerno-Sonnenberg and Sharon Isbin. His awards include the Academy Award from the American Academy of Arts and Letters, the Stoeger Prize from the Chamber Music Society of Lincoln Center, a Guggenheim Fellowship, a Rome Prize, a Bearns Prize and a New York Foundation for the Arts Award. In 1998, he won the Pulitzer Prize in Music.*

Aaron Jay Kernis is a master composer and, like many of his fellow Manhattanites, a master at using every square inch of his apartment. As I entered on a wintry day in early 1997, I noticed that nearly every surface was covered with his tools — scores, sketches, keyboards, recording equipment, tapes. Yet from this apparent chaos have emerged deeply felt compositions with their own internal logic and order. Kernis composed answers to questions in the same way he writes — trying out different ideas and modes of expression, then reshaping them until they say what he means. As we cleared away two places for us to sit, the conversation turned to his latest work for guitar.

THEN AND NOW

Jim Tosone: How did Concerto for Violin, Guitar and Orchestra come about?

Aaron Jay Kernis: Nearly three years ago, Sharon Isbin approached me about writing a piece for her and Nadja Salerno-Sonnenberg. At that time, I was talking with David Tanenbaum about writing a guitar concerto for him. But I decided to give their concerto a shot.

JT: The premiere was originally scheduled for April of 1996, but was postponed until February of 1997. What happened?

AJK: I blocked out five months to write the piece. For three of those months I was empty, not knowing what to write or how to go forward. I finally finished the second and third movements, and was pushing myself hard on the first. But Nadja decided at a certain point that there just was not enough time and that the premiere would have to be postponed. I wound up throwing out the first movement I was working on and writing an entirely different first movement, one that I feel good about.

JT: What happened during the month before the February premiere?

AJK: Everyone was traveling at exactly different times, so I wasn't able to meet with the soloists before we arrived in St. Paul. Most of the work with the soloists took place during the first couple of rehearsals there. Hugh Wolff, the conductor, is an incredible leader who was forceful in pulling the piece through rehearsal. Because I spent a lot of time over the past year perfecting the piece, the changes I made at rehearsal were minimal.

JT: And the premiere itself?

AJK: The premiere was in the Ted Mann auditorium at University of Minnesota, while the second and third performances were at the Ordway in St. Paul. The first performance was my favorite. Ted Mann auditorium has a clear and dry sound, with good balance. The performance was a bit more intimate than at the Ordway, since the soloists were not yet playing in the most bravura way and were particularly careful to listen to each other.

I was pleased at how well I could hear the soloists at all times. The piece received a very warm response from the players and the audience.

Inspiration and Influence

JT: Many of your pieces, like *100 Greatest Dance Hits* or *Colored Fields*, have rich stories or imagery behind them. What images do you associate with Double Concerto?

AJK: Well, I first saw Nadja perform on Johnny Carson's *Tonight Show*. And as I was writing the Concerto I kept getting flashes of the opening theme music. That's part of the reason there's a showy, big band jazz element to the piece. Also, when I began writing it I thought I might portray the difference between Nadja's flamboyant personality and Sharon's more inward-looking persona. But once the music took off on its own, it became instead a piece about the violin and guitar. It's actually more abstract than most of my other works.

JT: Are there jazz composers or performers that have influenced you?

AJK: I have not listened to jazz since my first year of college. I've had no interest, except for some of the *avant-garde* jazz downtown at places like Knitting Factory. So it was surprising to me that the jazz element comes through so clearly in this piece. I think it comes partly from an image of Nadja and Sharon onstage together playing actively, and involving music that isn't so mannered — in a classical sense — but has a more popular sensibility.

JT: Did you listen to any other guitar concerto recordings or attend any guitar concerto concerts to see how other composers approached this type of composition?

AJK: I listened to a lot of recordings. One thing that came out strongly was that most guitar concertos feature the orchestra more than the guitar. I wanted to remedy that imbalance, so Double Concerto is really a soloist's piece.

The Nature of the Piece

JT: What is its structure?

AJK: It's a thirty-plus minute work in three movements. Something I tried to do in the piece was vary the role of the instrumentalists so they could be shown as soloists, as duo partners and as oppositional partners. The first movement opens with a long phrase for the guitar — like two minutes — then a violin solo, followed by both playing together. Then the reverse — a violin solo, a guitar solo, then both together. After that, the

Aaron Jay Kernis (Daniel Vogel).

orchestra has a big tutti. The first movement for the guitar is almost exclusively single lines, with a couple of chordal passages.

Throughout most of the second movement, the violin and guitar play together as partners. The music is wildly extreme for both instruments. In the third movement, they are both soloists and partners. The guitar plays fast-moving sixteenth notes, but at the most insistent moments, it plays large chords for drama and weight.

JT: What about the musical language and the orchestration?

AJK: There's a lot of '50s and bebop jazz, a little bit of funk and elements of big band. I've written so many dark, tragic pieces in the last five years and I see this as more of a lighter piece, even though seventy percent of it is in a minor color. It belongs more to a dissonant jazz world than a lyrical consonant world. The piece is scored for a large chamber orchestra with strings, double winds, three percussion, harp, synthesizer, celeste and honky-tonk piano.

JT: Toru Takemitsu was commissioned so often in part because he gave the complex material to the solo instruments and kept the orchestration simple, because orchestras don't have lots of time to rehearse. Does this influence how you orchestrate?

AJK: It should, but it doesn't [laughs]. This piece is easier to rehearse than some of my straight orchestral pieces, although some bits are quite tricky for the orchestra. But the nature of the orchestration grows out of what I am trying to express, as opposed to extra-musical factors. One thing I did worry about is that orchestras don't have a strong feeling for jazz, that they don't have a strong affinity for the rhythms and syncopations. I had to be pretty specific in writing the music down, so swingy triplets were played as swingy triplets and straight eighth notes were played as straight eighths. I counted on the drum-kit player and the double-bass soloist, who often have this material, to bring it to life. They came through at the premiere with no difficulty.

PICKING UP THE GAUNTLET

JT: You've written three other works for guitar: a suite, a guitar and ensemble piece and *100 Greatest Dance Hits* for guitar and string quartet. Has it gotten any easier to write for the instrument?

AJK: I'll tell you the truth, every time I start writing for guitar, it's like I've never done it before. On the guitar, if you want to make sound, you have to write six-note chords. So sometimes I'll have to include an open-string drone note that I don't really want in the chord, just so the guitar can project. It took a while, especially in *Dance Hits*, for me to get used to the idea that I might have to include an occasional note that I don't really want in the texture. Other times, the more notes I took away and the simpler I kept the texture, the more effective on the guitar. There's no simple answer. So much can blot out the guitar, even the solo violin. Dealing with the balance between the two solo instruments and the orchestra was definitely the hardest aspect of the piece. One thing that surprised me was that Sharon's amplification created a "conflict" in sound production between the amplified guitar and the unamplified violin. Although I wouldn't suggest it, I almost wish the violin were slightly amplified — not for volume, but for sound production.

JT: Did you use any special guitar techniques in writing the piece?

AJK: I didn't, because of the need for the guitar to project. For instance, there are maybe two harmonics in the entire piece. Even the violin doesn't play a single pizzicato [plucked note], which is very unusual for my music. Generally, I include these types of textures, but here projection of the solo parts above the orchestra was more important. I wish I had had the freedom to use other playing techniques, but the piece needed to be about rhythms and development.

JT: What kinds of suggestions did Sharon make as you were working together?

AJK: Mostly taking out impossible shifts and filling out chords that needed an additional note to be playable. I used [guitarist] Michael Lorimer's guitar neck chart while I was writing. I couldn't have done it without that.

JT: Will you write more for the guitar?

AJK: It's a tough instrument to work with and it was such a hard work to write. But since this piece was a good experience, I'd like to do more.

Name That Tune

JT: I understand you held a contest at the premiere to name the piece. What was that all about?

AJK: The title is something that's confounded me for some time. It pains me greatly to call this piece Double Concerto. It's such a faceless, ordinary title. But I didn't want to call it "blue" this or "hot" that or some other typical jazz title. I had the title contest not only because I was curious to see how the audience verbalized their impression of the piece, but also because I wanted to entice them to focus closely. I must have gotten 500 little pieces of paper with suggestions. Some of my favorites were *Concerto for Two Strong Women*, *Mutual Admiration Concerto* and *Fire and Ice Concerto*. Two titles I did not understand were *Tiananmen Square Uprising* ...

JT: Maybe they thought they were at a Tan Dun concert.

AJK: ... and *Ass-Kicking Concerto*.

JT: Which would have made it the first concerto to get a parental advisory label.

AJK: [laughs] Yes. Anyway, I'm still going to call the piece Double Concerto.

Concert Reviews

Sharon Isbin, guitar
Nadja Salerno-Sonnenberg, violin
New York Chamber Symphony, Gerald Schwartz
Alice Tully Hall, New York City
April 20, 1997

An important new work was added to the guitar literature in 1997. Aaron Jay Kernis' Concerto for Violin, Guitar and Orchestra had its New York premiere on April 20 by guitarist Sharon Isbin, violinist Nadja Salerno-Sonnenberg and the New York Chamber Symphony.

Kernis has emerged as one of America's foremost composers in recent years, writing substantive yet readily accessible works. His collaboration with noted instrumentalists Isbin and Salerno-Sonnenberg resulted in the long-awaited Double Concerto. It is a jazz-influenced work that combines imaginative orchestration with guitar writing that fits the instrument without being overly idiomatic.

Salerno-Sonnenberg, clad in a stylish tuxedo-like outfit, and Isbin, wearing a multi-colored sparkling blouse, commanded center stage throughout the performance. Both were musically and technically in top form.

In the first movement, *Fast and Jazzy*, the orchestra's handling of the rhythmically complex percussion was precise yet fluid. The second movement, *Adagio molto*, is an expansive section filled with thematic ideas. It begins with beautiful melodies and harmonies for the violin and guitar, played well by Isbin and Salerno-Sonnenberg. In the more pastoral sections, the orchestra produced a lush sound.

The piece all comes together in the last movement: *Presto, sempre ritmico*. The passing of thematic material from violin to guitar to orchestra was handled deftly by the soloists and the orchestra. This movement in particular showcases Kernis' ability to write music that grabs you from the first note and doesn't let go until the final notes fade. It is the kind of music you can put your head, heart and soul into.

There were two minor acoustical flaws that lessened the enjoyment of Double Concerto. The first was a slight delay in the sound coming from the snare drum and cymbals, which gave the effect of them originating behind the audience. The second was that Isbin's amplified classical guitar was too loud and bright in the first movement. Amplification is certainly justified in this situation, where the guitar must compete with both the violin and orchestra. But in this case the volume of the guitar, combined with the fact that Salerno-Sonnenberg was in an acoustically dead spot on stage, produced an imbalance between the two instruments.

Nonetheless, the response from the audience was very enthusiastic. The soloists and conductor were called back three times. A lady sitting next to me said, "I love modern music, jazz and classical guitar. And I love this piece." Madam, I couldn't agree more.

Recording Reviews

American Landscapes
Sharon Isbin, guitar
St. Paul Chamber Orchestra/Hugh Wolff, conductor
EMI/Virgin Classics 55033

American Landscapes is a landmark recording. Not only is it the first recording of American guitar concertos, but the three concertos on the disc were written by major contemporary composers who had not written previously for the guitar.

John Corigliano's *Troubadours (Variations for Guitar and Orchestra)* is a unique guitar concerto in that it reaches back to medieval France for its thematic and scoring inspiration. It consists of free variations within a slow-fast-slow framework. *Troubadours* makes imaginative use of ancient instruments and orchestral textures. Its modal harmonies and phrases that repeat at whole-step higher intervals also suggest music from the distant past. The piece begins at a leisurely pace, but the fun begins in the central section when full-tilt brass and percussion playing is used to depict a medieval fair. *Troubadours* builds in drama until, after a solemn interlude, it gives way to an inventive guitar cadenza written in a way that gives the illusion of two guitars playing.

From Afar ... A Fantasy for Guitar and Orchestra by Joseph Schwantner was inspired by a personal distance. Schwantner was a guitarist in his youth, but had not played for many years. As he was writing the guitar concerto, he renewed his acquaintance with the instrument and recalled memories from that earlier time in his life. The piece was composed at the guitar and encompasses several guitar styles, including jazz. *From Afar* makes use of guitar techniques such as rasgueado and tremolo. It has rhythmic variety, dissonant harmonies, contrasting colors and waves of percussion, leading to a thunderous ending.

Lukas Foss' *American Landscapes for Guitar and Orchestra* draws its inspiration from American folk dances as well as fiddle tunes such as jigs and reels. The first movement uses material derived from the folk song *Jefferson and Liberty*, while the second movement is based on the spiritual *The Wayfaring Stranger*. The last movement is a hoedown rooted in the songs *Cotton-Eyed Joe* and *Stay a Little Longer*, with a finale that has the guitar playing its own tune while the orchestra plays excerpts from *America the Beautiful*.

The performances of these concertos can be considered definitive, given that Isbin worked closely with the composers from conception to realization. The playing is both musically and technically superb, with cohesiveness between the guitar and orchestra in both rhythms and tonal colors.

Nightshade Rounds
Sharon Isbin, guitar
EMI/Virgin Classics 45024

The historically male-dominated world of classical guitar continues to benefit from the emergence of a world-class group of women performers, as demonstrated on this latest recording from Sharon Isbin.

Isbin possesses a distinct musical perspective and a formidable technique, both of which continue to evolve. Her 1994 disc, *Nightshade Rounds*, represents her foray into the world of 20th century English and American guitar music. It contains a mixture of standard works (William Walton's *Five Bagatelles* and Benjamin Britten's *Nocturnal*) and new works written for Isbin (Bruce MacCombie's *Nightshade Rounds* and Joan Tower's *Clocks*).

The disc begins with *Five Bagatelles*, which was written for Julian Bream. Isbin's strong, yet well-controlled attack captures the lively nature of the first and fifth Bagatelles. In the quiet and introspective second and fourth Bagatelles, she imparts a sense of forward motion that makes the pieces come alive. This is one of the best performances of the Bagatelles that I have heard. Other noteworthy recordings include Carlos Bonell (*Twentieth-Century Music for Guitar*, EMI CDC 7 49512 2) and Julian Bream (*Twentieth-Century Guitar I*, Julian Bream Edition, Vol. 12, RCA 09026-61595). *Nocturnal* by Benjamin Britten was also written for Bream. There are a number of excellent recordings of this piece on disc, including Norbert Kraft (*Guitar Music*, Chandos CHAN 8784), Jan Wolf (*Guitar*, Partridge 1115-2) and the 1993 re-recording by Bream (*Nocturnal*, EMI CDC 7 54901 2). Isbin's interpretation of the work is a welcome addition. Of particular note are her performances of the second movement (*Very Agitated*), the fourth movement (*Uneasy*) and the Passacaglia. In the latter, she provides a distinctive contrast between the diatonic bass and the chromatic melody.

The main attraction of this disc is first recordings of *Nightshade Rounds* and *Clocks*. *Nightshade Rounds* was inspired by the deadly nightshade flower, with a series of unfolding arpeggiated patterns representing emerging petals. It has similarities to Steven Reich's *Electric Counterpoint*, in that its melodic and harmonic patterns evolve slowly over the course of the piece. *Nightshade Rounds* also recalls the blocks of modal arpeggios in Leo Brouwer's Etude No. 20. Isbin uses a number of techniques to maintain the listener's interest, including meticulous shaping of the patterns, precise changes in tonal color and a careful varying of the dynamics.

Tower's *Clocks* is a significant addition to the guitar repertoire. Its opening repeated pulse reflects the focus of the piece on musical time. It gradually accelerates into fast scales and leaping arpeggios, concluding with a set of arpeggios on top of an extended pedal point. The atmosphere of *Clocks* reminds me of Rodrigo's *Invocation et Danse*. The piece requires great stamina and Isbin is clearly up to the task. Her strummed chords in the final section are a model of intensity and clarity.

Rounding out the disc are excerpts from George Gershwin's *Three Preludes* and John Duarte's *English Suite*. The first two of the *Three Preludes* were arranged by Carlos Barbosa-Lima. The Preludes are not easy to transcribe to the guitar; they were clearly composed for the piano. It is difficult to capture the natural bounce in first Prelude, but Isbin gives a credible performance. The moody atmosphere of the second Prelude works very well on the guitar and Isbin has captured it perfectly.

Duarte's *English Suite* was dedicated to Andrés Segovia and his wife on the occasion of their marriage. The second movement (*Folk Song*) is a gentle tune based on a traditional English melody. Isbin's interpretation is very pleasing and her rhythm, dynamics and phrasing are all on the mark. I wish she had recorded the first and third movements as well, which are well suited to her spirited style. In addition to the classic Segovia recording of this piece (*Segovia on Stage*, Decca DL 710140), there is a recording by Neil Smith (*Plays John W. Duarte*, Guitar Masters Records GMR 1006).

The liner notes for this disc are substantial and well written. I particularly like the fact that they include a list of the performance editions used on the recording. I would like to see this become a standard part of all liner notes.

Discography

Dreams of a World
Teldec Classics International 3984-25736-2
Duarte: *Appalachian Dreams (op. 121)*; Ruiz-Pipo: *Canción y Danza*; Tárrega: *Recuerdos de la Alhambra*; Lecuona: *Canta Siboney*; San Sebastion: *Preludio (Dolor)*; Takemitsu: *Londonderry Air*; Shemer: *Four Songs by Naomi Shemer*; Theodorakis: *Two Epitafios*; Gismonti: *Agua y Vinho*; Thiago de Mello: *Varre-Vento*; Lauro *Virgilio, Romanza*; Ramón y Rivera: *Brisas del Torbes*; Granados: *Dedicatoria*.

Double Concerto for Violin & Guitar (by Aaron Jay Kernis)
Argo/Decca 460226-2

Kernis: *Double Concerto for Violin Guitar* (with Sharon Isbin, guitar; Cho-Liang Lin, violin; Saint Paul Chamber Orchestra/Hugh Wolff, conductor). Includes other non-guitar works.

Wayfaring Stranger
Erato 3984-23419-2
with Susanne Mentzer (mezzo-soprano)
Granados: *Spanish Dance no. 5*; Sainz de la Maza: *Zapateado*; Tárrega: *Capricho Arabe*; Rodrigo: *Aranjuez ma pensee*; Schubert: *3 Lieder*; Sieber: *4 French Folk Songs*; Martini: *Plaisir D'Amour*; Trad.: *4 French Bergerettes, 5 American Folk Songs*.

Journey to the Amazon
Teldec Classics International 0630-19899-2
with Paul Winter (saxophone), Gaudencio Thiago de Mello (percussion)
Almeida: *Historia do Luar*; Thiago de Mello: *A Hug for Pixinga, Chôro Alegre, Lago de Janauacá, Chants Nos. 1 & 2, Cavaleiro sem Armadura*; Savio: *Batucada*; Vianna (Pixinguinha): *Cochichando*; Montaña: *Porro*; Brouwer: *Canción de Cuna*; Canonico: *Aire de Joropo*; Lauro: *Waltz no. 3, Seis por Derecho, El Marabino*; Barrios: *Julia Florida, Waltz (op. 8 no. 4)*.

American Landscapes
EMI/Virgin Classics 55083
with Saint Paul Chamber Orchestra (Hugh Wolff, conductor)
Corigliano: *Troubadours (Variations for Guitar and Orchestra)*; Schwantner: *From Afar ... A Fantasy for Guitar and Orchestra*; Foss: *American Landscapes for Guitar and Orchestra*.

Nightshade Rounds
EMI/Virgin Classics 45024
Walton: *Five Bagatelles*; MacCombie: *Nightshade Rounds*; Gershwin: *Preludes 1 and 2*; Tower: *Clocks*; Duarte: *Folk Song (from English Suite, op. 31)*; Britten: *Nocturnal*.

Rodrigo: Concierto de Aranjuez
EMI/Virgin Classics 59024
with Lausanne Chamber Orchestra (Lawrence Foster, conductor)
Rodrigo: *Concierto de Aranjuez, Fantasia para un gentilhombre*; Vivaldi: *Concerto in D major*.

Love Songs & Lullabies
EMI/Virgin Classics 61480
with Benita Valente (soprano), Thomas Allen (baritone), Gaudencio Thiago de Mello (percussion)
Montaña: *Porro*; Villa-Lobos: *Estrela e lua nova*; Jobim: *Canta mais*; Brahms: *Wiegenlied*; Lorca: *El café de Chinitas, Nana de Sevilla, Sevillanas*; Anon.: *Salley Gardens, Drink to Me Only with Thine Eyes*; Britten: *I Will Give My Love an Apple*,

Sailor-boy; Niles: *I Wonder as I Wander, Go 'Way from My Window*; Foster: *Jeanie with the Light Brown Hair*; Schubert: *Wiegenlied*; Goldfaden: *Rojinkes mit Mandlen*; Bonfa: *Manhã de Carnaval*; Thiago de Mello: *Cunhã-tan do Andira, Varando Furos*; Ginastera: *Canción al arbol del olvido*; Seiber: *Le Rossignol, Marguerite elle est malade*; Martini: *Plaisir d'amour*; Madriguera: *Adios*.

Road to the Sun/Estrada do Sol: Latin Romances
EMI/Virgin Classics 59591
Sainz de la Maza: *Zapateado*; Rodrigo: *Invocacion y Danza*; Barrios: *La Catedral*; Paz Abreu: *Quejas*; Jobim: *Estrada do Sol*; Tárrega: *Capricho Arabe*; Brouwer: *El Decameron Negro*; Villa-Lobos: *Sentimental Melody, Etude no. 8*; Albéniz: *Mallorca, Asturias*.

J.S. Bach: Complete Lute Suites
EMI/Virgin Classics 59503
Bach: *Suite in E Major (BWV 1006a), Suite in G Minor (BWV 995), Suite in E Minor (BWV 996), Suite in C Minor (BWV 997)*.

Rhapsody in Blue/West Side Story
Concord Concerto CCD 42012
with Carlos Barbosa-Lima (guitar)
Bernstein: *I Feel Pretty, Scherzo/Somewhere, Cha-Cha/Meeting Scene, Something's Coming, Maria, America, Cool, Tonight, I Have a Love/Finale*; Gershwin: *Jasbo Brown Blues, Liza, Prelude no. 3, Rhapsody in Blue*.

Brazil, with Love
Concord Picante CCD 4322
with Carlos Barbosa-Lima (guitar)
Jobim: *Luiza, Gabriella, Chovendo na Rosiera, Garoto, Felicidade, Estrada do Sol*; Vianna (Pixinguinha): *Passatempo, Vou Vivendo, Pretencioso, Carinhoso*; Nazareth: *Brejeiro, Apanehi-te, Caraquinho, Bambino, Odeon*.

Black Topaz (by Joan Tower)
New World 80470-2
Tower: *Snow Dreams* (with Sharon Isbin, guitar; Carol Wincenc, flute); other non-guitar works.

Websites: www.sharonisbin.com
www.schirmer.com/composers/kernis/bio.html

2

Eliot Fisk: An American in Europe
February 1996

Eliot Fisk was born in Philadelphia, Pennsylvania, on August 10, 1954. He studied guitar with Oscar Ghiglia, Alirio Diaz and Andrés Segovia. While at the Yale School of Music, he studied with harpsichordist and Scarlatti scholar Ralph Kirkpatrick. Fisk founded the guitar department at the Yale School of Music and currently teaches at the Salzburg Mozarteum in Austria and the New England Conservatory of Music in Boston. Having lived in Austria and Germany, he now resides in Granada, Spain. His recordings include transcriptions of works by Bach, Beethoven, Haydn, Mozart, Scarlatti and Paganini, as well as new works by composers such as Robert Beaser, Luciano Berio, Nicholas Maw and George Rochberg. His passion for chamber music is fulfilled through his many collaborations with artists such as Paula Robison, Victoria de los Angeles, Gidon Kremer and the Juilliard and Shanghai quartets.

My interview with Eliot Fisk took place in four languages (one of which I actually speak). Fisk's multilingual, rapid-fire sentences made me feel like I was sitting in a UN Security Council meeting without headphones. Had I not brought the conversation to a close after more than two hours, Fisk would have surely outlasted the Energizer batteries in my tape recorder. The combination of intellect and emotion, assuredness and constant questioning, and tradition and experimentation that permeate his performances, recordings and conversations have their origins in his deeply held views about music and the world at large.

Those Who Can ...

Jim Tosone: In the fall of 1996, you returned to teaching in America by joining the guitar faculty at the New England Conservatory of Music. You've held a rather unique series of teaching positions over the past twenty years and I'd like to understand your thinking and the events behind them. To begin at the beginning, you started the guitar department at Yale in 1977. Why did you want to create a new guitar department, instead of going to an established one at another school?

Eliot Fisk: Well, I was a 22-year-old ignorant fool. But I did have the idea that the guitar belonged at Yale and that it should be associated with a university as prestigious as Yale. Of all the Ivy League schools, Yale has had the richest music tradition. I was fortunate in that at that time there was a wonderful, progressive dean named Phillip Nelson. If it hadn't been for him, the guitar probably would never have gotten started at Yale. But it did and they stuck with it, thank goodness. Of course Yale being Yale, the first thing they did once they had a competent music administrator was to fire him. That's absolutely typical of Yale. They like incompetence in arts administrators because they don't want the arts and the music schools to get too big for their britches. After Phil Nelson came a great decline. I must say I am very proud of the teaching I did at Yale, even though I was at the start of my career and compared to the way I teach now, really didn't know what I was doing. But interestingly, a number of students who studied with me at Yale in those early years turned out to be successful in other musical fields. Composers Arthur Levering and Sebastian Currier were both former students of mine.

JT: How has the guitar department fared since you left in 1982?

EF: I'm delighted with the manner in which Ben Verdery has taken over the program, developed it and kept it going. I admire so much his enthusiasm and capacity to be active in so many different styles. He has a wonderfully human way of working with the kids and getting them charged up. He did me a great honor when he said he wanted to start an Eliot Fisk prize at Yale. I said, "All right, under one condition. I will give you a check for $1,000; you match that and I will also play a benefit concert at some point. We will take in more money and use it as seed money so the fund will be self-sustaining." Originally, Ben was going to take the money out of his salary. Find yourself a colleague who'll do that. He's already matched the $1,000, and all we have to do now is find a time when I can give the benefit concert. It's not gonna be any great shakes of money in the prize kitty, but it will be enough so some student can buy his books for the year or [laughs] eat at Naples Pizza.

JT: You then took a position at the Hochschule für Musik in Cologne in 1982. How did that appointment come about?

EF: Indirectly. Around 1980, [guitarist] Oscar Ghiglia, who I studied with in the summers at Aspen and who was then in Europe, said to me, "You really should come to Europe. You ought to be known there. Why don't you come to the contest in Gargnano, Italy?" So I went and did this little guitar contest, which turned out to be the only guitar contest I ever won. The reason was because two of my former teachers — Ghiglia and Alirio Diaz — were on the jury, so I felt at home and was able to play well. In the audience were two German guitarists: Thomas Müller-Pering and Ansgar Krause. They told me about the teaching job in Cologne and said, "It's up for grabs. Why don't you try out for it?" I thought, "I don't really want to go to Germany to teach." But I decided to stop off there anyway and play a concert, just in case they might want me for the job. I didn't know that about forty people had applied. I was the last and a complete unknown. Well, the concert was a huge success and I was offered the job right after it.

JT: Was it a hard choice, to leave America?

EF: The reason I decided to leave America in the early '80s was that when I'd get together with musician friends, I wanted to talk about what they thought about a certain piece or musical esthetic or other philosophical questions. But so many of them wanted to talk just about who your agent was and how many concerts you had lined up. It was so ass-backward. So I thought, "I have this great opportunity in Germany. I could live on the salary and I'll get my German into shape." I expected to go for a year or two, but then I met my wife and everything changed.

JT: Recently, you tried to start up the Andrés Segovia Institute at the Mozarteum in Salzburg.

EF: Yeah. It was actually promised to me. I went through a whole lot of chicanery — countless meetings and attempts to get funding. It just went on and on with no end in sight. I finally got sick of being jerked around. Basically, it was a political thing. They have other institutes there and the other institute leaders didn't want any resources being diverted from them. I tried very hard but never did get it through.

JT: But you're still doing something in Salzburg.

EF: I don't really have an institute, but I do have a fantastic class and an assistant named Joaquin Clerch. Joaquin has transformed Hallein, this little town outside of Salzburg where he lives, into a guitar center. He founded a festival there and we're also doing all kinds of outreach programs. He's a brilliant player and a wonderful teacher. He's so generous with his students. When he started in Salzburg he had no money at all, but every student that came through stayed at his house — often for days on end.

There are about fifteen countries represented in my class. But it's only possible for me to carry that kind of student load because Joaquin is there when I'm away. A lot of the students are really advanced — what we in America would call at the tutorial level. Some are in their late twenties, even early thirties, and come from very far away — like Madrid, Berlin, Florence and Barcelona. It's flattering that they make enormous sacrifices to come and work with me.

JT: Are they hoping to have professional performing careers?

EF: They're not deluded about that. I tell them straight off the way things are. They're aware that they will have to survive mostly from teaching and the occasional concert. I push them to be versatile. I say, "If there's any kind of rock or jazz or anything like that you can play — do it. If you can collaborate with a dancer, with someone doing film, with a theater group — do it!" Anything you can do, any place you can get the guitar in, any angle you can use — use it! The guitar can be used across a broad range of cultural activities. You know, students today are saying, "What can we do? There are no jobs." But you have to create the jobs. Some musicians still dream about having an impresario handle everything. Those days are gone. The artist must give direction to his career, get people charged up and constantly check up to see if things have really been done. What musicians now have to do is a harbinger of what everybody's going to have to do in the twenty-first century. If musicians are alerted while they're in school to the need for them to be inventive, flexible and versatile, they're not going to be so much worse off than lawyers or doctors. Security is in the skills you can bring to the table and in your ability to react to opportunity.

JT: So to bring things full circle, why did you return to teaching in America?

EF: I just missed America. Also, I felt I could bring the deeper understanding I had acquired of the European cultures, which produced much of the guitar repertoire, to the American students. American youth are wonderful to work with because they are utterly fearless. They don't know a lot about the European cultures, but neither are they in awe of those traditions. And finally, I'm always trying to put good people from different countries, including America, in touch with each other to try to create a worldwide melting pot of musicians.

JT: And why the New England Conservatory of Music [NEC]?

EF: I knew the former president of the conservatory, Larry Lesser, from the Festival of the Two Worlds — which is held partly in Spoleto, Italy and partly in Charleston, South Carolina. I participated in both during the '80s. Also, my chamber music partner [flutist] Paula Robison teaches at NEC. Most importantly, NEC was willing to be flexible around my crazy schedule.

Eliot Fisk and flutist Paula Robison following a performance of George Rochberg's *Muse of Fire*, Philadelphia, May 1997 (George Fisk).

A Tale of Two Continents

JT: You've been in Europe for fifteen years now. How does America look when viewed through the prism of Europe?

EF: In Europe, government interference stifles initiative. Taxation, which can reach fifty to sixty percent, kills it. There's no comparison between America and Europe in terms of individual initiative and creativity. Government subsidy of the arts, which has been much greater in Europe, is being decreased. Since Europe has less tradition of individual initiative, it's going to be an absolute black hole when the government support goes; whereas in America everything's being cut to smithereens, but things come back. For example, the Syracuse Symphony disappeared and came back from nothing. It's still in there struggling.

JT: The *New York Times* recently reported that, as some of the government support subsidies are decreasing in the United States, community groups are stepping in to fill the void.

EF: That would be much better. It's infinitely preferable for people to be actively involved in their own destiny than to have a government handout.

JT: I heard an interesting comment when the French went on strike last year because of the proposed cuts in their retirement benefits. Someone said, "In France, the people go on strike against the government, but in the U.S., the government goes on strike against the people."

EF: I was in Paris during that strike! I had to record Luciano Berio's *Sequenza XI* for Deutsche Grammophon. The whole transportation system was shut down. I got to the Arc de Triomphe by bus and couldn't get any further. I could hardly cross the street because the cars were bumper to bumper. So I had to walk for two hours with all my bags. Next morning I had to get up and record *Sequenza* with Berio sitting in the control booth. But it went very well. Sometimes adversity breeds something good.

JT: One of the criticisms in the U.S.—I don't know if this applies in Europe as well—is that subsidies often go to the groups or organizations that have the most political clout or are the most prestigious. So the money's not going to some small classical guitar program, but to the Kennedy Center, the Lincoln Center, the Metropolitan Opera. And the original goal of supporting artists who need a leg up and haven't already established their careers has been subverted.

EF: I don't know enough about the financing in the U.S., but in Europe, that's true. They sponsor the big established artists. The city of Cologne spends millions of marks every year for their opera.

JT: David Tanenbaum said that the city of Munich's art budget is bigger than the entire NEA budget.

EF: Yeah, but who's getting it? It's being dished out to a very small group of people. It's very elitist and not necessarily so halcyon as it looks on paper. Also, frankly, the quality of the musicians in Europe is not as high as it is in America. If you're a musician in America, you're a musician 'cause you are hopelessly in love with music. There's little room for subsidized mediocrity in America. So in Europe, American musicians have a very good reputation. Europeans say, "How come so many good musicians?" I say, "Very simple; in America, you're great or you starve." And that's why in Europe so much junk gets subsidized.

JT: Do you think there's a bit of defeatism when you go the subsidy route, perhaps a sense that art cannot be self-supporting in the marketplace?

EF: Well, art's never been self-supporting. It's always had some patron. The problem with self-supporting art is that the job of the artist is to be a bit ahead of people. If art is too accessible, if the common denominator is too low, you lose a lot of the very purpose of doing art. So you have this paradox that, yes, we'd all love for art to be self-supporting, but if you simplify it too much, you obviate the need for making art. Paganini handled this dilemma by having different categories of artistic creation. He dedicated the Caprices "alli artisti" ("to the artists"), to the conoscenti, the people who really know what is going on. Then he dedicated all the guitar quartets "alle amatrici di Niccolò Paganini" ("to my female fans, to my lady admirers"). Those pieces were house music. Paganini played first violin and had his fun while his lady friends or "amatrici" played with him. And then he had the violin concertos for the big concert stage. So he had three levels: one where he was out in front of the field, one which was a sort of middle ground and one which was strictly popular.

JT: It sounds to me like Richard Rodney Bennett's solution. He writes serious music, what he calls his "personal" music. He also writes movie soundtracks that provide much of his financial support. And he plays jazz piano in cabaret-type settings. Another model is the Charles Ives solution — you can write whatever kind of music you want, but you have to sell insurance during the day to support yourself.

EF: I always cite Ives as a good example of how tough America is on its artists. Other countries have embraced their artists and supported them *because* they are from that country. In America, it's almost the opposite. If you're an American artist, we act like you can't be any good and so you have to go someplace else to make it.

JT: So how do you guide students in this complex environment?

EF: In the career development of young players, I tell them that what they're learning in the conservatory is mostly "alli artisti." Your performances there are for the conoscenti. It's different when you give concerts that reach out to the general community. When I do outreach programs, I may play *Recuerdos de la Alhambra*, a fast study by Villa-Lobos, the Bach Prelude in E major, maybe some Lauro and a Paganini Caprice at the end. I don't play Petrassi's *Nunc*, Bach's Third Lute Suite or other pieces that are difficult for the average person to grasp. I try to gauge the public without being condescending.

JT: Let's turn to another European-American topic. In the '50s, '60s, and '70s, the British and other European composers dominated the contemporary classical guitar repertoire...

EF: Because Julian Bream and John Williams were active in Britain, people writing for them were also there.

JT: ...but in the '80s and '90s, there's been a shift in focus to the American and non-European schools of music. What's your view of the current state of contemporary music in Europe?

EF: Europe is slowly coming out of a dinosaur age where everything in contemporary music had to be incomprehensible and difficult. Think about those reams and reams of experimental music that were supported by tax dollars, which were played once and never again. All that horribly academic crap that had only snob appeal and no intrinsic esthetic value. Europeans have this mania about originality and a bias against the Postmodern composers, who are now writing tonally again. Hans Werner Henze once wrote an A minor chord and was practically lynched by his colleagues.

JT: I can imagine how they must have reacted to Terry Riley's *In C* [laughs].

EF: Strangely enough, Minimalism caught on. Why? Because it was an "'ism." It was definable, it had a school and it could be pigeonholed. So Minimalism was accepted as a movement. But not Postmodern music, which defies categories. Now Europe is slowly emerging into a new populism.

LOST IN THE TRANSLATION

JT: The great composers of the Classical and Romantic periods have been difficult or impossible to transcribe for classical guitar. Why is it so hard to preserve the integrity of this music yet make it playable and natural sounding on the guitar?

EF: You've put your finger right on it. That was a period in music history where the guitar went out of fashion because it wasn't very well suited to the style. Sonata form is a bit antithetical to the guitar's possibilities, in the sense that it's dealing with transpositions of a fifth of specific musical material. That can be a problem on the guitar, since it often takes you out of the realm of the open strings. For example, Schubert's music has many modulations that play in a virtuosic way with enharmonic possibilities. He uses third-related keys and the extremes of the flat and sharp keys. Composers for the guitar during this period, like Sor and Giuliani, did the best they could but couldn't transcend the limitations of the instrument. In Sor's case the result was melodic monotony; in Giuliani's, harmonic monotony.

JT: Does anything from that period work on the guitar?

EF: Certain aspects of the classical and romantic forms can suit the guitar well. Beethoven could have written a set of Bagatelles or Schubert a *Ländler* suite. The Intermezzi of Brahms or the world of Schumann's *Kinderszenen* would've suited the guitar brilliantly. Unfortunately, there was no contact between those composers and the guitar subculture. I often dreamed of doing Schumann. As Segovia demonstrated, some pieces from Schumann's *Album für die Jugend* [*Album for the Young*] can be done — and perhaps some of his occasional pieces.

JT: Yet you've been able to make successful transcriptions of Haydn, Mozart and Paganini. What's your secret?

EF: Actually, I wasn't able to do much Haydn, Mozart or Beethoven. They are extremely resistant. Haydn is more malleable because he comes out of the Baroque style. But the jeweled perfection of Mozart's creations is such that there's almost nothing you can do. Altering a single note affects the integrity. You can transcribe some of his occasional pieces or his Divertimenti for solo guitar, but only if you simplify them a lot. Beethoven is another composer who is extremely difficult to arrange for guitar. I have arranged some of his smaller pieces or early sets of variations. But again, the organic integrity of the pieces is such that changing even the slightest thing gets you into trouble. Paganini is a different case. His violin playing was clearly helped by his guitar playing, by the guitar's chordal nature, by its arpeggiated style. He took a lot from the guitar, like scordatura and left-hand pizzicato. He's a composer whose way of writing is more receptive to the guitar than any of the other classical composers.

JT: Do you think you'll do any more transcriptions like the ones you did of Paganini?

EF: I think some of the transcriptions I'd like to make in the future may be more in the way of creative transcriptions — more like arrangements than my earlier, more literal, transcriptions. I'd like to take pieces by de Visée or Corbetta and really jazz 'em up.

JT: You mentioned the Baroque style. Your transcriptions of Scarlatti harpsichord Sonatas are generally of pieces that haven't been done before by other guitarists, often because of their technical difficulty. Are there any techniques you use to make them playable while retaining their original flavor?

EF: In approaching the work of any composer, you must approach that composer individually. You've got a number of composers who were born around 1685 — Scarlatti, Bach, Handel, Weiss and Telemann — all with different styles. To understand any composer, the best source is the composer himself. Students ask me what book they should read about Bach ornamentation, but the best source on Bach is his music. He didn't write much about how to interpret his music; he was too busy writing the damn stuff! So the more pieces by Bach you know, the more you'll have a feel for his style of ornamentation and for what he might've done at any given point.

JT: How then, might you approach Scarlatti?

EF: With the Scarlatti transcriptions, I would, for example, look at how he sometimes creates a harpsichord dynamic by the number of notes he uses. More notes mean more sound and fewer notes mean less sound. Scarlatti's harpsichord writing is such that the dynamics are practically automatic on that instrument. But when playing these works on the guitar, the effects are no longer automatic and must be recreated by the performer. It's always a fine line between how many notes you leave in and how many you leave out. I may reach a point where, to make a piece playable, I have to leave out so much that it is no longer a good transcription. I have thrown out as much as I've kept. This is an important thing in the development of any artist — the ability to ruthlessly cut, to throw out what's not good, to criticize yourself. It comes with maturity. There is no shortcut. I have spent a lot of my life ruminating and wrestling with problems occasioned by transcription. I feel that some of my earlier transcriptions were too complicated. They need to be streamlined and made more fluent.

JT: It's almost like language translation.

EF: Transcription can be compared to the art of translation in language. An overly literal translation can become so cumbersome that the sense of the original is lost, while a freer translation may convey more of the sense of the original. Likewise in music. A freer transcription, particularly when arranging keyboard music for guitar, can create more of the sense of the original than if you just go note for note. We are always searching for the right answer, which may shift from day to day and from generation to generation. This is why every generation has to practically reinvent the wheel on its own terms. This is why the act of making my own transcriptions is not an act of disrespect towards past transcriptions. Quite the contrary, it's a recognition that I could never render a transcription in the way, let's say, Segovia or Tárrega were able to. As Dante put it at the start of *The Divine Comedy*, "Nel mezzo del cammin di nostra vita, Mi ritrovai per una selva oscura, Che la diritta via era smarrita." ["In the middle of the journey of our life, I found myself in a dark forest where the straight path was lost."] This is the beginning of artistry, when you first find yourself in the middle of that dark wood — lost — and you have to find your own personal way out. It's a constant search, a constant seeking, a constant reevaluation. This has been the thrust of my life in music.

Breaking New Ground

JT: Regarding new works for the guitar, you once said in an article on Berio, "Composers who hear really well, and can write what they hear, can write successfully for the guitar." In addition to Berio, what other contemporary composers have this ability?

EF: Robert Beaser, absolutely. He's the first composer I ever worked with. I met him at Yale when he was around eighteen or nineteen years old. I asked if he played guitar and he said, "No, but I think I can figure out where a C major chord is." So I kept asking him, "Bobby, where's my Sonata? Where's my Sonata?" The resulting piece he wrote for me, *Canti Nocturni*, he wrote by ear. It's a non-tonal piece, in an idiom like Henze's second *Tento*. I might have changed but one or two notes over eighteen minutes of music. He's a wonderful example of somebody who hears perfectly. I remember a concert at Yale in 1973 of works by student composers. Bobby's contribution was a piece of about one minute. In the program notes it said, "The composer has described this piece as 'short.'" When I heard it, it was like a pearl amidst sand. I thought, "Whoa, where did this guy come from? This is a major twentieth century composer." He's gone on to demonstrate that in pieces like *Notes on a Southern Sky* and *Mountain Songs* for flute and guitar, which have both received acclaim. I'm working with him now in commissioning a guitar concerto. George Rochberg is another composer who intuitively and writing by ear produced two works for flute and guitar for me, and then a wonderful set of pieces based on Tin Pan Alley tunes called *American Bouquet*. And my final example is Nicholas Maw, who wrote a mammoth work called *Music of Memory*, inspired by a string quartet of Mendelssohn. I think what unites these four composers, with whom I've worked intensively, is a seriousness of purpose. They are able to write entertainingly, but are looking for something thoughtful to say. I consider all the works that I have from these composers to be pieces that will stay in the repertory and will inspire and challenge guitarists for a long time to come.

JT: It's interesting that, except for Beaser, they were all born before World War II. Do you think there's a generational difference between pre- and post–World War II composers?

Eliot Fisk (right) and composer Robert Beaser at the Aspen Music Festival, Aspen, Colorado, 1975 (Charles Abbott).

EF: There is a difference. I try to keep up on the young composers and I admire a lot of them. I am interested in soliciting scores and getting to know them. I have often premiered works by younger composers when asked, but haven't fallen in love with the results.

JT: Speaking of Berio again, for many of his *Sequenzas* for unaccompanied instruments, he created a corresponding *Chemin*, which has additional material layered on the original work. You premiered *Chemin* for guitar and orchestra in September of '92. What perspective does this *Chemin* provide on the guitar *Sequenza*?

EF: As Berio has said, the best commentary on a piece of music is another version of that piece. If you know the *Sequenza* intimately, you can understand so many things about it through the *Chemin*. Of course not everybody has the orchestrational virtuosity of a Luciano Berio. But one of the fascinating things about the *Chemin* is the extent to which he echoes the guitar all over the orchestra. There's one place near the end of the *Sequenza* where he has a tremolondo lasting for a quarter note on B across two strings that first goes up to a B-flat on the first string, then up to C, and then up to a C-sharp. In the original these are single notes. I suggested and got Berio's permission to put two B's under each of those single notes. This makes much more of an accent. In the *Chemin*, he imitates that idea with the orchestra.

JT: So your intent was not for harmonic support but to get a bigger sound?

EF: Well, both actually. Berio writes sforzando, but he writes only one note. One note will never sound really sforzando unless it's played as a Bartók pizzicato. But that was not idiomatic. Adding the open B's were. The interesting thing was that in the *Chemin* he took up this idea that I had suggested to him and imitated it. There are other ideas I suggested to him about the *Sequenza* that are not in the published music of the *Sequenza*, but appear in the *Chemin*.

JT: I was at the concert when you premiered the *Sequenza* in New York and your music fell over....

EF: And my glasses flew off and my tie fell over the guitar! Wasn't that hysterical? I was strumming wildly and turning a page when my glasses flew off into the front row of the audience. I retrieved my glasses and I tried to get back into the piece but then this long tie of mine was hanging over the front of the guitar, muffling the sound. At that point everybody just started to laugh. I was in the middle of the piece, so I couldn't really go back to the beginning. So I just finished the sucker. What was I going to do? Everybody who was there remembers only that about that concert.

JT: The thing I remember most, actually, is that you played the piece again for the encore. It's an enormous work to do once, let alone twice. I guess you felt a special obligation to the piece given it was the New York premiere.

EF: You're exactly right. It was the New York premiere and I absolutely wanted the piece to be heard in its entirety. My manager said, "This is probably the only time in history that that piece has been played as an encore." I think Berio would've enjoyed that bit of theater. I mean, this is the same guy who wrote a *Sequenza* for trombone where the performer comes out dressed in costume and halfway through the piece stops and asks, "Why?"

JT: Your incident reminds me of the Aaron Jay Kernis concert at the 92nd Street Y. The Muir String Quartet was performing Richard Danielpour's Quintet for Piano and Strings. And just when they were getting to the most intense part, BAM!—the first violinist breaks a string. She runs offstage to change the string and, of course, there's that awkward moment while we all wait. Finally, the cellist stands up and says, "I'd like to ask the composer if he still feels that breaking the violin string at this point is structurally optimal."

EF: [Laughter] Well that's part of the fun. This has been a time in music where we view these mishaps — which can be very communicative — as horrible errors. It's ridiculous; they are part of being human. I remember a concert in Aspen where the late William Masselos was playing a Saint-Saëns concerto. He was playing it so well, then he had a memory lapse. He went over and had a brief look at the score and started right back in. When he got done everybody stood up and screamed with jubilation. 'Cause he came back from the memory lapse and played gloriously. It's something I won't forget.

JT: It shows a person's character, how they react when these things happen.

EF: That's it. *That's* what you love in an artist. And that's what we should be trying to develop in young people. I think there's been a tendency for people to define music making in negative terms, in other words, by not making mistakes. But I define something only in positive terms. Did somebody give me something? Segovia, when he'd come toward the end of his life, sometimes forgot or made small mistakes. But those Segovia concerts are etched in my memory forever. He would always do something that you just couldn't believe.

THE REDEFINED VIRTUOSO

JT: You crossed a great divide last year — your fortieth birthday. How has this affected your perspective?

EF: My focus as I approach middle age, which will hopefully be a golden age in my work, is to reach outward. My future plans will involve less solo work and more collaboration. At present, I'm trying to teach myself jazz and flamenco, which is a pretty tall order. I think it will make me more flexible and a better musician. I've been performing quite a bit with Paco Peña, who's been very patient in helping me through some basic flamenco. And when in the summer I go to my house in Granada there's a good friend of mine, Juan Gimenez, who helps me get into the compás. I just did a project with the Turtle Island String Quartet. They're helping me get into jazz.

JT: Is part of the reason for learning jazz to try to recapture the lost improvisational aspect of classical music?

EF: Absolutely. And also certain rhythmic things. Steve Erquiaga did a wonderful arrangement of *Green Dolphin Street* for me and the Turtle Island String Quartet. The rhythms are so difficult. They're always a little bit after the beat or a little bit before the beat. Ironically, I find classical music much freer rhythmically than flamenco or that kind of jazz. We learned from Segovia how a measure could expand or contract at will, which was an important part of sound. Flamenco sounds free, but it's not. Rhythmically, it's rigidly structured. Paco taught me by ear and wouldn't let me write anything down 'till I learned the whole thing by memory. It was brutal instruction, but I've found it so helpful. I also work with Burhan Ösal, a Turkish artist who plays saz, oud, tambour and all kinds of percussion instruments. And I play with Lusero Tena, who is probably the only castanets virtuoso in the world, and I've performed with tenor John Aler. It's funny. One of the first string quartets I remember playing with was the Juilliard String Quartet, one of the first violinists was Gidon Kremer and one of the first singers was Victoria de los Angeles. The first jazz guitarist I performed with in public was Joe Pass and the first flamenco guitarist I played with was Paco Peña. In each case I was in way over my head. But learning new things has always been kind of a crash course for me.

JT: I'd like to talk about a topic you've had to deal with extensively, but from a couple of different angles. First, Berio has said, "Virtuosos are not only of the fingers but of the mind." How do you react when people attribute your virtuosity to natural talent or, as they did with Paganini, to a pact with the devil?

EF: Well, it's a mixture. Paganini was obviously an enormous talent, but was also forced to practice when he was very young by his father. The old adage "ninety percent perspiration, ten percent inspiration" is pretty accurate.

JT: A guitarist once said to me in a discussion about you, "Sure, I'd be a virtuoso too if I had an eleven-inch pinkie on my left hand." To use an old cliché, does size matter?

EF: [Laughs] There are advantages and disadvantages. For example, you'll see my fourth finger is about a quarter of an inch longer on the left hand, just from working it. So I do have the advantage of a big stretch. But it isn't just the length of the pinkie; it's the extension that I can get between the third and fourth fingers. I can reach from F in the 1st fret on the bottom string to the C in the eighth fret on the top string. Also, I can reach four or five frets with a third-fourth finger extension. But on the downside, I can hardly play the opening chord, let's say, of the B-flat major study of Sor. I have to practically cross the left hand fingers. So that instead of using 1-2-3-4 on the second fret, I have to use 1-3-2-4, because I hardly have room for my fingers. I also have to struggle enormously in fugal playing to keep my fingers out of the way of the adjacent strings, particularly since I play with a strong attack that really gets the strings vibrating. It's very easy for me to cause a slight buzz, which can be a real problem when recording.

I just have a different set of problems than other guitarists. Pepe Romero, who's got a relatively small hand, shows that size is of no significance. You couldn't have a more perfect technique than Pepe.

JT: How does your Humphrey Millenium help and complement your style?

EF: Well, I play that instrument because of its versatility. The raised neck certainly helps me get up in the higher positions. Some pieces are only playable with that guitar. For example, *Music of Memory* by Maw I would not want to play with any other guitar. The Berio and certain difficult transcriptions are very conducive to that guitar.

JT: The scale length you're using is...

EF: Unfortunately, the "66" I play has the best sound.

JT: You'd prefer a 650mm scale length?

EF: Yeah. I think it's a more natural size. Even with my big hand, I don't like stretching any more than anybody else does.

ON THE SHOULDERS OF GIANTS

JT: In the Segovia tribute issue of *Guitar Review*, you characterized the Segovian legacy as one that is international in scope, has a repertoire that spans five centuries, seeks out non-guitarist composers and values publishing and teaching, as well as performing. Do you feel like you're carrying on his legacy?

EF: I'm trying as much as I can to carry on in that great romantic tradition. There is a place for someone who is really conversant with European culture. Of course not all the repertory that we have from Segovia is something that everybody wants to play. But we shouldn't underestimate composers like Ponce, Castelnuovo-Tedesco, Tansman and Villa-Lobos. I'm preparing a CD dedicated to Tedesco. He has a catalog for guitar that's enormous. But with few exceptions, nobody plays the stuff. It may not be the most profound music on earth, but it is exquisitely crafted, some of it's damn good, it's accessible to the public and it's fun to play. But talk about music that needs translation and alteration! Tedesco sometimes writes for the guitar as if the bottom string were tuned to both D and E in the same piece. So often what he's written is not playable without rewriting. That's part of the fun of interpreting him.

JT: Carrying on a musical legacy reminds me of Wynton Marsalis, who's trying to do a similar thing in jazz. He feels strongly that jazz composers and performers need to understand the lineage from Jelly Roll Morton, Ellington, Parker, Monk and Coltrane to Miles Davis in order to interpret and progress jazz.

Eliot Fisk and Maestro Andrés Segovia at the home of publisher and editor Rose Augustine, New York City (courtesy of Rose Augustine).

EF: Absolutely. I feel the same thing. Whether you want to or not, you're part of the tradition and should learn from it. In my case, I had the good fortune to directly know and work with Segovia, Ruggiero Ricci, Victoria de los Angeles and Lusero Tena. I very much want to pass on to my students the knowledge I gained from those experiences.

JT: Segovia's legacy has been the subject of debate for a number of years. Some say his almost godlike stature in the classical guitar world stifled its evolution.

EF: Segovia was an enormous figure. He was like Mount Everest. And being a strong personality, he formed everything around him. It's true that Segovia didn't get compositions from Bartók, Stravinsky, Prokofiev and a lot of composers we would like to have pieces from. Maybe he was in a position to have done that, but on the other hand, who among us has done as much as he did? If other people were interested, they could've tried to commission them. Besides, this criticism of Segovia is pointless. If you disagree with what Segovia did, take that energy and go out and do something positive. Otherwise, shut up. Now, it's different when John Williams, who studied with Segovia, says he wasn't a good teacher and the like. There I see a difference in generation. I said to John, "Look, you had a much more difficult time with Segovia than I did. You had a father-son thing with him, while I had a grandfather-grandson thing." I didn't have Segovia butting into my life, telling me to do this and do that. That's why John needed to rebel violently. I had no rebellion against Segovia. My rebellion is in truth against Bream and Williams; because I have to confess I'm a bit disappointed in both of them. From time immemorial, it has been the practice of one generation to pass on to the next what it learned. But my generation has almost no guitar fathers. Ghiglia and Diaz taught and were accessible, but Bream and Williams were not.

JT: You're talking primarily about teaching? After all, both of them have worked hard to commission new works and get composers to write for the guitar.

EF: They've both given immensely. But growing up, I was very saddened by their inaccessibility. I feel that my generation lost a lot because of that. In a way, we all need to rebel. The next generation will rebel against us. It's one thing I encourage when teaching. I want to give my students the strength to tell me to go to hell. 'Cause if they can tell me to go to hell, they can tell the world. Ultimately, that will help them, not to be difficult but rather to have conviction for the long struggle.

JT: What about the other major figures that contributed to your musical development?

EF: My first teacher, William Viola, wasn't even a professional guitarist. He was an engineer at IBM. That was the only regular guitar instruction I ever had, from age twelve to fourteen. The rest was trial and error and good fortune. I studied in the summers, first with Oscar Ghiglia, then with Alirio Diaz and finally with Segovia. I also worked with [harpsichordists] Ralph Kirkpatrick and Albert Fuller at Yale.

JT: Ralph Kirkpatrick was one of the foremost authorities on Scarlatti. What did you take away from your relationship with him?

EF: Number one, I was fortunate with Ralph in that I did not play his instrument. Number two, I met him toward the end of his life when he was much softer. So my relationship with him was benevolent, whereas his effect on many of his earlier students was often quite harmful. He really cut into them at times. What I learned most of all from him was the ability to find the fundamental structures beneath the florid ornamentation of the baroque style. We worked a lot with figured bass and reducing ornamentation to its simplest elements so I could understand and reconstruct the underlying form. I also have a very close relationship with Oscar Ghiglia. Although I went through the father-son rebellion with him very strongly, any disagreements we might have had are in the past. Oscar's the kind of person who, for example when I studied with him in Aspen, would buy everyone ski lift tickets. He'd pay for everything 'till his money ran out. Ralph Kirkpatrick never took a cent from me. And Segovia? All the lessons I had with Segovia, I never paid. If you had dared breathe the idea of paying him, it would've been the end of the relationship. I know people who've studied with famous musicians who certainly got their pound of flesh out of the students, typically when the student was at the worst point in his career

Eliot Fisk (right) and guitarist Oscar Ghiglia at the Aspen Music Festival, Aspen, Colorado, 1975 (Charles Abbott).

economically. I think if you've reached a certain level, it behooves you to be generous to your future colleagues.

SPANNING THE CENTURIES

JT: I went back and I looked at the musical periods represented on your albums. You have at least half a dozen composers from all of the major musical periods on one CD. Why do you think your interest is so broad, instead of more focused?

EF: Well, I don't come from a musical family. I'm the first artist in the history of my family. I wish I had had better musical training earlier. I didn't really learn music theory till I got to Yale. But I have a broad cultural base and have always been attracted to different eras. As Berio says, anyone worthy of being called a virtuoso has to be capable of addressing the music of the past and the present. To really understand Western music you've got to go back in time and place. This is one of the advantages of our era, this ability to traipse across the centuries. I've walked the streets of Rome, Paris, Berlin and Granada. When I play *Granada* by Albéniz, I have the city in my head. When I listen to *Don Giovanni* by Mozart, I look at the Italian libretto, and I can taste what they're saying.

JT: Direct sensory experience is very important to you.

EF: Indispensable. The solar plexus decides. Ralph [Kirkpatrick] always said that.

JT: But at the same time, you have an affinity for structure. Even on your albums that are mostly collections of pieces, you organize them into a logical framework.

EF: I definitely think structurally when I'm doing a CD, particularly in terms of numerical balance and weight. And I often play numbers games. I use threes or sixes, or sometimes a mirror structure like 1-3-4-4-3-1 or 1-3-1. In the case of the *Fantasies* record, I tried to use the idea of three, since it contained the three *Tentos* by Henze. My CD *Segovia* is based on the principle of four. The four pieces that bear Segovia's name act as pillars that separate sixteen (4 × 4) folk song settings, twelve (3 × 4) transcriptions and four Preludes or Studies. But these programming ideas have to work viscerally as well as in the abstract. If I were to record any of my records again, I might go with completely different structures and orders.

JT: Very Bachian.

EF: I think it helps to communicate. When I'm devising a program with a student, I always say it's got to make psychological sense. Something that, when I go home, I can remember. In the case of the Rochberg *Caprice Variations* CD, there are fifty-one variations. How can you structure fifty-one variations? Rochberg published them in a particular order but said to me, "You make your own order." So I used the grouping 1-24-1-24-1, where Variation 1 begins the recording as kind of a Prelude, Variation 9 (after Brahms) is the mid-point of the recording and Variation 51 (Paganini's theme) is the close. The two groupings of twenty-four are each divided into four suites of six variations. Unfortunately, the way they printed it in the record jacket, that's not clear.

JT: You mentioned in the liner notes that you don't play them in the same order or play the same "suites" in each concert. And you say that listeners can even program their CD players....

EF: You know who first gave me that idea about programming the CD? It was Ruggiero Ricci. He came up with this idea to make a recording of violin concertos by Brahms and Beethoven, where he recorded sixteen or seventeen cadenzas for each. So you can program whichever cadenza you want. Here's a guy seventy-five years old who comes up with an idea for using the technology that's more creative than any of the young violinists.

JT: Do you program things differently now that we're dealing with

Eliot Fisk and composer George Rochberg (left), Portland, Oregon, July 1998 (Judy Blankenship).

sixty to seventy minutes of continuous music on a CD, as opposed to a forty-minute record with two sides?

EF: Honestly, I think sixty minutes is too long, although we have to do it now because of the technology. People want their "money's worth." But my mind stops after about forty to fifty minutes of music, I have to confess. There is something psychologically more right about that amount of time. On the other hand, I love the idea of being able to structure music over sixty or seventy minutes.

JT: The programming on your *Sequenza!* CD is interesting. Other performers generally program the guitar *Sequenza* with other Twentieth Century works. Why did you program it with Scarlatti, Paganini, Mendelssohn and other Berio pieces?

EF: I wanted to make a recording that I myself might like to listen to. And I don't always like listening to a lot of things in the same tonal language in one sitting. Also, I try and program in a way that gives the audience a chance to understand. Take *Music of Memory* by Nicholas Maw. It's a huge work based on various fragments from a Mendelssohn string quartet. In concert, I invariably program it after something by Mendelssohn. I may also put it on the same program with Britten's *Nocturnal*, since that's also a variation piece by a major English composer. And *Nocturnal* I like to program following some Elizabethan stuff, since it is based on a piece by John Dowland. I think programming is important because the audience doesn't always have the previous experience needed to understand a work.

JT: You mentioned your new CD a few moments ago.

EF: I'm going to be recording some Segovia pieces that Mrs. Segovia found amongst Maestro's papers. They will be part of a CD I'm recording in May called *Segovia*. I hope to have it out by Christmas 1996. It will include three different genres of his work — some transcriptions, some original studies and etudes, and most interesting of all, a collection of folk songs that he completed in Montevideo [Uruguay] in 1941. Because it was wartime, they were never published. The countries of origin are very interesting — not only England, Scotland, Ireland, Russia, Finland, but Slovakia, Poland, Serbia, Croatia and Slavonia. I'm playing a benefit for Amnesty International in Salzburg in May and I want to play these pieces in that concert. I will put the Serbian and Croatian songs one after the other to show that at least the music of these two countries is compatible!

JT: Recently, a *Best of Eliot Fisk* CD was released. And boxed sets have become quite popular both in popular and classical music, like Julian Bream's twenty-eight–CD set. If you had an opportunity to do an Eliot Fisk boxed set, how would you organize and package it?

EF: Well, one thing I have to say is that on the re-releases of Segovia's recordings, MCA screwed up the whole point of Segovia's programming by grouping pieces by composer and period. It's ironic that in an age when authenticity means so much in music — playing pieces on original instruments and the like — that such a thing could happen. As for my own retrospective set, there are still a lot of things I'd like to record, so it would be horribly incomplete now. I'd like to do a tribute to baroque guitar music and I want to get around to the Bach's Sonatas and Partitas for solo violin and his 'Cello Suites. I'd also like to do a Weiss CD and a Ponce CD, the latter including the concerto and perhaps some transcriptions of his songs.

JT: I guess we'll have to wait until you've reached Segovia's age and they release the Eliot Fisk fifty–CD set?

EF: That would be nice [laughter].

JT: With all this violin music playing in the background of the restaurant, I have to ask you about the thread of violin-based pieces — Bach, Paganini, Rochberg — that runs through your career. Do you secretly yearn to be violinist?

EF: Yeah. I always said I'm a Jewish violinist who happens to play the guitar [laughter].

JT: In a letter you sent me, you said, "I have so much to say that I don't know where to begin." What haven't you said yet?

EF: There are probably a lot more things, but I honestly can't think of any at the moment.

JT: Maybe I should change the title of the article from *An American in Europe* to *Eliot Speechless!*

EF: *Eliot Speechless!?* I think I prefer *An American in Europe* [laughter].

Concert Reviews

Eliot Fisk, guitar
Metropolitan Museum of Art, New York
December 6, 1996

Eliot Fisk warmed up a December evening in New York with a blazing program of guitar music from Spain. He began with Joaquín Turina's *Fantasia Sevillana*, propelling the piece forward with a powerful rasgueado. Then came three pieces by Regino Sainz de la Maza—*El Vito, Petenera* and *Zapateado*. Although not as well known as Turina, Sainz de la Maza's works were equally engaging. In *Petenera*, Fisk used vibrato to etch clearly the melody in the bass, while in *Zapateado* he brought out the lyrical and fluid nature of melody line.

The highlight of the program was *Nine Canciones Populares*, from recently discovered arrangements of sixteen folksongs by Segovia. Although musically simple, the songs required substantial technique to handle the left-hand bars and stretches while maintaining the necessary legato and rubato. As usual, Fisk was up to the task.

The first half of the program ended with Robert Beaser's setting of the folk song *Shenandoah*. It contains harmonies reminiscent of his *Mountain Songs*, including a section of dense chords with the melody moving through the middle register. Fisk's playing of this difficult piece was a model of expression and precision. Beaser was in the audience, so the appreciative listeners had an opportunity to applaud both composer and performer.

The second half of the program began with Manuel de Falla's *Homenaje, "Le tombeau de Claude Debussy."* Fisk's performance was uncharacteristically cautious, made less effective by a lack of tonal variety. It was followed by de Falla's *Danza del Corregidor* and *Danza del Molinero*, the latter played with a vitality and abandon more characteristic of flamenco or rock than classical guitar.

Joaquín Rodrigo's *Invocación y Danza* is subtitled *"Homenaje à Manuel de Falla."* Since it quotes from deFalla's *Homenaje*, it was fitting that it followed de Falla's piece on the program. Fisk navigated the technically difficult scale, arpeggio and tremolo sections in *Invocación y Danza* with his usual aplomb. He made effective use of tonal colors throughout — dark and distant one moment, bright and powerful the next. His hardy attack and Humphrey Millenium guitar made it possible to hear clearly the tonal and dynamic contrasts throughout the auditorium.

The formal program ended with three pieces by Isaac Albéniz. In *Torre Bermeja* the tempo was correct, but the piece somehow felt hurried — perhaps due to the bright articulation. Fisk's performance of *Granada* was beautifully executed, with the characteristic Segovia sonority and rubato in full employ. *Asturias* was exhilarating rhythmically, although the sound was a bit thin for my taste.

The performance ended with three encores — including a replay of *Shenandoah* — and a cheering audience.

Recording Reviews

Segovia: Canciones Populares
Eliot Fisk, guitar
MusicMasters 67174

Andrés Segovia, in his *A Note on Transcriptions*, wrote, "One who assumes the responsibility of transposing works for the guitar should not only be a magnificent instrumentalist, who knows all the resources of the instrument, but he should be trained in all the rules of music." Eliot Fisk's most recent CD, *Segovia*, showcases Maestro Segovia's talents as both a transcriber and a composer. The disc contains sixteen folk songs he arranged, twelve pieces he transcribed, four Preludes/Studies he composed and four pieces written in his honor.

The recently discovered arrangements are of folk songs from European regions as diverse as Ireland, Poland, Croatia and Spain. Segovia's settings of these songs are simple, but by no means simplistic. His harmonization of the melodies brings out their joy and sadness. Fisk has done a remarkable job of capturing Segovia's interpretive style — the elastic phrasing, the tonal variety resulting from playing notes in alternative positions on the fretboard. At the same time, he avoids the broad the Romantic gestures that typified early twentieth century guitar performance practice.

Segovia's transcriptions of classical works span five centuries of the guitar and its predecessors, but most of the twelve transcriptions on this disc are from the eighteenth and nineteenth centuries. They include Preludes by Brahms and Debussy, two pieces for organ by Franck and a Waltz by Brahms. Segovia's recordings of most of these transcriptions can be found on *The*

Segovia Collection — Vol. 9, The Romantic Guitar (MCAD–10281). Comparing the performances of Segovia and Fisk yields some surprises. In the performances of Luys de Narváez's *Canción del Emperador*, Segovia has (as one would expect) the warmer sound, while Fisk uses stricter tempos and sharper articulation. But the opposite is true in their performances of Schumann's *Romanza*. And in pieces like Franck's *Two Pieces for Organ*, the performances are similar.

Rounding out the disc are four compositions written in tribute to Segovia by prominent twentieth century composers. Mario Castelnuovo-Tedesco, who wrote one of the first twentieth century guitar concertos, composed *Tonadilla sur le nom de Andrés Segovia*. Tedesco combined a classicism with a feel for Mediterranean music to create a soulful work that captures the spirit of Spain, the guitar and Segovia. Fisk's interpretation takes a gentler approach to the work than does Segovia's. The remaining tribute pieces are by Alexander Tansman, the first major composer to write a piece for Segovia and by the French composers Roussel and Milhaud.

Those who first discovered the classical guitar through the recordings and performances of Segovia will, on hearing this recording, be transported instantly back to that time. The music of the man who shaped the guitar in the twentieth century will live on as the guitar moves into the next century.

Paganini: 24 Caprices
Eliot Fisk, guitar
MusicMasters 67092

Mention Niccolò Paganini to music lovers and their first thought is "violin." But classical guitarists think also of his Duos for Violin and Guitar and his 100–plus pieces for solo guitar. Although charming, Paganini's guitar pieces lack the musical depth and technical fireworks of his violin compositions. So it was only a matter of time before guitarists turned their attention to transcribing for their instrument works like Paganini's *24 Caprices* for violin. John Williams paved the way with his recording of Capriccio No. 24. Inspired by that undertaking, Eliot Fisk took up the challenge of transcribing and recording the entire set on his CD *Paganini: 24 Caprices*. With guidance from violinist Ruggerio Ricci, who has made three recordings of the complete set, Fisk has made a credible case for performance of the Caprices on guitar. Admittedly, there are spots where the transcriptions reveal the limits of the guitar, including the difficulty in reproducing the legato of the violin in rapid scale passages and the string noise resulting from difficult left-hand position shifts.

The performance bolts out of the gate with Capriccio No. 1, a piece comprising rapid multi-voice scale passages and high-speed arpeggiated chords in which the melody is outlined in the upper voice. Within the packed two minutes, Fisk uses shifting tonal colors — bright and pointed to warm and rounder — to bring out the dimensions of this Capriccio. Also noteworthy are Capriccios No. 2 and 9, which work as well on the guitar as anything Sor or Giuliani wrote. Interestingly, it is Caprice No. 24 — which contains the famous Paganini theme, 11 Variations and Finale — where the struggle for musicality on the guitar is most pronounced and where the outcome is not entirely convincing.

Nonetheless, Fisk has produced a recording that provides an exhilarating and gratifying listen, while augmenting the guitar repertoire and pushing the envelope of guitar technique.

Rochberg: Caprice Variations
Eliot Fisk, guitar
MusicMasters 67133

Paganini's Caprice No. 24 has been the basis for piano works by Brahms, Liszt and Rachmaninoff. George Rochberg, one of America's leading composers of chamber and orchestral music, adds to that lineage with his *Caprice Variations* for solo violin. Composed in 1970, the seventy-five minute work of fifty-one variations serves as a miniature chronicle of the Baroque, Classical, Romantic and Modern musical styles. Rochberg worked with Fisk to arrange the work for guitar, going so far as to construct a special version of Variation No. 41 that is playable on the guitar. Given Fisk's high level of musicianship and technical ability, the success of the recording depends heavily on the transcriptions themselves. More often than not, they work.

Five of the variations (Nos. 9–13) were inspired by Brahms. The music of Brahms is generally difficult to realize on the guitar, so it comes as a pleasant surprise to find that Variations 9–13 do sound natural on the guitar. In Variation 10, this is made possible through the strategic use of harmonics. Variation 12 uses harmonics in the melody to bring out the music box feeling in the piece. In Variation 13 the long left-hand position jumps used by Fisk create an agitation that brings out the fierce energy of the work.

Two variations (Nos. 7 and 21) were inspired by Beethoven. In Variation 7, Fisk uses heavy vibrato on the dense chords to highlight the Romantic element of the piece. Variation 21 contains echoes of the original Paganini theme and is one of the Allegro variations in the set that works particularly well on the guitar.

Schubert, Mahler and Webern were the inspiration for three other variations (Nos. 8, 44 and 41, respectively). Like the Brahms, the Schubert variation sounds natural on guitar, using alternations of natural and harmonic notes to create tranquil colors and harmonies. The Mahler variation is pleasant but uninteresting. The harmonic language used in the Webern variation works well on the guitar. Other noteworthy performances are Variation 20, with near-perfect precision in the phrasing and articulation, and Variation 35, which Fisk approaches as he does Berio's *Sequenza XI*.

As with the recording of the Paganini Caprices, Fisk has teamed up again with producer John Taylor. Together, at the Parish Church in England, they have created an accurate and uncolored rendering of Fisk's confident and energetic playing.

[Note — the variation numbers in this review refer to Rochberg's variation numbers, not to the order in which the variations appear on Fisk's CD.]

Sequenza!
Eliot Fisk, guitar
MusicMasters 67150

This disc has as its centerpiece a recording of Luciano Berio's *Sequenza XI* for guitar. Berio has described his thinking behind this piece in this way: "I love the guitar, but I was afraid of it. There is a very idiomatic component to guitar writing, a kind of music that goes with the instrument. You cannot destroy this; what I tried to do was use it, to present it in a different context."

Berio clearly succeeded. The fourteen-plus minute work, written in a combination of flamenco, classical and Berio's modern language, pushed the envelope along all dimensions of the guitar. Rapid changes from pianissimo to fortissimo and from dolcemente to violento occur throughout. Both percussion and pitch are used, in the form of tambour, Bartók pizzicato, four different kinds of rasgueado, lightning fast repeated sequences and implied polyphony. *Sequenza XI* begins with a brief, quiet introduction of the intervals that form the basis of the piece(a minor third, a fourth and a tritone).

I had an opportunity to speak to Berio at his 70th Birthday Celebration concert about this disc. Berio said he has heard Fisk's recording of *Sequenza XI* and thinks it is "very good."

Fisk's performance of the *Sequenza* is outstanding. His technical abilities are certainly well suited to the piece, his rasgueado is second to none and he takes the composer's violento markings very seriously. Particularly noteworthy is the way Fisk creates seamless transitions between disparate phrases and the precise control he exercises over the very short crescendos and diminuendos.

Eduardo Fernández's recording of this on his CD *Sequenza* (Victoria VCD19063) is characterized by clear definition of tambour and harmonics, carefully shaped phrases and an ending section that is particularly beautiful. The only drawback to his performance of the *Sequenza* is the need for more agitation in the both rasgueado and repeated sequence parts of the work. Njal Vindenes turns in a credible performance of *Sequenza* on his CD *Avant-Garde Guitar* (Decca 433 076), but his lighter, uneven rasgueado detracts from the overall impact of *Sequenza*. The rest of the Fernández and Vindenes discs are devoted to other Twentieth Century works.

Fisk took a different approach to the programming on his *Sequenza!* disc. He framed *Sequenza XI* with his transcriptions of two other Berio pieces—*Brin* (originally for solo piano) and *Aldo* (for two violins). Fisk also used Berio's statement that "a virtuoso has to be a musician capable of moving within a broad historical perspective" as the basis for his selection of the other compositions on this disc. These included transcriptions of three Sonatas by Scarlatti, *Six Songs Without Words* by Mendelssohn and *Variations on a Theme by Paisiello* by Paganini/Beethoven. The liner notes by Fisk are very informative.

Discography

Canciones Latinas
MusicMasters 67193
with Paula Robison (flute)
Villa-Lobos: *Aria, Canto do cisne negro*; Trad.: *Quirpa Guatireña, Pues ya saben Ustedes Señores, Tus ojos son mi encanto, Nagzdagañu*; Ponce: *Rumba, Estrellita*; Peramo: *Ogguere, La Comparsa*; Quintón: *El Coquí*; Casals: *Cant des ocells*; Piazzolla: *Nightclub 1960, Bordel 1900*; Ovalle: *Azulão*; Ginastera: *Cancion a la luna lunanca, Cancion a arbol del olvido, En la cuna blanca*.

Bach: The Six Trio Sonatas
MusicMasters 67182
with Albert Fuller (harpsichord)
Bach: *Trio Sonata for Organ no 1 in E Flat Major (BWV 525), Trio Sonata for Organ no. 2 in C Minor (BWV 526), Trio Sonata for Organ no. 3 in D Minor (BWV 527), Trio Sonata for Organ no. 4 in E Minor (BWV 528), Trio Sonata for Organ no. 5 in C Major (BWV 529), Trio Sonata for Organ no. 6 in G Major (BWV 530)*.

Segovia: Canciones Populares
MusicMasters 67174
Tansman: *Segovia*; Segovia: *Estudio sin luz, La Macarena, Preludio no. 14, Estudio, Canciones populares de distintos paises — Inglesa, Checa, Vasca, Escocesa, Irlandesa, Polaca, Rusa, Serba, Sueca, Finlandesa, Croata, Bretona, Eslovania, Polaca, Catalana, Catalana (Andante)*; Narváez: *Canción del Emperador*; Roussel: *Segovia (op. 29)*; C.P.E. Bach: *Marcia, Siciliana*; Castelnuovo-Tedesco: *Tonadilla sur le*

nom de Andrés Segovia (op. 170); Haydn: *Menuet and Trio*; Chopin: *Preludio (op. 29, no. 7)*; Brahms: *Walzer (op. 39, no. 8)*; Mussorgsky: *Pictures at an Exhibition — The Old Castle*; Franck: *Two pieces for organ*; Debussy: *La fille aux cheveux de lin*; Milhaud: *Segoviana*; Scriabin: *Prelude (op. 16, no. 4)*.

Best of Eliot Fisk
MusicMasters 67151
with Orchestra of St. Luke's, Paula Robison (flute)
Paganini: *Caprices for Violin solo (nos. 5, 15 and 24)*; Scarlatti: *Sonatas (K. 32, K. 62)*; Vivaldi: *Concerto in D Major for Lute (Largo), Trio Sonata in C major (Allegro)*; Beaser: *Il est né, le divin enfant, Mountain Songs — Barbara Allen, Quicksilver, Cindy*; Locatelli: *Capriccio in G major (op. 3, no. 18), Fuga*; Soler: *Sonata in D major (M. 34, Allegretto con ayre)*; Bach: *Prelude in C minor (BWV 999)*; Mudarra: *Fantasia que contrahaze la harpa....*; Frescobaldi: *Partite sopra Balletto*; Mozart: *Divertimento (K. 439b, no. 4, Adagio), Finale (allegro)*; Barrios: *Un sueño en la floresta*; Sagreras: *El Colibri*; Rochberg: *Caprice Variations for Violin Solo (nos. 41, 11, 46 and 38)*; Weiss: *Fuge*.

Für Eliot
GSP 1008CD
Scarlatti: *Three Sonatas*; Martin: *Quatre Pièces Brèves*; Ponce: *Valse, Thème varié et Finale*; Raffman: *Für Eliot*; Paganini: *Four Capricci*.

Sequenza!
MusicMasters 67150
Scarlatti: *Sonatas (K. 175, K. 481, K. 482)*; Berio: *Brin, Sequenza XI, Aldo*; Paganini: *Caprice d'Adieu*; Mendelssohn: *Six Songs Without Words (op. 30 no. 3, op. 85 no. 2, op. 62 no. 4, op. 18 no. 4, op. 38 no. 4, op. 18 no. 6)*; Paganini: *Sonata no. 23*; Paganini/Beethoven: *Variations on a Theme by Paisiello*.

Rochberg: Caprice Variations
MusicMasters 67133
Rochberg: *Variations nos. 1–51*.

Baroque Guitar
MusicMasters 67130
Frescobaldi: *Balletto*; Bach: *Ciaccona*; Scarlatti: *Sonatas (K. 380, K. 531, K. 322, K. 323, K. 213, K. 159)*.

Eliot Fisk
MusicMasters 67128
Scarlatti: *Sonatas in G Major (K. 146, K. 391; K. 390)*; Bach: *Suite in E Minor (BWV 996); Prelude, Fugue and Allegro (BWV 998)*; Froberger: *Suite no. 15 in A Minor*.

The Latin American Guitar
MusicMasters 67127
Ponce: *Theme, Variation and Fugue on Folias de España*; Sagreras: *El colibri*; Barrios: *Danza paraguaya, Aire de Zamba, Maxixe*; Lauro: *Seis por derecho, Angostura,*

Carora, El niño, El marabino-El totomo de Guarenas); Sojo: *Venezuelan Pieces no. 2 (Aguinaldo)*; Mi Teresa-Estrella del mar-Mi Teresa; Anon.: Merengue.

Vivaldi Concerti
MusicMasters 67097
with Orchestra of St. Luke's, Albert Fuller (harpsichord), Louise Schulman (viola d'amore), Frederic Hand (guitar)
Vivaldi: *Concerto in C Major for Mandolin and Strings (RV. 425), Sonata in G Minor (RV. 42), Concerto in D Major (RV. 93), Concerto in G Major for Two Mandolins and Strings (RV 532), Concerto in D Minor for Viola d'Amore and Lute (RV. 540), Trio Sonata in C Major (RV. 32)*; Bach: *Concerto in D Major for Keyboard After Vivaldi (BWV 972)*.

Paganini: 24 Caprices
MusicMasters 67092
Paganini: *Caprices nos. 1–24 (op 1)*.

Bell' Italia
MusicMasters 67079
Scarlatti: *Sonatas (K. 274, K. 32, K. 377, K. 62)*; Frescobaldi: *Aria detta "La Frescobalda"*; Locatelli: *Two Capricci (op. 3, nos. 24 and 18)*; Petrassi: *Suoni Notturni, Nunc*; Fiorillo: *Capriccio no. 28*; Paganini: *Sonata no. 4*; Castelnuovo-Tedesco: *Capriccio Diabolico (op. 85)*; Giuliani: *Le Rossiniane (op. 119)*.

Mountain Songs
MusicMasters 7038
with Paula Robison (flute)
MacDowell: *Woodland Sketches— Will-o'-the-Wisp, To a Wild Rose, A Deserted Farm*; A. Richards: *The Smile of Contentment and Love*; Foster: *Jennie's own Schottisch, Beautiful Dreamer, If You Only Have a Moustache*; Corea: *Children's Song no. 2*; Schumann: *Orpheus and his Lute*; Ives: *Waltz, We Are Climbing Jacob's Ladder*; Beaser: *Il est né, le divin enfant, Mountain Songs— Barbara Allen, House Carpenter, He's Gone Away, Hush-You-Bye, Cindy, The Cuckoo, Fair and Tender Ladies, Quicksilver*.

Guitar Fantasies
MusicMasters 7008
Bach: *Prelude in C Minor (BWV 999)*; Couperin: *Les barricades misterieuses*; C.P.E. Bach: *Rondo in A Major*; Weiss: *Menuet, Fantasie, Fuge*; Molinaro: *Fantasia I*; Milan: *Fantasia XXII*; Mudarra: *Fantasia que contrahaze la harpa....*; Piccinini: *Toccata XI*; Dowland: *Forlorne Hope, Fantasia from Varietie of Lute-lessons*; Mozart: *Adagio for Glass Harmonica in C Major (K. 617a), Funeral March for Piano in C Minor (K. 453a)*; Sor: *Introduction, Theme and Variations on a Theme from Mozart's "Magic Flute" (op. 9)*; Henze: *Drei Tentos*; Roussel: *Segovia (op. 29)*; Poulenc: *Sarabande*; Barrios: *Sueño en la floresta*.

Website: www.eliotfisk.com

3
Richard Rodney Bennett: Composing for the Guitar
February 1996

Sir Richard Rodney Bennett is one of the most celebrated British composers of the twentieth century. He was born on March 29, 1936 in Broadstairs, Kent, UK. Bennett received a scholarship to the Royal Academy of Music in London where he studied with Lennox Berkeley and Howard Ferguson. In 1957 he won a scholarship to study in Paris for two years with Pierre Boulez. Bennett's works during the late '50s and early '60s for piano, voice, orchestra and chamber ensemble led to his selection in 1965 as Composer of the Year by the Composers' Guild of Great Britain. In the early '70s he was a visiting professor of composition at the Peabody Conservatory of Music in Baltimore. Bennett also held the International Chair of Composition at the Royal Academy of Music.

He has written in numerous musical forms, including chamber, orchestral and jazz. His film credits include the soundtracks for more than fifty films, including Far from the Madding Crowd, Nicholas and Alexandra, Murder on the Orient Express, Enchanted April, *and* Four Weddings and a Funeral — *three of which resulted in Academy Award nominations. Bennett also helped orchestrate Paul McCartney's 1997 symphonic poem,* Standing Stone.

For many guitarists, Richard Rodney Bennett's Five Impromptus for solo Guitar *was their introduction to twelve-tone or serial music. The year 1996 marked the 25th anniversary of the publication of the* Impromptus, *the 26th anniversary of the completion of his* Concerto for Guitar and Orchestra *and the 10th anniversary of the London premiere of his* Sonata for solo Guitar. *It was also the year he turned sixty — a good time to reflect on his guitar works.*

I had wanted to interview Richard Rodney Bennett for a long time. Although he lived on the West Side of New York City and I worked on the East

Side, I never managed to cross that great divide. Then one day while I was on business I stayed at a hotel in Philadelphia. As I was checking in, I noticed a flyer for a jazz cabaret show to be held in the hotel that evening. The featured pianist was none other than Richard Rodney Bennett. I cornered him after the show and made my pitch for an interview. Several months later we sat down in his apartment, among the piles of manuscripts and two cats, and began to talk.

Through the Past, Briefly

Jim Tosone: How did your concert music originate?

Richard Rodney Bennett: I was friendly with Elisabeth Lutyens, one of the few twelve-tone composers in England in the '40s and '50s. I say "friendly with" with a slight hesitation, because she was a very difficult lady. But she influenced me a lot and through her I got to know the music of Schoenberg, Webern and Berg.

JT: In point of fact, your twelve-tone compositions are closer to Berg than Webern, perhaps best described as a neo-romantic serialism.

RRB: Yes, but the twelve-tone element of my music is very unimportant, except that it's easy to trace and understand if you're looking at the music. But it's never been the *raison d'être* of my music.

JT: When you were a student at London's Royal Academy of Music in the early '50s, you studied with Lennox Berkeley and Howard Ferguson. Was it there that you got to know the music of Pierre Boulez?

RRB: It was. Boulez's music absolutely bowled me over, so much so that in 1957 I went to Paris and studied with him for two years. And in the way that one does when one is young and doesn't yet have one's own voice, I assumed some of his compositional mannerisms. Then I started to find my own voice. Serial composition can be a very academic way of writing, but my music was never academic.

JT: Now, nearly thirty years later, your music is becoming tonal again.

RRB: My compositional style has changed a lot. Recently, I was commissioned to write an orchestral piece. The commission came after a dry period, during which I was getting away from atonal music and back to tonality. The piece that came out — Partita — was well liked by players and audiences. Not just because it was easy to listen to, but because it strikes them emotionally. Even so, it's not easy changing compositional styles. It's not like taking off one suit of clothes and putting on another. You have to speak the tonal language with total confidence and your own personal touch. I don't want to write music that is indistinguishable from hundreds of other composers' tonal music.

Richard Rodney Bennett (Novello & Co., Ltd.)

JT: Key to understanding you, as a composer, is the variety of musical styles in which you enjoy writing and playing. In addition to your concert music, you are a prolific composer of music for film, children and amateur performers. How does your approach to writing concert music differ from your approach to writing tonal popular music?

RRB: I never take on commissions to write music for children or to write light music. I do them because I feel like writing something simple and melodic, and I don't demand much of myself. Film music, which I've been writing since I was nineteen, is more demanding but doesn't exercise my mind like writing an orchestral piece. I recently finished the music for a film called *Swann*, based on a novel by Carol Shields, the author of *The Stone Diaries*. It's an intense score for a small group of strings. I had to write half an hour's music and orchestrate it in ten days. I could never do that with my concert music, including my guitar music. There I ask a great deal more of myself and am very self-critical. Writing a half-hour concert piece is a very tough, demanding thing.

JT: What is the relationship among your different musical styles?

RRB: Perhaps my different musical persona are coming closer together. In 1990, I wrote *Concerto for Tenor Saxophone, Timpani and Strings* for [saxophonist] Stan Getz. That was the first time I was able to bring my knowledge of jazz into the same arena as my concert music. I never thought I would be able to write an extended concert piece that spoke the language of jazz — but it worked!

FIVE IMPROMPTUS FOR SOLO GUITAR

JT: You were eighteen when you first met [guitarist] Julian Bream at the prestigious Dartington Summer School, where many notable contemporary musicians have taught and performed.

RRB: From the moment we got to know each other, Julian bullied me to write him a Concerto for guitar. I guess he knew I was a composer who would respond to the guitar. It's one of those instruments that you can't write for with any sophistication unless you know how it's played. So there was no way I was going to write a Concerto for Julian right off, because I didn't know enough about how the guitar worked. Instead, I wrote *Impromptus* for him in 1968, about fourteen years after we first met. They were little exercises towards writing a Concerto. I tried out various technical things — the different colors of the guitar, what happens when you tune a string down, harmonics. I was so anxious for it to be playable that I wrote it with a guitar in my hands. Although the score says "Fingering by Julian Bream," a lot of the original fingering was mine. It gave me a strong feeling of what it felt like to play the piece. William Walton once said that he could play his Violin Concerto, but it would take him three weeks to get through it. Well, I could play *Impromptus* but it would take me several months.

JT: How do you view *Impromptus*, twenty-five years after their publication?

RRB: When I began writing the piece I didn't know where it was going. It wound up being five modest character pieces that exploited a lot of colors and moods. They don't overreach what they set out to do. I had no idea it would become standard repertoire for the guitar, but it's been played and recorded a lot and I'm very touched by that.

Concerto for Guitar and Orchestra

JT: Your Concerto for Guitar and Orchestra is more in the character of an eighteenth — rather than nineteenth — century concerto, in that the guitar is more of a participant in an ensemble rather than a soloist. Many believe that it is one of the finest orchestrated guitar Concertos.

RRB: Perhaps, but it did not turn out exactly as I expected. When I wrote the guitar Concerto, I thought rather naively that if I used a scoring with three winds, two brass, three strings and percussion, it would be so light that the sound of the guitar would not be covered. What I learned was that although forty strings will not cover a guitar, a solo oboe will. Still, it's a nice little orchestra and I like the instrumental combination. Since the orchestra tends to cover the guitar, I prefer that the guitar be amplified. The thing I remember about performances of the Concerto was that historically Julian Bream would never use amplification. Then he was scheduled to play the Concerto at Lincoln Center in New York. The publishers delivered the parts in an extreme state of disarray, so Julian and the orchestra didn't have time to work on the balance. So for the first time Julian played with amplification. I think he was pleased. I would say anybody who wants to play my guitar Concerto should use a certain degree of amplification.

SONATA FOR SOLO GUITAR

JT: The origins of your Sonata for solo Guitar can be seen readily in the *Impromptus*. The opening row of the Sonata is a rising motive beginning E-A-D-F, which harkens back to the E-A-B-C opening of *Impromptus*.

RRB: I wanted to write an extended guitar piece that would take me much further than *Impromptus*. The Sonata was a piece I really wrote for myself. I mean, I wrote it for Julian but he didn't commission it.

JT: The first performance was given by Julian Bream in 1985 at Town Hall, Cheltenham, as part of the Cheltenham Festival. The Sonata's London premiere, also by Bream, was in 1986 at Wigmore Hall. Bream did the final editing and fingering.

RRB: Yes. But the original editing and fingering was done with [guitarist-composer] David Leisner, who was enormously helpful. I also liked David's performance of it. I don't know if the Sonata is successful, but I enjoyed writing it and I like it very much.

COMPOSING FOR THE GUITAR

JT: Bream describes you as the kind of composer that you can't suggest things to, that you give people the feeling you know exactly what you're doing and don't take kindly to suggested alterations.

RRB: I'm a composer who decides the notes I want, and that's that. I don't mean that I'm rigid or academic. But if I put down a note on the page it's because I've chosen that note rather than any other.

JT: According to those who have performed your works, you also understand the special characteristics of the guitar and how to relate them to your compositional style.

RRB: My musical nature has always been that of a romantic and the guitar is a romantic instrument — its resonance and sound is very lyrical. It's a tonal instrument because of its tuning and therefore not ideally adapted to serial music, which in the past has been my musical language.

JT: The trend in guitar composition is towards tonal music. Since the guitar is tonal and your music is now tonal, a natural question is why you have not written recently for the guitar.

RRB: I have to say that I don't have a strong affinity for the guitar. I haven't written anything since the Sonata and I don't have any plans. Also,

Richard Rodney Bennett (left) and guitarist David Leisner reviewing the score of *Sonata*, New York City, March 1999 (Ralph Jackson).

guitarists apart from Julian have never commissioned pieces from me, and my whole musical life has been writing to commission. It's not just a question of money; it's a question of the date. I generally need to have a date for a performance or delivery before I can write an extended piece of music. Otherwise it will fall by the wayside. Another reason I haven't written more for the guitar is that I've always been influenced by heroes in music and there are not that many works for guitar that I regard as heroic. There are no towering masterpieces in the twentieth century, apart from Britten's piece [*Nocturnal*]. I wish Debussy had written for the guitar. Wouldn't that have been something? Debussy's Ballet *Jeux* is one of the most important pieces of music in my life. If I'm feeling depressed and can't think of anything to write, I will look at Debussy and that makes me love music all over again.

JT: So why devote the time that you did to writing two major works for the guitar?

RRB: The reason I wrote for guitar, as well as for saxophone, marimba and percussion, is because those instruments need repertoire. I have no interest in writing another violin or piano Concerto. I write for specific instruments because I want to give music to those players. At present, I'm writing a piece for solo viola that will be the set piece for an international competition.

JT: How can guitarists attract composers to write for the guitar?

RRB: Certainly a guitarist who needs a large abstract work for recital purposes would be of interest to a composer. Also, many composers are turned on by virtuosity. I don't mean Paganini-like, but a performer with passion and dedication as well as extraordinary ability. For example, I wrote *Concerto for Alto Saxophone and Strings* and *Sonata for Soprano Saxophone* for John Harle. He is a great virtuoso and one cannot help but be turned on by somebody like that. It is immensely important for young composers to get hands-on experience with the instruments they're writing for. And to have players talk about the instrument and tell them about technique and what does and doesn't work. I'm sure two-thirds of composers have no idea what the guitar is, apart from how it's tuned. Guitar music comes from the players, not just the composers. There wouldn't be a guitar repertoire if it weren't for Julian Bream. It's very important that guitarists be in touch with composers, encourage them to write and show them how to write for the instrument.

JT: I understand you don't think much of the scores for guitar music, in that they go into such detail about left- and right-hand fingerings.

RRB: It's like it was written out in Braille, as though you couldn't possibly play it unless your fingers did exactly those things. The violin, viola, cello and double bass all work the same way across the strings, but no string player would be able to read string music if it was written like guitar music. Guitarists have to be told every finger in both hands and every string to play on. They're only reading one stave, for goodness sake! Sight reading is a thing that a child of five can learn. Guitarists should be able to read. We're not asking them to reduce an orchestral score at sight. I can't understand it.

It's Alive!

JT: What do you think of the different performances of your works?

RRB: I have to say that I'm not that interested in my pieces after they've gone out into the world. Once they have a life of their own, I'm too busy wondering whether I can write the next piece. Nonetheless, I understand the critical role a performer has in bringing a score to life. Julian does some things in the guitar Concerto that are not in the score. For example, there's a rasgueado he does which I didn't write. But he likes the idea of playing it his way and he was determined to do it. I'm not complaining, because he's a genius. Julian's performance may be eccentric, but it has depth and poetry. John Williams played the Concerto extraordinarily, with no difficulty at all. He is a marvelous player and I even hesitate to say this, but John's performance didn't have the poetry of Julian's.

JT: What is the worst thing a performer can do to a composer's music?

RRB: Play it at the wrong speed. Very often players simply don't bother to find out the speed at which the composer meant it to be played. I'm not bothered about notes. If the occasional note goes wrong, it's no big deal. But a wrong speed is a terrible thing to do to the music. Often the music can't sustain the weight of being played too slowly or the details are incoherent if you play it too fast. For example, I've had people play the last *Impromptu* [*Arioso*] incredibly slowly. The guitar is not resonant enough to support that speed. It also lays too much weight on the music. The *Arioso* is a lyrical, quiet piece, but it's not an elegy for the end of the world. That being said, one's demands with regard to one's own music do change over the years. That is, when I wrote a certain piece, I had no doubt that I wanted it to be played at that speed. Now I'm more flexible. I might hear a performance that was slightly slower or faster and it would feel right. Unfortunately, I've heard performances of my music which were so disastrously wrong in terms of what I originally wanted that it was like those terrible dreams when you're trying to run, but your feet are stuck in glue and you can't move!

SERIAL KILLER

JT: Having devoted much of your life to composing using serial techniques, what is your perspective regarding their impact on present-day classical music?

RRB: It's the same legacy one gets from studying counterpoint. Nobody writes strict counterpoint anymore and nobody in his or her right mind would write strict twelve-tone music today. But serial techniques occupied me for so many years because of the idea that you could take a small group of notes and write a symphony. That is an admirable way of composing—nothing wasted, nothing random. The technique can be used with enormous fantasy, invention and imagination or it can be just a mechanical manipulation of notes. The freedom has to come from a solid grounding in technique. It's simply not possible for an untutored composer to write a coherent piece of music lasting half an hour. It's still terrifying for me, even at my age, to write a half-hour orchestral piece. But I know ways of doing it, having been through the intense discipline of twelve-tone technique.

JT: Once twelve-tone music reached the end of its evolution, it gave way to a variety of compositional styles, including Postmodern and Minimalist music. What trends do you see in compositional styles?

RRB: Minimalist music is starting to settle down and acquire its own viewpoint. At first, it tended to be simple-minded endless repetitions of the same material. Then composers realized it was possible to do something more intelligent. Sometimes you must to go to an extreme before you can write something acceptable. Boulez, for example, constructed a piece based entirely on a mathematical series before he could break away from that. A lot of Minimalist composers went to the extreme of repeating mindlessly before they could start to create something important. Composers like John Adams, Aaron Jay Kernis and Michael Torke have learned from Minimalist music. The new perspective that they write from would not have been possible without the music of the Minimalist composers. Even so, Minimalist music is not my thing. Although it was a healthy reaction against serial technique, I think it's too easy a solution. I'm not particularly interested in what's going on nowadays in contemporary music. There are a lot of empty fashions and no major composers. I don't have many musical heroes in the world of composition anymore.

ALL THAT JAZZ

JT: In the 1970s, you began accompanying jazz and cabaret headliners, beginning with singer Cleo Lane. Since then you have achieved distinction as one of the most refined and stylish pianists in the cabaret arena. Your playing has a classical sensibility—from the thoughtful approach to phrasing, dynamics and articulation to the creation of interesting inner voices—that still manages to retain a feeling of freedom.

RRB: Yes, my approach is never cold-blooded. There are one or two pianists in jazz who are incredibly cold-blooded purveyors of technique and of perverse manipulations of the material. I'm not that kind of pianist at all. But I think the way I voice chords has something to do with my classical background. But it's not "Bach meets jazz." I can't stand that! It absolutely gives me the creeps. I would never introduce any echo of classical music into my cabaret or jazz performances — no. There are many giants in jazz piano, such as Bill Evans and Oscar Peterson, and it's enough to be influenced by them.

JT: One of the high points of your evenings of cabaret is when you sing and accompany yourself.

RRB: I enjoy singing very much. I've worked with singers for years and I always knew the lyrics of the tunes I was playing. Then one of the singers I was working with in England persuaded me to start singing. I must say it was a big leap from looking into the piano and playing to looking at the audience and singing lyrics which are highly charged emotionally. It is a very naked feeling. It's not a question of having a serious voice, because a lot of great jazz singers did not have great voices. It's a question of putting lyrics over in a way that moves people. I know I can do that because I understand the emotion behind the lyric. And I find it much more rewarding to sing and play rather than just always play.

JT: Does performing help you avoid the ivory tower syndrome that afflicts some composers?

RRB: Yes. I love to perform; I need to perform. I can't just write music. I like the distractions of getting out on the road and playing.

An Englishman in New York

JT: You were born in England, but have lived the last sixteen years in New York City. Do you plan on staying?

RRB: I regard New York very much as my home. I've always lived in cities. My friend and fellow colleague Peter Maxwell Davis lives on the remotest possible island off the north coast of Scotland. I can't imagine that. I love being in my apartment in the middle of the city and not going out for days at a time because I'm so wrapped up in the music I'm writing. But once it's over, or if it's going badly, I can rush out into the street and there I am with a hundred things to do.

Life, the Universe and Everything

JT: What would you like to accomplish in the coming years?

RRB: I don't view things in those terms anymore. My accountant said to me, "Richard, when you retire you'll have a nice pension waiting for you." And I said, "Listen, composers don't retire." Because in general they don't. But then I was talking to a friend of mine about this conversation, and I said, "Maybe I could retire. I'm not driven to write anymore." This was around the time I was struggling with my return toward tonality. But I have at present six commissions I have to do, so [laughs] I guess I'm not retiring.

Julian Bream on Richard Rodney Bennett
February 1996

Julian Bream is the best known classical guitarist alive today. Born in London on July 15, 1933, Bream studied piano, cello and composition at the Royal College of Music. Since there were no college-level curriculums for the guitar at that time, he learned classical guitar through private instruction. From 1948 to 1997, his numerous recordings and concert tours — along with radio and television appearances — have brought him worldwide acclaim. Bream was the first to commission leading twentieth century British composers to write for the guitar, including Malcolm Arnold, Richard Rodney Bennett, Benjamin Britten, Hans Werner Henze, Michael Tippett and William Walton. He studied Renaissance lute and helped contribute to its revival through his solo recitals and through the Julian Bream Consort. In the 1970s, Bream's recordings and concerts with fellow guitarist John Williams helped create an interest in, and an appreciation for, the guitar duo.

Without Julian Bream there probably would be no guitar works by Richard Rodney Bennett. Bream's perspectives are a key element in understanding Bennett's work. Recently, Bream and I had a chance to discuss his relationship with Bennett, which began more than forty years ago.

Jim Tosone: You met Richard Rodney Bennett at Dartington Summer School. He says that from the moment you met him, you "bullied" him to write a Concerto for guitar. What did you see in Bennett that led you to believe he had some guitar pieces in him?

Julian Bream: Well, I always admired the best of Richard's music very much indeed. He knows exactly what he wants to say and he says it in a lucid way. He's is also a highly disciplined composer who does his homework and finds out how an instrument works.

JT: The first work he actually wrote for guitar was not the Concerto, but *Impromptus*. It's been twenty-five years since their publication. On reflection, how do you view them and their place in the guitar literature?

JB: The *Impromptus* are occasional pieces that have great charm and create a beautiful atmosphere. They were preludes, in a way, to his bigger guitar pieces — the Concerto and the Sonata. The *Impromptus* were his way of exploring the expressive possibilities of the instrument.

JT: He believes you have to deeply understand an instrument to write for it.

JB: Yes. Most great composers have understood intimately the instrument for which they were writing. Some composers write notes that get played on the guitar, but Bennett writes notes specifically for the guitar. He understands the instrument as well as any composer I know.

JT: Bennett mentioned that when writing *Impromptus*, he was influenced by Hans Werner Henze. And that although the last movement, *Arioso*, was based on a twelve-tone row, it had a strong tonal influence. How do you see the influence of Henze's music on Bennett?

JB: Well, they're very different composers, aren't they? The one thing they do have in common is they are both contrapuntal composers. But Henze is more of a romantic composer. Richard's music is more aesthetically conceived and clearly delineated. Henze's music has a more complex texture. There's an emotional intensity in Henze's music, whereas Richard's music doesn't have great emotional leaps and falls. But it is often dramatic and sometimes intensely lyrical.

JT: Although Bennett himself says he's a romantic at heart. It's interesting to see how composers view themselves versus how their interpreters view them.

JB: I think Richard's romanticism is implied rather than actual. But it's certainly there, particularly in the last *Impromptu*.

JT: I have here the original autograph manuscript of the Sonata, which Richard was kind enough to lend me.

JB: The Sonata is a very substantial piece. The writing for the guitar is more developed than even in the Concerto. With the Sonata, Richard was more adventurous and willing to take risks with the musical material, the texture of the music and how it lies on the instrument. He's got a near infallible ear and what he hears, works. Both the Sonata and the Concerto are, in my opinion, pieces of considerable significance.

JT: Did you have to change anything in order to play the pieces?

JB: I didn't change very much in the Concerto, just one or two little things that I thought could be more effective as they related to my conception of the piece.

JT: Bennett's compositional style for classical music has returned to the tonal realm after many years of being atonal or twelve-tone. In my interview with him, he described the guitar as a tonal instrument. Do you think there's a tonal guitar piece in Bennett that we might be able to get out of him?

JB: There may be. He writes a lot of music and when you've been through the disciplines of atonal or serial systems, I should think it's a piece of cake to write a tonal work. Whatever people say about the serial systems of the '60s and '70s, it did give those composers a language and a discipline. Eventually, though, it constrained them — so they broke it. The problem was what was going to happen after the serial system was discarded. We are now in the middle of that crisis.

JT: The Postmodern or the Minimalist movements were to some degree a reaction to serial systems, just as the Rococo period was a reaction to the late Baroque period. What is your view on the Postmodern and Minimalist schools of composition?

JB: [Laughs] Well, it's a way out certainly. There had to be some redress of style after the serial system collapsed. I suppose it's a brave effort. But today's music is very difficult aesthetically for me to come to terms with. I find it often mechanical and it nearly always overstays its welcome. I don't think there's anybody in the younger generation of composers that I really admire. I sometimes like their music, but that's different from having an admiration for it. The musical world has changed considerably in the last twenty years. I don't think it's as interesting or stimulating as it was. But I'm getting older and perhaps I am not so receptive. It's very difficult to have a good perspective on what's happening. All I can say is that most music that comes my way these days is often stylistically incoherent, harmonically insecure and melodically undistinguished.

JT: How have you approached interpreting Bennett's guitar music and communicating it to the public?

JB: With contemporary music, the performer must first have a musical point of view about a work to communicate it to an audience. The player has to feel the music deeply and to search for the character of the music. I'm not an analytical musician; I tend to do these things intuitively. And sometimes I get it wrong. But when I do something, at least I do it with conviction. Only then do I have a reasonable chance of communicating and convincing an audience that the composition in hand is worth listening to.

David Leisner on Richard Rodney Bennett
March 1996

David Leisner was born in Los Angeles on December 22, 1953. He studied guitar with John Duarte and David Starobin, as well as composition with Virgil Thomson. Leisner was a prize winner at the 1975 Toronto and 1981 Geneva International Guitar competitions. He is currently on the faculty of the New England Conservatory of Music and the Manhattan School of Music. His record The Viennese Guitar *contributed to the rediscovery of guitarist-composer Johann Kaspar Mertz. From 1984 to 1991, a hand injury interrupted his performing career. During that period, he turned his attention to composing and produced works such as* Passacaglia and Toccata, Dances in the Madhouse *and* Billy Boy Variations. *Since his full recovery from the hand injury, he has returned to the concert stage and recording studio.*

David Leisner had an important role in bringing Richard Rodney Bennett's greatest guitar work, Sonata, *to fruition. Leisner drew upon both his performance and composing experience in helping to prepare* Sonata *for publication. Julian Bream, in turn, added his touches when he prepared* Sonata *for its world premiere.*

Richard Rodney Bennett

David Leisner

Jim Tosone: How did you become involved in bringing Richard Rodney Bennett's Sonata for guitar into the world?

David Leisner: Many years ago, I went to Richard and played his *Impromptus* for him, because I was going to perform them and wanted his feedback. I guess he retained that memory when, years later, he finished the

Sonata. He called me up and said, "I've written a piece for Julian Bream and since Julian is not here in New York and you are, would you consider helping me out with the piece?" It was my great honor to be asked and I was thrilled to do it.

JT: What would you say was your contribution to the piece?

DL: Well, Richard is a remarkable craftsman besides being a wonderful composer. When he presents a piece to an instrumentalist the work is basically done. He has an unerring sense of instrumental writing. The score he gave me was already in superb condition, almost like an engraved score. That tells you something about his personality — very meticulous. When I discussed this aspect of Richard's writing with Julian Bream, he said that Richard was similar to Benjamin Britten in being one of the few composers who presented such perfectly finished works in manuscript. So what I did with the Sonata was provide right- and left-hand fingerings. I made only a few note changes. My overall approach to this kind of work is to get in the way as little as possible. Julian tends to be a bit more creative. Sometimes it's genius and sometimes it moves the work away from the composer's intention. But Julian is aware of that and feels that when he does it, he's making the piece more playable.

JT: What was it like working with Bennett?

DL: Richard has always been kind and generous to me, and I am very grateful for that. From the beginning, he treated me with respect. I think we worked well together. We're kindred souls in the area of rhythm, for example. Rhythm is very important to Richard and he was pleased that I could play his rhythms accurately. That led him to trust my input. He is also open to suggestions, but at the same time is firm about those aspects of his composition that he feels should not be violated.

JT: As a composer, what have you learned about composition from Bennett and his works?

DL: Richard is one of the most consummate technicians I've ever encountered. His approach to structure and overall coherence of the material is awesome, in the truest sense of the word. Sonata, for example, should and will be considered a towering masterpiece in the guitar literature in terms of structure alone. Richard is also a wonderful orchestrator. That is true not only of his orchestral works but of the Sonata. There is orchestration going on throughout it. In other words, he knows what each note sounds like in different places on the guitar fingerboard and he uses that to create a certain timbre atmosphere. It's quite a remarkable gift.

Finally, Richard's metronome markings are admirable. When he writes a metronome marking, he means it. I remember playing the last movement of the *Impromptus* for him at a tempo that he felt was too fast. He showed me the tempo, and I said, "Gee, that sounds a little slow." We went to the metronome and sure enough, it was right on. It's a wonderful example of his unfailing sense of tempo. Here was a piece that he had written many years ago and I'm sure hadn't thought about again until that moment. He's like Stravinsky, in that way. When anyone asked Stravinsky for comments about a performance of his music, all he would say is "right tempo" or "wrong tempo" [laughter].

JT: What about the influence of Bennett's film music and his jazz piano playing on his guitar works?

DL: I think the jazz influence is very important with regard to the Sonata. There are all kinds of little jazz tunes and blues riffs tucked away throughout the piece. Although it is written in a free serial style, the melodic element uses the language of jazz.

JT: Bennett must be using it subconsciously, since he said he likes to keep definite boundaries between his popular and his serious music.

DL: That is, in fact, the most laudable way of incorporating popular-style music into one's own music. Do it naturally, almost without conscious use of the style. The language of jazz is so ingrained in Richard that he cannot help but incorporate it.

JT: Speaking of influences, do you see elements of the *Impromptus* in the Sonata?

DL: Definitely. The Sonata is like an extended version of the *Impromptus*, although much more sophisticated. It was the next logical step beyond the *Impromptus*.

JT: Can you comment on the twelve-tone or serial aspect of Bennett's guitar works?

DL: The beauty of Richard's work is that he was never rigid about the serial system. The Sonata is a beautiful example of free serial style writing. Richard will always bend the rules of serial technique to achieve the lyrical and sonic goals he is striving for. That's one of the reasons why I think his works will last.

JT: If that's correct, why isn't the Sonata played or recorded more often?

DL: Well, the piece is on the dry side, so it has been slower in finding its audience. Ultimately, its beautiful melodic qualities will overcome any reservations that people have. Also, it's monstrously difficult. But so was Britten's *Nocturnal* when it first appeared.

JT: And now it's hard to find a classical guitar CD without the *Nocturnal* on it!

DL: [Laughs] Exactly. Another piece that met a similar reception is Ginastera's Sonata, a fiendishly difficult guitar piece that few guitarists played in the beginning. Now it's starting to be played a great deal. The same thing will happen with Richard's Sonata. Then it will be recognized for the masterpiece that it is.

Discography of Richard Rodney Bennett's Works for Guitar

English Guitar Music
Maximilian Mangold, guitar
Musicaphon M 56824
Bennett: *Impromptus*; other non–Bennett guitar works.

Tippett: The Blue Guitar
Craig Odgen, guitar
Nimbus 5390
Bennett: *Impromptus*; other non–Bennett guitar works.

Lyrical 20th Century Guitar Music
Raphaella Smits, guitar
Accent ACC2 8966 D
Bennett: *Impromptus*; other non–Bennett guitar works.

Guitar
Jan Wolf
Partridge 1115-2
Bennett: *Impromptus*; other non–Bennett guitar works.

Dedication (Julian Bream Edition, Volume 14)
Julian Bream, guitar
RCA 09026-61597
Bennett: *Impromptus*; other non–Bennett guitar works.

Guitar Concertos (Julian Bream Edition, Volume 15)
Julian Bream, guitar
RCA 09026-61598
Bennett: *Concerto for Guitar and Chamber Orchestra*; other non–Bennett guitar works.

Websites: www.schirmer.com/composers/bennett/bio.html
www.davidleisner.com

4

David Tanenbaum: The Classical Guitar in Today's World

June 1995

 David Tanenbaum was born in New York City on September 10, 1956. He began his studies with Rolando Valdes Blain in New York and continued them with Aaron Shearer at the Peabody Conservatory in Baltimore. Tanenbaum won first prize in the Carmel Classical Guitar Competition (1977) and second prize in the Toronto International Competition (1978). In 1988 he became the first American guitarist to be invited to perform in China. In 1989, as president of the Second American Classical Guitar Congress, he commissioned five new works, including Rosewood for 100 Guitars *by Henry Brant. David Tanenbaum is a proponent of new guitar repertoire. Works have been written for him by Hans Werner Henze, Terry Riley, Aaron Jay Kernis, Roberto Sierra, and Tanenbaum's father, Elias Tanenbaum. As a chamber musician he has collaborated with, among others, the Kronos Quartet, Ensemble Modern, the Steve Reich Ensemble and guitarist Manuel Barrueco. Tanenbaum is currently chairman of the Guitar Department at the San Francisco Conservatory of Music and has been on the faculty of Mills College as well as artist-in-residence at the Manhattan School of Music. He has produced many editions of guitar music, including the* David Tanenbaum Concert Series. *He has also written a series of three books,* The Essential Studies, *which analyze the Etudes of Sor, Carcassi and Brouwer and complement his recordings of those works.*

 As we strode down Lexington Avenue on a beautiful Manhattan Sunday morning, Tanenbaum exclaimed, "I love walking around this city!" He had been in the recording studio until 5 a.m. the previous evening, but his boundless energy and intensity — a product of his New York origins — was still in full force. His comments were thoughtful, provocative and spirited as we covered topics ranging from composers to careers to learning — as well as what the future holds for Tanenbaum, who is emerging as one of the guitar's major figures.

THE ARTIST AND COMPOSER

Jim Tosone: Composer Terry Riley gave voice to the Minimalist movement in America. In your interview with *Guitar Review* in 1991, you said that you wanted to get him to write a piece for you. How did you go about making that dream a reality?

David Tanenbaum: Well, I've known Terry for many years. I first met him in the '70s and I've been both a friend and a fan of his music. I've always felt there was a good guitar piece there, so I nagged him in my gentle sort of way. But I think what actually broke the camel's back was his son becoming interested in the guitar. Terry began writing the piece, *Ascensión*, in the summer of '93. Since I knew he was writing it, I scheduled the premiere concert for January '94. But he got stuck with the ending, and by November I still had no piece. Then Terry went off on a tour. He does these Keith Jarrett–like solo piano improvisation tours. Well, in the middle of one concert he was improvising something and it hit him that this was the end of the guitar piece. When he got home from the tour, he stayed up for three jet-lagged days and finished the piece. I got it just in time. Now Terry's completely into the guitar and he's talking about writing twenty-six pieces, one for each letter of the alphabet. *Ascensión* is the first.

JT: What's the nature of the piece?

DT: It's like spending an evening with Terry listening to his CD collection, in that it's very eclectic. There's some free jazz–like music, a long raga-like middle section and an ostinato section at the end. He takes from a lot of different worlds, but it's always tonal and you can almost always tap your foot to it. I think it's a very beautiful piece.

JT: Riley says that performers should "own the music they're playing," in the sense that they should feel free to shape it. How have you shaped Riley's piece?

DT: I worked very closely with Terry on *Ascensión* and I've also performed it thirty or forty times. I've developed a sense of when an audience is with me and when it isn't. As a result, we've made two cuts in the piece. Basically, I was able to identify places where the listeners were taken through too many twists and turns and lost their moorings. So we tightened it up.

JT: How do you work with composers who are writing their first guitar piece?

David Tanenbaum (right) and composer Terry Riley, Berkeley, California, April 1999 (Julie Tanenbaum).

DT: I like to teach composers about the guitar by giving them fingerboard charts and playing pieces from the guitar repertoire for them. But I don't like to hinder their imagination. I want them to really feel free to express their ideas — and then, later, refine it.

JT: Riley feels that western music is melodically and rhythmically deficient, because it's so harmonically dominated. Are melody and rhythm what attract you to Riley's pieces?

DT: Well, Terry's done extensive study of Indian music, which is melodically and rhythmically based. So that's always reflected in his music. There's a good sense of line in *Ascensión*, but he was also thinking vertically in that piece. The whole opening is very harmonically based. But I must say my attraction to it is beyond analysis of separate musical dimensions. I just really dig it.

JT: A couple of years ago, you recorded Lou Harrison's *Harp Suite* and his *Serenade for Guitar and Percussion*. The latter was written for guitar with interchangeable fingerboards, each in a different intonation. Harrison places a great importance on an artist playing a composer's works with the intonation asked for. Harrison's lifelong passion has been "just intonation." Did you use "just intonation" when you recorded his pieces?

David Tanenbaum (far left), composer Lou Harrison (center) and San Francisco Symphony Music Director Michael Tilson Thomas (second from right) at the "Celebrating Lou Harrison" festival, San Francisco, February 1997 (Bob Adler).

DT: I did not. Part of the reason is that I haven't yet heard a guitar that I felt had a great sound with interchangeable fingerboards. Lou, as you know, really loves just intonation. He's always saying to me, "You play so beautifully, but damn that equal temperament."

JT: He calls it "dull, industrial gray."

DT: Really? On the other hand, there's [composer] Ingram Marshall who says, "Oh, come on, it's *just* intonation" [laughter]. But I'm a fan of equal temperament. I'm perfectly comfortable in that landscape.

JT: Harrison is very spontaneous and once said that he's "never consciously done anything." That's a very different approach to life than yours. How do you relate to someone who, in that respect, seems so different than you?

DT: Well, that's the beauty of being a performer. We're like actors and we take on different roles. I certainly don't want everything I play to sound like music I would write. I love delving into a composer's world and getting to know the person behind the music. Lou, for example, is a very interesting, broadly based person. He recently published a book of poetry, he curates art exhibits and he's growing hemp in his yard to use as paper. He's also studied a lot of Asian music and has said that he wants to make every single note he writes as beautiful as possible. Those kinds of things are what's really interesting about working with today's composers.

JT: You've also recorded Steve Reich's *Electric Counterpart*, although with acoustic guitars. It's interesting that Reich has cited both Terry Riley and Lou Harrison as influences. For example, Reich said that he wrote *It's Gonna Rain* while under the influence of Riley's piece *In C*. In what ways do you see Riley's influence on Reich?

DT: *In C* was very influential. Steve was already interested at that point in Eastern music and African drumming. The composers we're talking about — Terry, Lou and Steve — are really influenced by a lot of different cultures, particularly Eastern ones. That's something Minimalism has that Modernism, being more insular, did not have as much of. I think La Monte Young produced the first bud of Minimalism. Then Terry wrote *In C* and it ignited Minimalism as a movement. Steve was the next important figure in that school. What Steve did was clean it up. He's a perfectionist and his music is incredibly precise. If you look at the score of *Electric Counterpoint*, it's absolutely carefully and precisely written. When he writes a crescendo on the second eighth note, he wants it *there*.

JT: Do you feel that these three composers are helping to reintegrate classical music back into the culture?

DT: I think so. For one thing, they've made classical music fun again. We're now seeing a generation of younger composers who grew up with pop music and some Minimalism in their ears. Very few are writing in hard-core Modernist languages anymore. Many composers and performers are trying to create art that has real depth, but is also fun and accessible. I think that's very possible to do.

JT: Which composers do you think have been particularly successful at achieving that?

DT: Aaron Jay Kernis, Steve Mackey and Michael Torke are three. Steve wrote an electric guitar concerto for Bill Frizell that was just premiered by the Los Angeles Philharmonic. It's basically a lot of rock and roll. We're going to see more of that from many young composers. I think the Minimalism of Terry, Lou and Steve opened the door for them.

JT: Speaking of Kernis, you're in New York this week to record one of his pieces. Can you tell us about that project?

DT: Sure. Aaron Jay Kernis, who I've been friends with for a long time and, who I think is one of the great young composers, wrote a piece for me two years ago called *100 Greatest Dance Hits*. It's for guitar and string quartet. I recorded it last night with the Chester String Quartet as part of a Ker-

David Tanenbaum (left) and composer Aaron Jay Kernis, New York City, March 1999 (Barbara Hennerfeind).

nis CD. It's the only guitar piece on the disc. The origin of the piece was that Aaron likes to write big, sometimes heavy, pieces and follow them with more fun ones. He was writing a piece that was very intense and noticed that he would spend his entire day in his New York apartment composing in isolation and then go out at night and hear a very different aural environment — ghetto blasters, kids rapping on the subway — than what he had been hearing all day. And he asked himself, "Why can't some of that material be used in a piece? Why this dichotomy between what I compose and what's on the street?" So he wrote a piece that uses many different popular dance styles, that has easy listening music in it and that has the string quartet doing rap and percussion.

JT: Do you see this as a new idea or does it harken back to earlier time periods, when folk music formed the basis for more stylized, formal compositional dance suites?

DT: That's a good question. I think both. I mean, that's obviously a long tradition. But there was a separation when Modernism came along. We're in a Postmodernist period now, where it's much harder to define borders in all fields — fiction and non-fiction, for instance. That's true in classical music as well. You have a whole school of composers like Andrew York and Carlo Domeniconi where you listen and think, "What exactly is the style?" That reflects the world we're in now. It's harder to define what classical guitar is than it used to be.

JT: When I interviewed John Williams, he said the most important trend in contemporary music was that the assumed superiority of the European classical music tradition was being questioned, and that, more and more, that tradition was being viewed as only one of many wonderful musical cultures that are blending together.

DT: I think that's very true. European classical music is an incredibly rich tradition, one that I really love. But as Williams has also said, we guitarists don't have our Brahms and our Beethoven, regrettably; but as a result, we're not tied down to that era. We are in a lot of ways more free to explore the twentieth century and all the different styles that are going on. We play the instrument of more peoples of the world than any other and it's an incredibly adaptable instrument. This is a great time to be a guitar player.

MAKING MODERN MUSIC

JT: Lou Harrison has described himself as being in the "research and development end" of composing, meaning he sees himself as an innovator of new compositional forms and techniques. Do you consider yourself to be in the research and development end of music performance and if so, in what way?

DT: I think what Lou means is that he's always a student. In that sense, I feel absolutely that way.

JT: Along those lines, you've performed and recorded several pieces using guitar in combination with prerecorded tape—*Electric Counterpoint* and Shirish Korde's *Time Grids*, for example. What do you find rewarding about performing those kinds of modern works?

DT: It's amazing if you work hard how much freedom there is in playing with a tape. I find it really rewarding to look for ways to be flexible around what the tape is doing. I think in *Time Grids* the relationship with the tape, especially in the second movement, is quite free. So it comes out different every time. When I recorded it I did three or four takes with different pacing and expressive ideas. Later I picked the one I liked best.

JT: What effect has your father's work in composing pieces involving electronic music had on your interest in this area?

DT: Well, for one thing, I grew up listening to the most *avant-garde* music. In our living room there were these huge speakers, and my father would be playing Stockhausen as loud as you can imagine. I find myself doing that now with my three-year-old son. So my father's influence was very strong in that way. He was in a period where everything he wrote included tape, but I was interested in him getting away from tape a little bit. So, in fact, he's never written a piece for me that includes tape. But certainly, I got used to taped parts and synthesizers from being around him.

THE LEARNING TREE

JT: You mentioned your son, so I'd like to turn to the subject of learning about music and about the guitar. Music instruction in grammar school seems like something that would be critical to the creation of a musically literate society, as well as the development of world-class performers. Yet most grammar school programs seem to fail in this endeavor. I know you feel strongly about the importance of early education in the creative arts experience. What do you think is needed to address this problem?

DT: I think you can't take music out of grammar schools without it really having a negative effect. I'm seeing in master classes that basic musical skills are not where they should be. I'm also starting to see a greater disparity between the level of students in Europe and the students here in the U.S. I think we're getting students applying at the conservatory level who are less musically educated than they used to be. In Europe, there are many community music schools where students can get lessons for free after school. That provides a lot of work for musicians and makes music so much a part of the culture. That's one reason why the European music tradition is so strong, because it's supported by real tax dollars. There are some interesting programs in Berkeley, California, where I live, to make sure that music stays in schools—benefit concerts, for example.

JT: Speaking of master classes, which continue to be an important vehicle for musical instruction, what are some of the more important suggestions you've made in master classes?

DT: That's a good question, and a big one. One thing I always try to do in master classes is to engage the audience. So when a student comes up and is about to play a piece, I'll give some context or perspective by talking about the composer and where the piece fits in his output. I think that's something that has been helpful for students, to understand that you need to not just get a score and learn some notes, but to look at each piece in a larger musical and sociological context. I try also to talk about performance aspects as well, and deal with the performance that I just heard. If a student gets up there and is playing, shaking his head and showing frustration, I try to encourage him to build good habits and not just assume things are going to change when he gets on stage. That's another thing that has drawn some immediate results.

There's also something relating to technique I see in a lot of master classes that is almost epidemic in the guitar world. I often see students having trouble with the "a" finger [the ring finger on the right hand], where it's not quite as fluent as the others. I think some of that comes down to overuse of the tip joints. It's really important not to use the tip joints too much because it's very hard to move independently from there. For instance, if you try to move from the tip of "m" [the middle finger] it carries "a" in with it. I think a lot of the problem with the "a" finger has actually to do with the "m" finger. Because "m" is longer, people tend to flex its tip a lot to clear the next string. So I try to get students to play with less tip flexion. That can sometimes give them more possibilities with the "a" finger and loosen the hand up.

JT: Have you gained any new insights into teaching from watching your son grow and develop?

DT: I've gained insights in terms of discipline. I was less good at that when I was closer in age to the students. But getting a little older and having my son has taught me about drawing lines when they need to be drawn. I really think I'm a better teacher now than ever. In terms of students coming to a conservatory, I'm entering into a contract with them. I'm saying to them that I feel they have a sufficient level of talent and if they work and listen, they have the potential to become great guitarists and musicians. They're putting their education and future in my hands. That's a great responsibility, so I need to be firm and say what's necessary. Guitarists are very collegial, but I sometimes think that goes a little too far between students and teachers.

JT: Chairing a guitar department at a leading conservatory provides a unique opportunity to shape a learning program for students. What do you feel is special about the program you've created at the San Francisco Conservatory of Music?

DT: Well, I do think it is pretty special. I have thought about that program a lot. My idea behind the program is that we owe it to students to be very conscious of the world they're going to face when they get out of school. It's no longer a world of the superstar soloist. Working musicians now have diverse musical lives. They do some teaching, play chamber music, solo repertoire, concertos — all of that. I want to train them in all the skills they're going to need, besides making them good guitar players. So for one thing, I hired guitarist Dušan Bogdanovic, who broadens the scope of the program. He's an expert in world music, improvisation and jazz. He's also a composer, so the students play his music, including a little suite he wrote for the students. We have a fretboard harmony improvisation class, a pedagogy class and a transcription arrangement class. There's also a lot of performance opportunity and a lot of focus on chamber music, particularly chamber music with other instruments.

JT: Any further innovations in mind for the coming years?

DT: I have more ideas for the pedagogy class. We currently bring in students from other schools, who the conservatory students teach in a classroom setting, and then we all talk about the lesson. That's going to be developed more. I'm doing more work with sight reading, which is now a required part of juries at the end of each year. I also want to bring the guitar department out into the world more. We're going to do a concert next year in San Francisco which will feature the guitar department in Henry Brant's *Rosewood for 100 Guitars*. Guitarists from all over northern California from age ten and up will be playing in that. And we'll do *Electric Counterpoint* again — we were the first group to do that live. I also want the four students that Dusan wrote the suite for to each play it out in the community. There's a great program at the conservatory called community service, where the conservatory arranges gigs for students.

JT: There are fundamental principles that are constant when teaching all styles of music, but what must be done differently in the teaching process to help students internalize contemporary music as they learn it?

DT: In general, the range of expression is greater in twentieth century music. Part of the key is to teach students to delve into the language and develop a sense of context. In other words, if they're given a piece by a composer they don't know, they need to learn where this composer came from, what the composer's about and listen to his other music. Some students are very cautious about being inventive or are insecure with new techniques. Others, in the search for perfect playing, compress the dynamic range or limit the color. So some of my teaching is geared toward helping them develop their own sense of courage. In a lot of Modernist scores, you have to get aggressive and to some degree throw caution to the wind.

WE ARE NOT ALONE

JT: Earlier, you cited the influence of rock-and-roll on contemporary classical music. As you well know, Manuel Barrueco released a new recording in August called *Manuel Barrueco Plays Lennon-McCartney*. In addition to the solo and orchestral settings, the disc includes duets arranged by Leo Brouwer and performed by Barrueco and you. What pieces did you record together?

DT: We did *Penny Lane*, *Fool on the Hill* and *She's Leaving Home*.

JT: Can you tell us about the character of Brouwer's arrangements?

DT: As composers often do when they're arranging, Brouwer seems

David Tanenbaum (right) and composer Toru Takemitsu, San Francisco, October 1990 (Kingmond Young).

very confident when making arrangements and not quite so tight about staying close to the score as guitar arrangers sometimes are. Also, as in so much of Brouwer, they feel great on the instrument.

JT: How do they differ from Toru Takemitsu's solo arrangements of Lennon-McCartney?

DT: With Takemitsu you can always hear a little bit of Debussy and French impressionism. So the rhythm in Takemitsu's arrangements is not as driving as in Brouwer's. Takemitsu is really into beautiful, sonorous harmonies. His arrangements are pretty close to the originals, but they stop and start more than Brouwer.

JT: It's interesting that you mention rhythm, because one of the reasons Barrueco says he thinks so highly of your playing is that you have good rhythm. What's the key to having good rhythm?

DT: I don't have any idea. I think real rhythm is innate. There are certain things that are very difficult to teach and rhythm may be one of them. You can develop some rhythmic sense, but you just have to feel it.

JT: Did you do anything special, either musically or technically, when playing with Barrueco?

DT: We felt very natural playing together and we heard phrases in a similar way. But I really wanted to blend into his style because, except for the three duets, the rest of the CD is all Manuel. So I studied his stylistic ways — for instance, his fast vibrato — and made an attempt to go over to his style for blending purposes.

JT: A lot of guitarists have difficulty playing in ensemble settings, whether it's duets or with a string quartet. Why do you think you're so successful at ensemble playing and why do you enjoy it so much?

DT: Well, I love the social integration and I love it for the sound. It was great to play with a string quartet all week and hear the integration of sound. Why am I good at it? I had basic musicianship skills very early. I read music before I read English, so skills like that are innate for me. On the other hand, the guitar is solo-oriented and there's something in me that's very private. Even though I love ensemble music and concertos, I like solo playing the best. It's just temperament, I think. But it's fantastic for musicianship to play ensemble music. It's also become more important financially, which will drive more guitarists in that direction.

THE BUSINESS OF MUSIC

JT: I did want to talk to you about the business side of music, which you've just alluded to. Classical guitarists are perhaps the ultimate independent entrepreneurs, in that they run their own businesses and they're also the product. From a business perspective, what have you done to have a successful career as a performing classical guitarist?

DT: I feel like I've made tons of business mistakes and have played as well as possible to try to overcome them. When I was starting out, I didn't even understand how to use the phone effectively. I just sent a lot of things out in the mail and expected people to answer. Also, if I were to do it again, I would make a professional quality tape a lot earlier. I did five years of affiliate artist work, in which I was playing in small towns for people who might never see me again and don't live near big record stores, so I could have sold a lot of tapes. They can serve as business cards as well as help out financially. Sometimes I go to festivals just to meet people and network. I met [Hans Werner] Henze at a festival in California, which ultimately led to the concerto [*An Eine Aölsharfe*] he wrote for me. One thing that Manuel and I used to do when we were first starting out was to devote an hour or two a day to careers — 9:00 to 11:00 or something like that. You had to think of something or you just sat there. That often generated ideas.

JT: Is there anything in the San Francisco Conservatory program that helps students with the business aspects?

DT: There is something in the general program. Also, at least once a year in the guitar department we have a special event where we bring in people like artist managers, who have been exceptional at marketing. They talk about things like networking. I hope that more and more schools will train guitarists and other musicians in the basics of business, so that obvious mistakes can be avoided.

JT: You've had relationships with several recording companies and publishers over the years, including New Albion and Guitar Solo Publications. What do you look for in these relationships and how do you try to structure them to achieve your goals while also meeting their needs?

DT: Well, I look for as much money as possible, as much creative freedom as I can get, and as much distribution as I can get. And I usually get very little of any of that [laughter]. Seriously, New Albion has been very good because, particularly with *Acoustic Counterpoint*, I had a concept and they just let me do it. After that, they went in a direction that was more composer-oriented than performer-oriented. But they've gone back a bit recently, because certain performers have done well for them. They're planning to release a retrospective of my work, for example. There's been a real push from retailers in the record business to have single composer records, partly because it's easier to file them. That's really difficult for guitarists because not many composers have written sixty minutes of great guitar music. The only way for an artist to beat that is to get their own bin in the record stores.

JT: What, if anything, have you learned from reviews of your recordings and performances?

DT: Reviews can be very instructive and informative. If a reviewer has done some research, has thought about it and comes with some knowledge, they can be helpful in putting your work in context and teaching you some things. I've always thought that Andrew Porter, for instance, was a very good critic. He reviewed once a week for the *New Yorker*. Porter used to really study. When there was a premiere, he would get a score in advance and would come to the performance with some kind of context and perspective. I don't know how these people do it who review five times a week. I don't think it's possible for someone to be educated in opera, the symphonic literature, the piano literature and also our instrument, which is a whole different ballgame. I've also learned some things from reviews about programming. I mean, I always play a program through for myself a number of times and then for some friends to see how it's working. But someone who hears many concerts can sometimes tell whether something's working better than you can. Also, there are pieces that I may have really believed in, then I see a certain trend in reviews and I suddenly see it with new eyes.

JT: I noticed in a review of your CD *Great American Guitar Solo* the critic mentioned that the sequencing was good except for the Johanson piece at the end, which he felt would have worked better between two other pieces.

DT: I remember that review. I struggled with the order on that disc a lot. The five pieces are very different and I spent quite a few hours listening to them in different sequences. I still think the order is right. The Johanson is like a little epilogue. It was a creative choice and you have to make it at some point. But the review was thought provoking.

A Career in Progress

JT: Next year you'll be forty and will have been performing for nearly twenty-five years. What would you say have been your major accomplishments to date?

DT: Well, I think some of the music I've helped bring into the world such as the Henze concerto, the Riley piece and the Kernis pieces. Also some of the arrangements, like the Harrison pieces. And each time you perform, you change a few people's lives slightly. I played in Mexico last week and a very famous artist who came to the concert said he felt very inspired. Maybe a little bit of that feeling will get into his work and make its way into the world. I think concerts can have real power.

JT: What do you hope to accomplish over the next twenty-five years?

DT: I definitely want to commission and be involved in getting new music into the world, especially with composers of my age. Bream has said that it's important to get them to write the second guitar piece, because they've already learned the instrument. That's really important. I have my eye on quite a few composers who I think are going to write great guitar pieces. I want to commission Steve Mackey. And Aaron, I'd like to get guitar pieces from him for the next thirty years. Also, there are certain records that I cherish. My favorite is Glenn Gould's record of Renaissance music by [William] Byrd and [Orlando] Gibbons, which, in fact, was his own favorite. It's been a real constant in my life, something I go back to all the time. So I would love to make some discs that people really have as part of their lives and want to listen to a number of times. There are some of my discs, like the Piazzolla and *Acoustic Counterpart*, which for some people are important. It's nice to feel that you made something that people live with and cherish.

JT: The next twenty-five years are really just the second third of your career, if you think in Segovian terms.

DT: We'll see. I don't know if I'm Segovian that way! But I do want to continue to make more music, make some great CDs, play some great concerts and play with some great musicians. And also do other things that have nothing to do with the guitar.

JT: For example?

DT: Play around with my son, hike, play basketball. I love to read a lot. In my next life, I'm going to be a writer. I love writing.

JT: Do you find that when you're reading or writing you get perspectives or ideas that you carry back into the world of music?

DT: Yes. There's always been something very musical to me about writing and words. When I was very young, I read all the time. And I have novels that I wrote when I was nine or ten — boxes of them. This was ear training for me. In other words, I would read five James Bond novels and then would write a James Bond novel. So I was training my ear in the rhythm of the prose. Something akin to that still goes on. I don't process directly in that way, but I listen while I read.

JT: I assume your next recording will be one of those great CDs you're planning to make. Can you tell us about it?

DT: I'll be recording it at the end of the '95 summer. Kernis has written a twenty minute solo suite for me that will be on the record. The Terry Riley piece will also be on it, as will Three Preludes by Lewis Richmond. Finally, two [Alan] Hovhannes Sonatas that have never been recorded, which I think are very pretty. He's an Armenian-American composer who's become more and more popular in his eighties. Anyway, I want this next CD to be something that is serious fun — tonal and not too eclectic. I want the listeners to be able to create their own eclecticism.

THE OLDE WOODEN BOX

JT: You've played a number of different guitars over the years by some very fine makers — John Gilbert, Greg Byers and Thomas Humphrey. What thought process did you go through in deciding to move to a new instrument, and how did you go about selecting them?

DT: Each guitar has its strengths and weaknesses, and each changes a player's playing to at least a small degree, and sometimes, to a large degree. You do different things on different guitars. I was married to Gilbert's guitar for a long time. I also worked with Greg Byers on his instruments for many years. He sent me all of his new guitars and I told him things that I thought needed improvement. He remained open and flexible and is making some incredibly fine guitars. I felt like I had been part of the process with those guitars and something of my ears was in them. There's a real refinement to Byers' instruments, a wonderful fine craftsmanship and a beautiful sense of legato. They are incredibly musical instruments and they're very, very even across the range. I've used them for a number of my recordings and I love recording on them.

Then I got fascinated by and almost addicted to Humphrey's *Millenium*. I think that's such an important invention. I warn everybody out there, don't spend more than a few hours with this guitar unless you're ready to have your guitar playing life change a little bit, because I found it hard to go back.

JT: With the *Millenium*, is it the physical nature of the raised fingerboard or the volume and responsiveness across the whole range?

DT: With that guitar, I have to say that the ability to get above the twelfth fret without feeling like it's different territory is incredible for my whole thinking about the fingerboard. Before it felt like the fingerboard ended at the twelfth and then started again. Now, it physically feels like one cohesive entity. The *Millenium* is also a real player's guitar in that I can be really rough with it. I never feel like staying in one place with the right hand. It calls for using a lot of colors. I'm also into playing 650s [650mm scale length] right now, as a lot of people are.

JT: Why is that?

DT: I just feel very comfortable. And perhaps getting a little older, I don't want to work any harder than I have to.

The Guitar in Society

JT: Several times, you've talked about the guitar and music in relation to the larger world. You've toured both China and the former Soviet Union, which have been undergoing tremendous changes, both economically and politically. How do you see those changes impacting music and musicians?

DT: One of the ironic things is that the worse things get politically, often, the better the arts get. In some of the most horrendous times, art just flowers. There's a lot of suffering going on, though, in places like Russia. It's very difficult for musicians from what I hear. In China, there was a tremendous hunger for the guitar and I hear that's still happening. But there is very little money behind it. Given the opportunity, the guitar could flower there.

JT: There's currently a debate about whether taxpayers should be subsidizing artists through the National Endowment for the Arts. Even some artists who have been NEA grant recipients have spoken out against public funding of the arts, claiming that it's actually, in the long term, harmful to the arts community. As a musician and a recipient of NEA funding, what's your view?

DT: How is it harmful? I'm curious as to what that point of view is.

JT: Well, Leonard Koscianski, a two-time recipient of individual artist grants from the NEA, mentioned two things. First, grants have become a government seal of approval given by like-minded artists and academics to the "aesthetically correct," excluding whole categories of art — usually the more traditional and conservative — from serious consideration. And second, that grants are usually awarded to successful practitioners who are already doing fine without government support.

DT: If you think that's happening now, try making all the funding private and see what happens. Exxon is going to fund Pavarotti and things that make Exxon visible. It's going to be endemic. Look, I'm an old lefty. I think we should cut the defense budget by half, double all teachers' salaries and multiply by ten or even one hundred the funding of the arts by the government. I was just in Munich, where the budget for opera is greater than the whole NEA budget. In Europe, you can see how tax dollars go to the arts and the culture is enriched from that. Artists become national heroes who are funded and revered. Some of their big time, older generation composers like Henze and Berio live very well and they're more respected in their countries than, for instance, our dean of composers, Elliot Carter, who doesn't get the same kind of cultural support.

JT: In the private sector, people voluntarily part with their money to purchase your CD or to attend your concert. And they decide what part of their income they're going to spend on the arts and what specific organizations and artists they're going to spend it on. When taxpayers subsidize artists, they are effectively disenfranchised from both how much is spent and whom it is spent on. What do you say to the taxpayer who wants to decide for himself how much of his money is spent on the arts, and how it is spent?

DT: I say I just disagree. I think there's a certain priority that's expressed by a culture that puts their money into the arts from a government level. That's just my sense of values. I think it's a national disgrace right now. And it is going to get cut this year, I don't think there's any doubt about it.

JT: Do you find yourself approaching how you sell yourself and your idea to get an NEA grant or other public funding, versus the way you have to package and sell yourself in the commercial sector to get funding?

DT: When I do an NEA grant proposal, I try to do it based only on content. I don't get into the sexiness of it or the commerciality. Whereas, when you're making a CD, you're thinking more of those things. I like to think a serious panel of my peers will review my proposal based on artistic content and my background. It's a whole different ball of wax when it's market-based. The marketplace is affecting our artistic decisions all the time. I think, for instance, of a discussion I had with Takemitsu, who is one of the most commissioned composers by orchestras. He said he figured out quite a few years ago that orchestras don't have any time to rehearse because of money. So he was going to write simple orchestra parts and always give any sophisticated musical material to the soloist, who had time to practice. And orchestras caught onto it — "Hey, we can learn this stuff in a couple of rehearsals." He got commissioned like crazy. That's an artistic decision being made on a financial basis which is, I guess, a practical way to go.

Coda

JT: What do you feel is most important for guitarists to keep in mind as they continue their involvement with the instrument?

DT: For me, performing is one of the richest experiences, a way to process life through the guitar. I would tell guitarists to value the process, not just the end results. Also, don't be afraid to be an amateur. I think amateurism is wonderful. People become fixated on the end result, and if they don't get quite the result they want, they drop the whole thing. None of us should forget why we're playing in the first place. It's not just about getting the good grade or the most cookies. It's about each of us trying to make something happen in our small way.

Concert Reviews

David Tanenbaum, guitar
Manhattan School of Music, New York City
February 5, 1998

A February Nor'Easter was no match for the enthusiastic audience that came out for the second concert in the Augustine Regal Guitar Series. David Tanenbaum rewarded their dedication with a thoughtfully constructed, mostly contemporary program of guitar music.

To begin the concert, Tanenbaum reached back to the Baroque era, to the music of lutenist Sylvius Leopold Weiss and harpsichordist Domenico Scarlatti. His performance of Weiss' *Tombeau sur la mort de M. Comte de Logy* was both deeply expressive and meticulously crafted.

The three Scarlatti Sonatas that followed were all transcribed by Tanenbaum. The insight Tanenbaum gained in his youth from studying the 500–plus Scarlatti Sonatas at the keyboard clearly helped in both piece selection and transcription. Tanenbaum's careful attention to ornamentation and pulse helped bring out the essence of this music.

Next up were two movements from Aaron Jay Kernis' Partita. Kernis — who studied composition with Tanenbaum's father, Elias — wrote the piece 1981. He revised it in 1995 and added a new movement, *Echo*. This melodically engaging and rhythmically entertaining movement showcased Kernis' playful inventiveness as well as his understanding of the guitar. When Tanenbaum finished Partita, the composer — seated in the audience — rose and took a well-deserved bow.

The first half of the program ended with *La Folia Folio* by Bryan Johanson. This piece was constructed by taking the eight-bar motive from *La Folia d'Espagna* and, using modern guitar techniques, varying the harmonic progression thirty times. The result is an exciting and engaging piece. That part of Tanenbaum which admires the music of Piazzolla was evident in his performance of *La Folia Folio* — outgoing and connecting with the audience in a visceral, rather than intellectual, way.

The second half of the program began with the New York Premiere of *Piezas Breves* by Roberto Sierra. The five short pieces ranged from *Con gracia*, played as gently as a Caribbean breeze, to *Intensio*, played with controlled passion. Although *Piezas Breves* is structurally cohesive, the piece does not make a deep impression.

In contrast, Toru Takemitsu's *In the Woods* is a memorable work of deep beauty, one of the last that he wrote before his untimely death in 1996. Each movement of *In the Woods* gets progressively slower, depicting a walk deeper into a forest. Tanenbaum's realization of the tonal colors in the piece made the imagery come alive.

Terry Riley's *Barabas* is the second of twenty-four pieces in his planned guitar cycle. Anyone expecting the guitar equivalent of Riley's famous Minimalist work *In C* would have been surprised. This is an energetic work, from the constantly moving independent lines of the opening to the rasgueados and descending basses that follow. Tanenbaum, the guitarist who persuaded Riley to write for the guitar, mirrored the eclectic nature of the piece in his performance.

The program ended with Tarrega's *Jota*. This piece, by the founder of the modern school of classical guitar, provided perspective on the five contemporary works that preceded it on the program. Besides, it was a crowd pleaser. Tanenbaum saw to that.

David Tanenbaum, guitar
Luciano Berio — 70th Birthday Celebration
Tisch Center for the Arts (92nd Street Y)
New York City
November 15, 1995

November 15, 1995 was an evening of unparalleled music and musicianship — thirteen world-class soloists performing the *Sequenzas* of Luciano Berio, one of Europe's foremost contemporary composers. Written in Berio's highly individual musical language, the *Sequenzas* are technically demanding, unaccompanied works that examine interrelated concepts, expand the boundaries of their associated instruments and challenge our conventional image of each instrument.

Beginning with *Sequenza I* for flute in 1958, the set also includes works for harp, voice, piano, trombone, viola, oboe, violin, clarinet, alto saxophone, trumpet, guitar and bassoon. *Sequenza XI* for guitar was written in 1988 for Eliot Fisk and was performed at the 70th Birthday Celebration concert by David Tanenbaum.

Tanenbaum spoke to me about the events leading up to his performance at the celebration concert. He received a call in July to perform *Sequenza XI* at the concert. Although he had several other projects in the works at the time, his strong interest in the piece lead him to accept.

Tanenbaum learned the *Sequenza* from a final draft of Berio's manuscript, which he received before publication of the printed score. There are about twenty minor differences, such as notes in the manuscript that later became harmonics in the printed score. As Tanenbaum observed, "Using the original manuscript could be — in some ways — controversial. One can rightly assume that the printed score is the one approved by the composer," he explained, "and this score is very well edited. But I was intrigued by some of the details in the manuscript, and in working with Berio at the dress rehearsal he made some suggestions, but never said anything about the elements I used from the original manuscript."

Tanenbaum also worked with Berio the day after the concert because Mode Records asked Tanenbaum to record the piece as part of a planned double CD of *Sequenzas I through XI*. Mode wanted to make sure all of the artists had worked with Berio and that he was comfortable with their performances. "Berio's very involved in performances of his music and makes quite detailed suggestions," noted Tanenbaum.

Since the *Sequenza* is unmeasured, dealing with pulse and tempo are a challenge. Tanenbaum explained, "I spent a lot of time with a metronome to get a sense of the pulse, even though there's no consistent beat. I used accents where appropriate to help provide pulse, but not in the fast sequential parts that shouldn't have a feeling of pulse." Because there's so much in *Sequenza XI* that's aggressive, Tanenbaum's approach was to use whatever space was available, such as in the "tuning" section, as a place of repose. There are many technical things going on in the piece. So a good rasgueado (the type of strumming used extensively in flamenco music) is a must,

David Tanenbaum

David Tanenbaum (with guitar), composer Luciano Berio (second row, center) and the other musicians who performed Berio's complete *Sequenzas* at his "70th Birthday Celebration," New York City, November 1995 (Steve J. Sherman).

because Berio uses four different kinds and is very specific about them. Also, the repeated sequences must be even faster than the thirty-second notes used throughout. 'One can get easily sidetracked by the incredible amount of activity going on," cautioned Tanenbaum, "but I find the essence of *Sequenza XI* to be the interplay between the fast passages and the more sustained sections. Berio sequences many things, but only uses a small amount of basic material."

Composers writing their first pieces for guitar face a tradition strongly associated with Spain. Some composers, like Peter Maxwell Davies, address this by avoiding any reference to the Spanish repertoire. But Berio used the flamenco language, the classical language and his own inventions to create *Sequenza XI*. "What I admire about Berio is that he went right after the flamenco element of the guitar," Tanenbaum said. "He created an important piece packed with a variety of wonderful techniques and spectacular sounds that uses the guitar really well. Many guitarists have expressed disappointment with the piece, thinking it to be one-dimensional. I want to find as much dimension as possible in this *Sequenza* and see what I can do to change that perception."

The 70th Birthday Celebration concert was Tanenbaum's third public performance of *Sequenza XI*. He said the concert felt historic and noted that it was a very different experience hearing all thirteen *Sequenzas* performed together, in contrast to having *Sequenza XI* performed as part of a guitar program. One thing Tanenbaum learned from talking before the concert to the other performers, some who have been performing their *Sequenzas* for fifteen years, is that the pieces don't get any easier to play. "That wasn't too comforting to hear!" confessed Tanenbaum with a laugh. "But the performers all had a great admiration and fascination for their pieces and were very focused on giving the best possible performance."

As for the performance itself, Tanenbaum demonstrated a deep understanding and feel for the work. While the beginning was tentative, the middle was solid and the ending superb. And though some of the passages in the upper registers sounded unsteady, Tanenbaum's Humphrey Millenium was a good match for this piece, given the forays into the higher registers of the guitar and need for wide dynamics. Tanenbaum brought out all of the extremes in the work—rapid changes in dynamics from fortissimo to pianissimo, right hand changes from tasto to ponticello and transitions from dense chords to single-line passages. The audience clearly enjoyed the performance and called Tanenbaum back three times.

David Tanenbaum, guitar
Chester String Quartet
Aaron J. Kernis/ Richard Danielpour Today's Composers Concert
Tisch Center for the Arts (92nd Street "Y")
New York City
February 21, 1996

If composer Aaron J. Kernis were a chef, his cuisine would be undoubtedly New American. Kernis places a premium on originality, combining musical styles in a completely natural way and serving up concoctions both sophisticated and fun. He is one of the most auspicious young composers on the American music scene today. To date, he has written three works for guitar: *100 Greatest Dance Hits* for guitar and string quartet, Concerto for Violin and Guitar, and Partita.

Three of Kernis' works were presented as part of the *Today's Composers* series at the 92nd Street Y's Tisch Center for the Arts. His pre-concert interview with the director of the Tisch Center, Michael Barrett, provided a unique insight into his works, including *100 Greatest Dance Hits*. Kernis began by speaking about the composers who have influenced him, including Bach and Mahler. From Mahler, he learned how to express a wide range of emotions through music. He then talked about the inspiration he has received from popular music—everything from Jerry Lee Lewis to rap music. According to Kernis, the title *100 Greatest Dance Hits* was inspired by the old K-Tel Music commercials extolling albums with titles like *100 Greatest Motown Hits!* His advice to the string quartet on playing the first movement, *Introduction*, is particularly interesting. Kernis said they must "play percussion on the bodies of their instruments, let loose and hope they don't break their Stradivarius." He also explained that the title for the last movement (*Dance Party on the Disco Motorboat*) was inspired by the television dance show *Soul Train*.

As for the concert itself, Tanenbaum and the Chester Quartet produced a big, bold sound for *100 Greatest Dance Hits*. The first movement, *Introduction*, began with the guitar and the quartet drumming on their instruments, which segued into a call and answer between the guitar and the quartet. Both Tanenbaum and the Chester Quartet demonstrated their ability to deal with a variety of unusual instrumental techniques in this brief opening.

The second movement, *Salsa Pasada* (rancid or spoiled salsa), is rhythmic and highly syncopated. A single-note Latin-flavored melody for guitar gives way to sections for the quartet ranging in feeling from New Age to Romantic. Tanenbaum gave this section a playful bounce, while the Quartet provided a fanciful tone for the mood needed by their parts.

The third movement, *MOR Easy Listening Slow Dance Ballad*, takes its name from the old radio term "middle of the road." It is the longest and most lyrical movement in the piece. The sound created by the Quartet at the opening of this movement was exquisitely shaped—full and round, yet clearly defined. The interplay between the guitar and violin in the middle of this movement was well balanced.

The final movement, *Dance Party on the Disco Motorboat*, is a tour de force with musical influences ranging from disco and rap to Brazilian and easy listening. Parts of this movement had a sensual feeling, not unlike Piazzolla's music. A funky bass line in the guitar, the abandonment by the quartet of their strings for a drum, triangle and sandblocks that lead into a John Mayall–style vocal percussion. Then back to the strings for a quick ending. The performance was playful, but at the same time the interplay among the five performers was precise.

The remainder of the first half the program was dedicated to two other works of Kernis', *Still Movement with Hymn* and *Superstar Etude*, the latter of which appears on the Kernis CD *100 Greatest Dance Hits*. The second half of the program was devoted to a contemporary of Kernis, composer Richard Danielpour.

Recording Reviews

Lou Harrison: The Perilous Chapel
David Tanenbaum, guitar
William Winat, percussion; Scott Evans, percussion; Joel Davel, drums
New Albion NA055CD

David Tanenbaum continues his noteworthy contributions to the guitar on three recently released discs. His prodigious output over the last two years represents an artist in the prime of his career. The pieces on these discs all have their roots in the twentieth century. While *Great American Guitar Solo* features more formal compositional forms, Piazzolla uses Latin and jazz forms and Harrison uses Middle and Far Eastern forms.

The Perilous Chapel contains two works performed on guitar with percussion, the first being a transcription from the harp. These two works take up half the disc. The rest of the disc consists of four pieces for ensembles containing various combinations of flute, cello, harp and piano, together with a variety of percussion instruments.

Tanenbaum collected seven of Harrison's works into a *Harp Suite*, consisting of *Serenade for Frank Wigglesworth, Avalokiteshvara, Music for Bill & Me, Jhala, Sonata in Ishartum, Beverly's Troubadour Piece,* and *A Waltz for Evelyn Hinrichsen*. All these, except the last, have been published by Tanenbaum in the *Lou Harrison Guitar Book* (Columbia Music, 1994). The *Serenade for Frank Wigglesworth*, written in 1952, stylistically foreshadows works ranging from Brouwer's Etudes to New Age guitar music. Written as a melody with arpeggiated accompaniment, its harmonies are achieved almost exclusively without the use of simultaneously played notes. In this way it is reminiscent of the Bach 'Cello Suites. Tanenbaum's sensitive reading is distinguished by a warm sound and an even tonal color. In contrast, Benjamin Verdery's recording of this *Serenade* on his disc *Ride the Wind Horse* (Newport Classic NPD 85509) has his characteristically strong articulation and a wider tonal shading, particularly in the *Ritmico* section.

The next five pieces in the *Harp Suite* combine Eastern and Western musical forms. They are unmeasured and tend to focus on melody and rhythm, not harmonic structure. Three of the pieces—*Avalokiteshvara, Jahla* and *Beverly's Troubadour Piece*—have percussion accompaniment in the form of tuned water bowls, drums, finger cymbals and tuned bells. *Avalokiteshvara* uses a scale based on a Korean mode and makes heavy use of arpeggiated octaves interspersed with short scale passages. Tanenbaum captures the dance-like feel of the piece, in part through careful use of overlapping or ringing notes. *Jahla* and *Beverly's Troubadour Piece* have a similar feel as *Avalokiteshvara*. In contrast, *Music for Bill and Me* is a contemplative piece. In his transcription, Tanenbaum changed one of the passages in the deCapo section to harmonics and eliminated the lower notes in a subsequent octave passage. This results in a change of color and less weight at the end. His stated reason for doing this was because the octaves do not work as well on the guitar as they do on the harp. The *Sonata in Ishartum* has the feel of a two-voice fugue in flamenco mode. I particularly like this piece as well as Tanenbaum's performance, since his feel for Baroque counterpoint serves him well here. The final piece in the suite, *A Waltz for Evelyn Hinrichsen*, uses traditional Western rhythm and a dark harmony in A minor to achieve a feeling of sadness or loss.

The *Serenade for Guitar and Percussion* is based on eight-tone mode, with a flatted second and a raised fourth. Like several pieces in the *Harp Suite*, the *Serenade* has a Middle Eastern feel, with its monophonic writing and simple percussion. Tanenbaum's playing ranges from animated in *Round*, to mysterious in *Air*, to sultry in *Usul*. Of particular note in *Serenade* are the *Infinite Canon* and the Sonata. In these two pieces, Tanenbaum manages to bring out both their Baroque and Middle Eastern qualities.

Tanenbaum's association with Harrison has clearly helped in realizing the composer's intentions. In addition, Tanenbaum gets an excellent sound on this recording from his Greg Byers guitar. The liner notes, written by David Tanenbaum and Lou Harrison, are good.

Great American Guitar Solo
David Tanenbaum, guitar
NEUMA 450-84

One of Tanenbaum's important contributions to the guitar world has been his dedication to the promotion of new guitar works. Accordingly, the *Great American Guitar Solo* consists of five premiere recordings.

The disc gets off to a rousing start with the title track, *Great American Guitar Solo*, by Curtis Curtis-Smith. Its dramatic, strummed open-string "chord" leads into a series of chromatic descending sequences from E to B. The single-movement piece uses walking basses and blues-tinged melodies as it evolves over seven and one-half minutes to its logical conclusion on a strummed E major chord. Tanenbaum has a real affinity for this kind of piece. His love of this music and the music from which it draws its influences, along with the years he has spent studying and performing this type of music, really pays off here.

Marilyn Kind Currier's Sonata is a piece whose harmonies and sequences, though somewhat conservative, are firmly rooted in the twentieth century. Currier, primarily a composer for orchestra, has written this Sonata as her first piece for the guitar. It is a welcome addition to the repertoire and deserves a place alongside the twentieth century guitar Sonatas of Berkeley, Brouwer and Ginastera. Of particular note are the dark passages in the lower registers of this minor key–dominated work and the interesting arpeggio section in the first movement that is faintly reminiscent of the one in the Bach Chaconne. Tanenbaum's performance is right on the mark in bringing out both the beautiful and the physical nature of the piece.

William Bolcom is a composer and pianist whose works include symphonies and chamber music. *Seasons,* his first piece for guitar, was written more than twenty years ago but unfortunately never recorded until now. Tanenbaum's performance is splendid throughout. However, although two of the five movements —*Winter* and *Summer Sounds*— are consistently good, the other three movements are uneven in their writing.

Shirish Korde, who also produced this disc, is represented here by his first piece for guitar, *Time Grids.* It is a three-movement work for amplified guitar and computer synthesized tape. The second movement is particularly interesting in that the sound colors of the guitar are transformed by the tape into sounds similar to those of various string instruments from around the world. In the third movement — a kind of deranged *Electric Counterpoint*— the tape transformations are associated with polyrhythms. Korde's other works include *Goldbach's Conjecture for Flute and Tape.*

The disc closes which *Mortua Dulce Cano,* a small gem for the guitar by Bryan Johanson. Johanson's works for guitar include *Fresco 1* and *Labyrinth, Op. 30,* the latter having been transcribed by Tanenbaum. The performance here is characterized by a well-rounded sound, even in the upper registers.

Tanenbaum worked directly with all of the composers on this disc to ensure that their intentions were realized. He has made an important contribution by bringing to light in these premiere recordings several pieces that merit wider appreciation. The liner notes, some by the composers themselves, are informative.

Astor Piazzolla: El Porteño
David Tanenbaum, guitar
New Albion NA065CD

If you like Astor Piazzolla, the well-known Argentinean composer who transformed the traditional tango by adding new rhythmic and harmonic characteristics, you will savor David Tanenbaum's *El Porteño.* It is a somewhat new direction for Tanenbaum, an artist who does not see himself constrained by his previous areas of focus. So when New Albion gave him a chance to do a recording of pieces he particularly enjoyed, Tanenbaum chose Piazzolla.

El Porteño consists of two larger works and three single pieces. The first larger work, *Las Cuatro Estaciones Porteños*, is a collection of four pieces — *Otoño Porteño, Inveirno Porteño, Primavera Porteña* and *Verano Porteño*. The arrangement is by Sergio Assad and this is the first recording of his arrangement. The pieces work well on the guitar, although they are by no means easy to play. Here we are treated to the warm and sensual Tanenbaum, a side of him that we do not get to see as much in his performances of Baroque and formal twentieth century works. In addition to this recording, be sure to check out John Williams' recording of *Verano Porteño* on *Spirit of the Guitar* (CBS MK44898), a relaxed, sultry performance with his legendary tonal palette in full force.

The other larger work is *Cinco Piezas*, which Piazzolla wrote for guitar in 1980 after hearing Walton's *Bagatelles*. I especially like Tanenbaum's reading of *Compadre*, the last of the five pieces, in the way he contrasts the bright and mellow passages while seamlessly blending the percussive effects. Other recordings of *Cinco Piezas* include Oraison (Etcetra KTC 1023), Savijoki (Ondine ODE 781-2) and Aussel (Circe 87101).

Chau Paris is a charming piece arranged by Abel Carlevaro. Tanenbaum's interpretation is sunny and playful, yet always in control. The only other recording of this piece I am aware of is on Carlevaro's import LP *Recital de Tango* (Ayui A/M 17, LP Uraguay), which unfortunately may be almost impossible to find.

From the opening harmonics to the closing arpeggiated chord that fades into the distance, Tanenbaum's performance of *Milongia de Angel* is inordinately satisfying. A transcription of this piece by Horatio Malvicino, the guitarist in Piazzolla's Quinteto Nuevo Tango band, was published in the Summer 1992 issue of *Guitar Review* [GR 90]. I prefer the arrangement Tanenbaum uses, in both its choice of key and its choices of register. *Guitar Review* is planning to publish Tanenbaum's transcriptions of Piazzolla pieces in an upcoming issue. The only minor drawback to *El Porteño* is the brief liner notes, which are not very informative.

Discography

David Tanenbaum
New Albion NA 095
Kernis: *Partita for Guitar*; Richmond: *3 Preludes*; Reich: *Nagoya Guitars*; Riley: *Barabas*; Zappa: *Waltz for Guitar*; Hovhaness: *Sonata no. 2*.

El Porteño
New Albion NA 065

Piazzolla: *Chau Paris, Las cuatro estaciones porteños, Milonga del Angel, La Muerte del Angel, Cinco Piezas.*

Great American Guitar Solo
NEUMA 450-84
Bolcom: *Seasons*; Currier: *Sonata*; B. Johanson: *Mortua Dulce Cano*; Korde: *Time Grids*; Curtis-Smith: *Great American Guitar Solo*.

Estudios
GSP 1000
Carcassi: *25 Estudios (op. 60)*; Sor: *20 Estudios*; Brouwer: *20 Estudios Sencillos*.

Acoustic Counterpoint
New Albion NA 032
with The Shanghai Quartet
Tippett: *The Blue Guitar*; Reich: *Electric Counterpoint*; Davies: *Sonata*; Sierra: *Triptico*; Takemitsu: *All in Twilight*.

Henze: Royal Winter Music
Audiofon CD 72029
Henze: *First Sonata on Shakespearean Characters, Second Sonata on Shakespearean Characters.*

Manuel Barrueco Plays Lennon & McCartney
Angel 55228 2
Lennon-McCartney: *Fool on the Hill, She's Leaving Home, Penny Lane* (with David Tanenbaum, guitar); other Lennon-McCartney works for solo guitar and guitar/orchestra performed by Manuel Barrueco and the London Symphony Orchestra.

Last Letters from Stalingrad (by Elias Tanenbaum)
Albany TROY 247
E. Tanenbaum: *Shadows* (with David Tanenbaum, guitar; Chester String Quartet), *Last Letters from Stalingrad* (with Robert Osborne, baritone; David Tanenbaum, guitar; Tina Pelikan, viola; William Trigg, percussion; David Tanenbaum, piano); *Reflected Images* (with David Tanenbaum, guitar; Amy Hersh, flute).

100 Greatest Dance Hits (by Aaron Jay Kernis)
New Albion NA 083
Kernis: *100 Greatest Dance Hits* (with David Tanenbaum, guitar; Chester String Quartet); other non-guitar works.

The Perilous Chapel (by Lou Harrison)
New Albion NA 055
Harrison: *Serenade for Guitar and Percussion* (with David Tanenbaum, guitar; William Winant, percussion), *Harp Suite* (with David Tanenbaum, guitar; William

Winant, percussion; Scott Evans, percussion; Joel Davel, drums); other non-guitar works.

Le Miracle de la Rose, etc. (by Hans Werner Henze)
Ars Musici AM 0859-2
Henze: *An Eine Aölsharfe* (with David Tanenbaum, guitar; Ensemble Modern); other non-guitar works.

Beaming Contrasts (by Peter Scott Lewis)
New Albion NA 060
Lewis: *Beaming Contrasts* (with David Tanenbaum, guitar; Alexander String Quartet); other non-guitar works.

Website: www.davidtanenbaum.com

5

David Starobin: Making Modern Music
February 1999

David Starobin was born on September 27, 1951 in New York City. He began playing ensemble music at age eight and went on to study with Manuel Gayol, Alberto Valdes Blain and Aaron Shearer. Starobin has been involved in ensemble music since his studies at the Peabody Conservatory in Baltimore, and was the guitarist for the Theatre Chamber Players of the Kennedy Center. He has directed the guitar programs at North Carolina School of the Arts, State University of New York and at the Manhattan School of Music, where he holds the Andrés Segovia Chair. Starobin has been a pioneer in bringing new works for guitar to the public, in both solo and ensemble settings. He has had more than 300 works composed for him by such noted composers as Elliott Carter, George Crumb, Milton Babbitt, Lukas Foss, Poul Ruders and Mario Davidovsky. Starobin is the president of Bridge Records, which he founded in 1981. The recordings released by Bridge have received a number of nominations and awards, including the 1998 Cannes Classical Music Award for George Crumb's Quest and a 1999 Grammy Award nomination for Starobin's Newdance. He has been honored by Harvard University's Fromm Foundation for his commitment to modern music and the Lincoln Center awarded him the Avery Fisher Career Prize.

I first approached David Starobin about an interview in October 1998, at a reception following the U.S. (New York) premiere of George Crumb's Mundus Canis. In early 1999, he sat down to answer my questions.

On Stage

Jim Tosone: Ensemble playing has always been a central part of your career, whereas most classical guitarists put their solo careers first and foremost. Why did you choose this path?

David Starobin: I'm not so sure this was a choice I made consciously. When I was eight years old, I played recorder and guitar duets with my father. When I was nine, I began playing trumpet and later percussion in bands and orchestras. At age twelve, I was the lead guitarist in my neighborhood rock band, and by thirteen, I was going to summer music camp, and was playing guitar quintets by Boccherini. During my first year at Peabody Conservatory, I formed a duo with baritone Patrick Mason. We still perform together, thirty years later. While I was at Peabody, I was asked to join the Theater Chamber Players in Washington, D.C., and to be a participant at the Marlboro Music Festival. What I am getting at is that, early on, I was fortunate to have many excellent opportunities to play with others. The guitar's chamber repertoire is broad and challenging, and as any musician will tell you, there is nothing that surpasses the joy of communal music-making.

Since 1980, I've been a member of Speculum Musicae, a new music group here in New York City. With Speculum, I've played a lot of the contemporary chamber repertoire — everything from Boulez on. My work with Speculum has also given me an opportunity to develop an important and growing area of the guitar's repertoire — chamber concertos featuring the guitar. Some really terrific pieces in this genre have been composed for us, including George Crumb's *Quest*, Mario Davidovsky's *Festino* and Poul Ruders's *Psalmodies*.

JT: Given the large number of complex pieces that have been written for you, what techniques do you use to learn them quickly and get them to performance level?

DS: I divide my initial study period into work away from the guitar — reading through the score, noting any problems — and work at the guitar. At the outset, the work at the guitar is mostly rough reading, and formation of left-hand fingering, and later, right-hand possibilities. This fingering period — the physical and aural laying-out of the piece on the guitar — is the most creative stage. The large number of fingering choices and combinations available on the instrument determine phrasing, articulation and color in a profound way, perhaps more so than on any other instrument. I try to determine the most effective choices early on, but I tend to refine and revise as I work. Once I've got the piece fingered, I begin the more repetitive work of bringing the physical realization in line with an imagined ideal.

If all of that sounds complicated, I should hasten to add that the ancient desire "not to make a fool of oneself up there" is also a potent technique in inspiring focused work under pressure.

JT: Your own work performing the Nineteenth Century repertoire has led you to performance on the Viennese style guitar, exemplified by the nineteenth century instruments of Staufer, Sherzer, and even Herman Hauser, Sr. in the early part of the twentieth century. What are the advantages of playing the Nineteenth Century repertoire on this style of instrument?

DS: The slender neck and adjustable action of these guitars make them the ultimate "left hand" instrument. The ability to fine tune the Viennese guitar's action results in more accurate left-hand articulation than on the modern classical guitar, and the comparatively smaller scale enables the player of normal hand size to play with the singing legato that the music of this period demands. These old guitars also have the raised fingerboard that Tom Humphrey's recent *Millenium* guitars have made popular again. This design truly helps playing above the twelfth fret. I've recently acquired a 1923 Hauser built in the Viennese style — that is, it has a maple back and sides, a very slender neck and fingerboard, an adjustable mechanical action, and in this case, Hauser's 1921 patent bracing. The instrument is larger than a Staufer in body size and longer in string length — coming in at 638 cm. The guitar is powerful, ultra-playable, very clear, and sustains spectacularly.

JT: You have sometimes performed standing up, using a guitar strap. Under what conditions do you take this approach?

DS: [Laughing] I don't do it much now — it's probably a holdover from my rock days. I started doing it with a Gary Southwell copy of a Staufer guitar, when I was performing the Regondi Ten Etudes. These little guitars are not too different in size from a Stratocaster [electric guitar], and lend themselves nicely to a standing, and therefore, less cradled position. I used to do the Regondi as an uninterrupted forty-five minute set, and I think that both the Etudes and I breathed better when I was standing.

JT: Your focus has been on Nineteenth and Twentieth Century guitar music. What is the nature of your involvement with Renaissance and Baroque music?

DS: My main involvement is as a teacher and grateful listener. The sixteenth, seventeenth and eighteenth centuries gave us a rich foundation of excellent plucked music — music which lends itself easily and effectively to transcription on the modern six-string, nylon-strung, classical guitar. Most of my guitar students want to play the vihuela and lute repertoire, and they universally want to perform Bach. From Andrés Segovia onward, the overwhelming majority of professional classical guitarists have transcribed, performed or recorded this literature as a sizable portion of their work.

David Starobin (Waring Abbott).

JT: What musicians have inspired you?
DS: I've been a listener as far back as I can remember. I have a memory, as a little kid, of doing wild dances with my parents to recordings of Petrouchka and Nielsen's *Masquerade Overture*. I got to sit ten feet away

from the Budapest String Quartet one concert season. When I was fifteen, Varèse, Messiaen, Schoenberg and Stravinsky were gods. I got to see Jimi Hendrix, close up, a number of times. I remember a particular Mahler Ninth. I just love to be inspired by musicians—composers, performers, kids, masters. Music is the most intensely personal form of human communication that I know of. I can't put it better than George Crumb, who said, "Music surpasses even language in its power to mirror the innermost recesses of the human soul."

Performer and Composer

JT: Many composers, including Elliott Carter and George Crumb, have written several works for you. In what ways did Carter's and Crumb's latter pieces differ from their earlier pieces?

DS: I've been very fortunate to have long relationships with a number of composers. William Bland, Meyer Kupferman, John Anthony Lennon, Barbara Kolb, Poul Ruders, Milton Babbitt, and my brother, Michael Starobin, have repeatedly been willing to write for me. Elliott Carter and George Crumb are both composers whose music I've been involved with as record producer, conductor and guitarist for nearly thirty years. In fact, my most active involvement with both of their outputs has been as a record producer. I first met Elliott Carter in 1970, when I played his 1938 voice and guitar setting of *Tell Me Where Is Fancy Bred?* This simple song, on the surface, seems to have little to do with the atonal action-music of the solo guitar work *Changes*. And yet, in both of these vastly different works, bell sonorities play a central role. *Changes* is a challenging piece for the player and rewards the listener handsomely with repeated exposure. I had a conversation with the pianist and Carter authority Ursula Oppens last week and we both concurred that Carter's latest guitar solo, *Shard*, was virtually a perfect piece. There are not too many examples of this kind of inspired perfection in the twentieth century guitar repertoire — where not a single note seems extraneous or out of place, and the material fits the form like a glove.

JT: What about George Crumb's two guitar works, *Quest* for guitar and chamber ensemble, and *Mundus Canis* for guitar and percussion?

DS: These works could not be further apart in style. *Quest* is a reserved and introverted work of transfixing lyric beauty, while *Mundus Canis* is a slightly raucous and humorous rendering of five dog portraits. *Quest* evolved over a period of many years and was a difficult work for Crumb to finish. *Mundus Canis* was delivered right on time for the work's premiere.

JT: In the premiere of *Mundus Canis*, Crumb himself played percussion. What were the rehearsals like?

Composer Elliott Carter (courtesy of G. Schirmer, Inc.).

DS: The rehearsals were memorable. We were in Cannes, the food was wonderful, the weather was spectacular and the Mediterranean sparkled. The organizers in France had a difficult time coming up with some of the fairly arcane percussion instruments that George needed, and I remember several visits to the kitchen of our hotel to find proper beaters and other assorted implements. George is a good friend and colleague. We continue to tour together with this piece, and I enjoy his company immensely.

JT: What piece required the most back and forth interaction with a composer?

DS: I think that would be Elliott Carter's *Changes*. In fact, though the title has other meanings, the reference to incessant revision was definitely an inside joke at the time. This piece changed as it came into focus, both in its formal design as well as in its local detail. It began its life as a piece that was about half the length of what it eventually ended up as. I met with Elliott to play this early version and we both felt that it needed to be expanded. Then, in a series of meetings and a very extensive correspondence, sections were added and inner details worked on. I remember Elliott being very careful to make sure that all of the durations could be sustained and that the details of the guitar writing were notated precisely. I'm very pleased that this piece seems to have entered the instrument's repertoire. It's a work that I've recorded twice, and perhaps have played more than any other piece in my repertoire.

JT: You have had more than 300 new works composed for you. What composers would you like to have write a piece for you that have not already done so?

DS: I've requested pieces from a number of composers who either said "no" or "later." A few that I can remember are William Schuman, Pierre Boulez, Morton Feldman, Iannis Xenakis, Earle Brown, John Cage and Gyorgy Kurtág. The guitar is a quirky instrument, and some composers shy away from its intricacies, or need to wait until the right moment.

JT: What was the most unusual circumstance under which a composer wrote a piece for you?

DS: I'm not sure if this is unusual, but it certainly is different. The Danish composer, Poul Ruders, has a number of times come to live with my family for brief periods. During these visits Poul has written guitar music. He composed his Etude and Ricercare, as well has his Chaconne while at *chez* Starobin. I'd like to think it was the inspiring domesticity of our household that did the trick, but I suspect it was the availability of a nice guitar and an eager player to coo encouragingly at his efforts.

JT: Ruders has already written you a chamber concerto, *Psalmodies*, and now I understand there are plans for a new guitar concerto with orchestra.

DS: *Psalmodies* is a suite in eleven movements, with the guitar playing solo during three of them. In the other eight movements, the guitar interacts with different combinations of instruments. It's a wonderfully crazy work — stylistically, very free, but with masterful control over the instrumental resources. With Ruders, one never knows what to expect next, so the upcoming concerto is something that I'm sure will surprise me.

JT: Your brother, Michael Starobin, has written and arranged a number of works for you. Does your closeness affect the normal composer-performer relationship?

DS: If anything, it makes the relationship easier. Our shared background has always given me confidence about knowing just where the music was coming from. An example is Mike's recent piece, *The Snoid Trucks Up Broadway*. This little tune springs from our mutual enjoyment of the books by

David Starobin (right), brother and composer Michael Starobin and *Guitar Review* editor and publisher Rose Augustine (background, right) (Jessica Katz).

underground cartoonist Robert Crumb back in the late '60s and early '70s. I remember bringing them home and the giggles that resulted. While Mike was composing *Chase* for guitar and tape, we shared a studio on 72nd Street in New York City. He would write a bit, I'd come in and play it. And his lovely arrangements of songs from Stephen Sondheim's *Sunday in the Park with George* flowed right out of his work on the original production of the show. I remember attending previews, being entranced by the world of this piece, and simultaneously twisting his arm to convince Sondheim that guitar versions would be a nice idea. The work of Michael's that I identify most closely with is his *Joshua Variations*. This piece stems from a little tune that Mike and his wife Hannah would sing to their son Josh, right after he was born. The various events taking place in our lives during that time color my emotions every time I play it.

JT: Other than those that play guitar, which of the composers that have written for you have a particularly good feel for the guitar?

DS: The late Mel Powell wrote me a gorgeous solo piece, *Setting for Guitar*. And Mario Davidovsky's two guitar works — *Synchronisms #10* for guitar and tape, and *Festino* for guitar, viola, cello, and contrabass — are also superbly idiomatic works. In this era, numerous non-guitarist composers have learned to write good guitar music. With the entrance of guitarists into universities and conservatories everywhere, composers have had the opportunity to collaborate closely with guitarists who are eager to play new music. This new body of repertoire represents the flowering of aspirations that Andrés Segovia had for the guitar early in this century. We guitarists finally have before us a great canon — one which spans all styles and all genres. It is a truly satisfying experience for me to watch my students and their students perform this repertoire, which fifty years ago was only a hope.

The Next Generation

JT: Chairing a guitar department provides a unique opportunity to shape a learning program. What do you feel is special about the program you've created at the Manhattan School of Music (MSM)?

DS: We know that providing easier access to more information enables students to make more intelligent choices. I've been fortunate in having MSM's administrative support and assistance from the Augustine Foundation in developing MSM's guitar program into a center for serious guitar studies. In addition to its fine guitar faculty and curriculum, MSM presents the Augustine Guitar Series and also presents approximately ten master classes per year. In recent years we've had master classes by Julian Bream, the Assad Brothers, Leo Brouwer, David Russell, Aaron Shearer, John Duarte, Gordon Crosskey, Manuel Barrueco, The L.A. Guitar Quartet, Alvaro Pierri, Eduardo Fernández, Jorge Morel, Ben Verdery, Eliot Fisk, Eduardo Isaac and Roberto Aussel. The students and faculty benefit tremendously from these provocative encounters with vivid personalities and ideas.

JT: How do you help your students learn about and deal with the business aspects of a performing career?

DS: By virtue of their rapidly swelling ranks, the professional performing guitarists of tomorrow will face stiffer competition than ever. I try to guide my students into areas of music that they might enjoy, and which use their particular gifts. I try to be realistic about their possibilities as professionals, and in almost all cases, tell them that they should be developing auxiliary skills. Most of them, as children of the computer revolution, are miles ahead of me on this count.

A View from the Bridge

JT: How has your company, Bridge Records, been able to survive and prosper over the past two decades while other classical record labels — including some major ones — have foundered?

DS: Bridge has followed a fairly steady course. We've tried to develop our artists and recordings over long time periods and gradually develop a deeper catalog. In addition, we have steered a fairly conservative fiscal course, which has covered our rear ends — sometimes barely — at times of strain. We were very fortunate to sign a long-term contract with the Library of Congress in 1995; especially so, because at that time, the market for classical CDs took a downturn. This is a very tough, constantly shifting marketplace, and our competitors have often had resources far outweighing ours. Ultimately, it comes down to working hard to put out the most distinctive product that one can, and then doing the best that you can for it in the market.

JT: Bridge has released several discs that have been nominated for Grammy awards. What was special about those discs that you feel got them nominated?

DS: I've been privileged to produce studio recordings and a posthumous CD "in concert" series for the great American mezzo-soprano, Jan DeGaetani. Both of Jan's Grammy nominations for her Bridge recordings came after her death, and were testimony to the high esteem in which she was held by her colleagues. This year we received nominations for my disc *Newdance* and for Elliott Carter's *90+*, played by the pianist Charles Rosen. Carter's music, as performed by Charles Rosen, is classic, epic, twentieth century art — no less moving than a Jackson Pollock canvas or a Frank Capra film. My *Newdance* disc is a survey of eighteen composers writing eighteen short dance pieces in a wide range of styles.

JT: Bridge is coming up on its twentieth anniversary. How do you plan to celebrate?

DS: Our company is a family affair. My wife, Becky, is its managing director and both of our kids do work for the company. I'd like to celebrate by just spending a quiet evening at home with them. Maybe watch a "vid" together, diddle a guitar, read a book, play trivia games and gobble microwave popcorn.

George Crumb on Composing for the Guitar
April 1999

George Crumb was born in Charleston, West Virginia, on October 24, 1929. He studied at the Mason College of Music in Charleston and received his degree in 1950. Crumb continued his studies with Eugene Weigel, Boris Blacher and Ross Lee Finney. He then held several teaching positions before beginning a long association with the University of Pennsylvania, Philadelphia, in 1965. While at the university, Crumb was named Annenberg Professor of the Humanities in 1983. He subsequently retired from teaching in 1997. Crumb holds many honorary memberships and degrees, and has been the recipient of numerous grants and awards, including the Pulitzer Prize (for Echoes of Time and the River*). He cites Debussy, Mahler and Bartók as the principal influences on his music.*

The reception following the U.S. (New York) premiere of George Crumb's Mundus Canis *was clearly my lucky day, for it was then that I was able to get him to agree to an interview. Some six months later, on a pleasant spring morning, we had this delightful and engaging conversation.*

A FIRST TIME FOR EVERYTHING

Jim Tosone: How did you meet David Starobin?

George Crumb: Our acquaintance goes back to the early '70s. I was invited to the Peabody Institute in Baltimore as a visiting composer and David was a student there. Sometime after that he came to my house for dinner and I got to know him personally. I was impressed by David's intensity as a musician, his deep interest in new music and his love for the guitar.

JT: How did the request from David to write *Quest* come about?

GC: Very early on he asked me if I could write him a work for the guitar. He wasn't too specific about the context in which the guitar would appear — it could be solo, it could be a small chamber work. He arranged the commission through the Augustine Foundation.

JT: I understand it took a while to write.

GC: Composing the piece stretched out over five or six years. David had to wait about twenty-five years [laughs] from his original request for it to finally came to fruition! It was a very hard piece for me to write. I had not written for guitar before and the instrument had to carry the musical argument over a long space of time. So I decided to use a soprano saxophone with the guitar, creating two lead instruments within the chamber ensemble, which was a sextet.

JT: What is the musical language of *Quest*?

GC: I should say first of all that my compositional style has not changed radically since the early '60s, when I first began writing "my music." So *Quest* is related to my earlier music in every way — thematically, harmonically, rhythmically — as well as the gestural things, like an obsession with tambour, which is characteristic of my music.

David Starobin (left) and composer George Crumb, with one of the percussion instruments featured in *Mundus Canis* (Mark Brown).

JT: And the structure of *Quest*?

GC: Well, that was part of the difficulty in composing the piece. I had a hesitation as to the form, in part because of my lack of knowledge about the idiomatic aspects of the guitar. I wanted to have several contrasting sections which would show the different facets of the guitar's personality. At the outset, David gave me some indications of guitar idiom. He said, "Just remember we guitarists love to play repeated notes. This is something we can do in our sleep" [laugher]. The other thing he said was, "Don't forget that the guitar can play prestissimo tempos. It might seem like an ungainly instrument, but it's capable of very fast play." So I included these two ideas in the piece.

JT: *Quest* includes percussion, but not the typical percussion found in classical works. You specified rather unusual instruments such as the Appalachian hammered dulcimer, the African talking drum, and the Mexican rain stick. Why these instruments?

GC: In my works, I've tended to lean very heavily on world percussion sounds. Some of my works, like *Night of the Four Moons*, almost represent a United Nations of musical instruments. A student of mine wrote a work that included the Mexican rain stick and I had loved the sound of it. It seemed appropriate to include in *Quest*.

JT: I noticed that phrases from *Amazing Grace* appear at three points in the piece. What sort of imagery or programmatic ideas did you have in mind as you were composing *Quest*?

GC: That tune was a second thought. I had written an original bit of music in a quasi-folk style and was not happy with it at all. When I revised that section, I decided to use a real folk tune. I've used a couple of revival tunes in my other works and it is also a little homage to my Appalachian background. I think the music kind of expands in a way from the association that the listener brings to that passage.

It's a Dog's World After All

JT: What inspired *Mundus Canis (A Dog's World)*?

GC: David asked each of about twenty composers for a little solo dance piece. I started sketching one and found that I had too many ideas for one single little piece; it was developing into a suite of pieces. Then the idea came of memorializing the family dogs we've had over the years with little humoresque pieces. Each piece would feature the personality of one of the dogs. Composers like Ravel have written about cats, but dogs have not had great moments in music [laughter].

JT: How did you decide on the instrumentation? One guitarist and one percussionist is somewhat unusual.

GC: Part of that choice was again the fact that I felt uncomfortable in sustaining a work for solo guitar. Actually, I was quite pleased with the result because it gives the guitar a little more breathing space and creates a sense of dialogue between the instruments. In the beginning, I had in mind very minimal percussion — mostly just small instruments, like maracas. I then expanded it to include instruments like the frame drum. Each of the five pieces has its own percussion coloration.

JT: You're not a percussionist, but played percussion in the world and U.S. premieres of *Mundus Canis*. Why?

GC: Very early on I may have mentioned to David that I was writing the percussion *so* simply that even I could play it. David asked if I would be interested in actually performing it. I'm not a percussionist — piano is my instrument. But I've written so much for percussionists that sometimes people think I must play. So I became the percussionist in several concerts with David and it very much increased my respect for percussionists [laughter]. Some of the things I asked for seemed simple but they're not so easy to do. Like staccato on the maraca. I get a "dribbling" effect rather than a cleanly etched staccato.

JT: Should listeners familiar with the unusual sonorities of *Black Angels* or the spectral vocal settings in *Ancient Voices of Children* be surprised by the kind of happy-go-lucky nature of *Mundus Canis*?

GC: Well, yes. I suppose I'm not known for having written a lot of joyous or lighthearted music [laughter]. There's only the central piece in *Mundus Canis* that's a little more mysterious in style.

Putting Pen to Paper

JT: Did you listen to any other guitar recordings or study any guitar scores before writing your first work for guitar?

GC: One problem I had in composing for the guitar was that there were so few works that could serve as models. In the classical contemporary style, for example, there's no great Sonata by Béla Bartók for the guitar. David sent me many of his recordings, mostly of contemporary works. I listened to them, but many were not relevant to my style. I'm thinking of Milton Babbitt's piece [*Soli e Duettini*], which works very well in his own language but is not something innate for me. Mostly, I tried to draw some technical things from the recordings. And it helped just hearing the instrument.

JT: Was it any easier writing the second piece for guitar?

GC: Writing *Mundus Canis* was certainly much faster than *Quest*. It was done in a few months rather than several years. If I write for guitar again it'll speed up a little more, as I become more and more comfortable with the idiomatic side of the guitar. It's a conceptual thing partly, expressing our own voice through the very special voice of the guitar. I must say, as insecure as I felt when composing both pieces, I am happy with the results.

JT: What would you say is the most satisfying thing about writing for the guitar?

GC: The guitar is beautiful for the exploitation of timbre and color. The string bending effects are pretty. And each of the strings seems to have its own personality [laughter]. Also, the pitch range is so wide. You get a quasi-bass with the low E and the harmonics can take you up very high. The musical space that the guitar encompasses is quite vast.

JT: What's the most frustrating thing about writing for the instrument?

GC: Establishing a presence for it. The guitar's a soft-edged instrument. Since I wanted to use it with other instruments, I was always thinking about how I could help it exert itself. I did suggest a bit of amplification, which would not undermine its integrity as an acoustic instrument, but would make it possible to compete with the other instruments.

JT: Yet in *Quest* you paired the guitar with a soprano saxophone. At first glance, this reminds one of the satirical P.D.Q. Bach work *Sinfonia Concertante for Bagpipes and Lute*.

GC: [Laughter] It sounds surprising that I included soprano saxophone, which has a hard-edge sound, but nowadays there's a growing capability for pianissimo playing on the saxophone. But part of the compositional problem is staying out of the way of the guitar, allowing open space where the guitar could sound, not writing on top of the guitar, and not writing textures that entrap the guitar. One thing that worked beautifully in *Quest* was including harp, dulcimer and contrabass. There are passages in the concluding movement where the harp, dulcimer and pizzicato bass augment the guitar to give the sense of hearing an extended cosmic guitar.

JT: What would you tell a composer who is writing for the guitar for the first time?

GC: When I was a student in the 1950s, the guitar was not included when we studied instrumentation. Now, many of my students have had practical experience playing guitar, so they have at least a little technique on the instrument and a kind of a built in understanding of it. There's also a lot more music that they can look at now, like the Benjamin Britten piece [*Nocturnal*], which is beautifully conceived for the guitar. One thing I did do was pick up a very cheap guitar. I can't play guitar but have always had instruments of this type — like the mandolin and the banjo — to explore sounds and to make sure the chords I write are possible on the instrument.

JT: What can guitarists do to attract composers to write for the guitar?

GC: More concentration on the chamber aspects of the guitar. There's already an awful lot of solo guitar music.

Tomorrow Never Knows

JT: You once wrote an article called "Music: Does It Have a Future?" I like to ask you the question "Guitar Music: Does It Have a Future?"

GC: I have a strong conviction that instruments are constantly reinvented for each period. I've often felt that the piano at any point in history might have seemed exhausted, and then it was reinvented. Who could have predicted that the flute would become so important in twentieth century after the clarinet practically displaced it in Romantic music? Yet it came back in a dozen new ways. I think the guitar is at the outset of an enormous progression of development. So many composers are interested and the literature is exploding in both quantity and quality.

JT: Will you write more for the guitar?

GC: I've been writing a little less in recent years. I hope I can get back into more sustained work and perhaps guitar can figure in once again. Maybe one day I'll find the courage to write a solo piece.

Concert Reviews

David Starobin, guitar
Manhattan School of Music, New York City
October 1, 1998

The Manhattan School of Music was the backdrop for a special evening of premieres and other works from guitarist David Starobin. This concert was the first in the Augustine Regal Series, for which Starobin is also the program director.

An important aspect of Starobin's career has been the commissioning of new works from the finest contemporary composers. Tonight was no exception, beginning with a set of five new dance pieces—*Shameless Sarabande, Reflexiones Latinas, Da'Ase, Serenita* and *Shard*—the last four featured on Starobin's latest CD, *Newdance* (Bridge 9084).

Jorge Morel's *Reflectiones Latinas* is exactly the kind of piece one would expect from Morel—Latin American rhythms, simple melodies and colorful harmonies that capitalize on the color palette of the guitar. Starobin's treatment of the rhythm layered a sublime rhythmic bounce over a steady pulse, while his handling of the middle section was a model of sonority.

Da'Ase by Richard Wernick was a marked contrast to Morel's piece. Based on a Yemeni wedding dance in seven beats, its asymmetric single lines created cross-rhythms that challenge Western notions of dance. Starobin found within the piece a covert playfulness that the audience responded to enthusiastically.

In 1983, Elliott Carter wrote *Changes* for David Starobin. *Shard* has much in common with *Changes*, in that it is built on a series of concise, sharp episodes. In Starobin's hands, *Shard* was a two-and-a-half minute burst of energy that radiated throughout the hall.

Starobin's interest in nineteenth century guitar music and ensemble playing was showcased in Fantasie, Op. 54, one of twelve guitar duets written by Fernando Sor. As is typical of Sor's duets, one guitar had a high single melody line, while the other played chords and arpeggios in the lower registers. Starobin and his student Jorge Caballero played as one, giving a lively performance befitting the Romantic atmosphere of the piece.

Starobin also performed Sor's Twelve Pieces, Op. 31, taken from a collection of twenty-four studies for the guitar that appeared in 1828. His reading was clear and well-articulated, with the play in the rhythm adding to the interest of the piece.

The grand finale was the U.S. premiere of George Crumb's *Mundus Canis (Five Humoresques for Guitar and Percussion)*. The piece was written about a year ago and is about five dogs that Crumb has owned during the course of his life. Crumb himself played percussion during the performance, with different percussion instruments portraying the temperament of each dog. Although Crumb pointed out that he is not a percussionist, what he lacked in refinement he more than made up for in theatrical gestures. The crowd loved the performance and called the duo back for an encore of the last movement.

All-in-all, it was another ear-opening concert from one of the guitar's true pioneers.

David Starobin
Manhattan School of Music, New York City
March 21, 1996

From the moment David Starobin strode onto the stage it was clear that the audience's conventional wisdom about the guitar, its repertoire and performance practices was to be challenged. For Starobin played standing up, read from the printed score, used amplification and wore a guitar strap.

But the bottom line, from a musical perspective, was that Starobin's unique approach worked for him. He used the freedom that standing provided to reinforce his musical expression with physical gestures. The amplification was unobtrusive and sounded natural. And Starobin used the scores primarily for occasional reference during the more complex pieces and musical passages.

The program opened with Elliott Carter's *Changes*, one of the major twentieth century compositions for guitar. Commissioned by David Starobin and dedicated to him, *Changes* is an intense work built from contrasting moods. Starobin's use of the printed score was particularly wise here, since it is difficult to accurately render Carter's intentions from memory. Starobin captured superbly the wide range of colors and dynamics at the heart of the piece. While the rapid starts and screeching halts of *Changes* often command the most attention, Starobin was particularly effective in bringing out the softer, warmer elements in the closing *Lento tranquillo*.

Next on the program was *Five Anecdotes* by Andrés Segovia. In addition to his epic role as a performer, Segovia penned close to fifteen pieces for guitar. Unfortunately, he never recorded them and they are seldom performed. Starobin redressed this neglect by playing *Five Anecdotes*. In the first *Anecdote*, one can clearly recognize Segovia's playing style — the clear definition of notes, the warm sound and fluid pulse — built into the fabric of the piece. Starobin highlighted these elements through his phrasing and articulation. The second piece is lively and sunny, very much in the spirit of Spain. Here Starobin brought out the sonorous textures while preserving the lighthearted feeling.

The third *Anecdote* was soulful, while the fourth had the traits of a lullaby or Nocturnal. Starobin approached the fourth in a way that brought out its kinship with the Iberian music of Albéniz and Granados. The dancelike fifth *Anecdote* was enchanting and showed that Segovia had an ear for guitar composition as well as a heart for performing. Starobin's performance of *Five Anecdotes* reminded the audience of yet another aspect of Segovia's contribution to the guitar. (The *Five Anecdotes* were originally published in 1947 by *Guitar Review*.)

David Starobin is well known as a performer of contemporary guitar music. So finding two prominent composer-guitarists of the nineteenth century, Fernando Sor and Giulio Regondi, on the program might seem surprising. It should not be. Starobin's efforts to bring this era's guitar works to the public, by playing them on a guitar akin to a nineteenth century guitar, made it possible to hear Sor and Regondi's music in a "new" way (that is, closer to how the composers heard their works).

Giulio Regondi's Ten Etudes for guitar is a forty minute, technically demanding work from the peak of the Romantic period. Although meant to be performed as a set, Starobin played only Etude #8, the most mellifluent of the Etudes. His push and pull of the timing within the relatively fixed pulse was key to making the opening melody and the rhythmic development come alive. Starobin's performance of Regondi's tremolo study, *Reverie-Nocturne (op. 19)*, was characterized by an even, natural-sounding tremolo and good balance across the registers.

Opening the second half of the program were three instrumental works by Fernando Sor — Andante (op. 35, no. 9), a simple melody played over an arpeggio, Etude (op. 6, no. 3), an exercise built over left-hand pull-offs and a simple chord progression, and Galop (op. 32, no. 6), a lively piece whose performance triggered a burst of applause from the audience. The other two works by Sor were for voice and guitar — *Seguidilla: "Las Mujeres y Cuerdas"* and *Seguidilla: "Muchacha y la Vergenza."* Here Starobin was joined by baritone Patrick Mason, a frequent duo partner of Starobin's over the last twenty-five years. In both pieces the humor in the lyrics made the *Seguidillas* worth hearing.

Two of the program's high points involved Mason and composer-arranger Michael Starobin. Starobin's 1995 composition *Four Stevens* (based on the text of Wallace Stevens) is one of a handful of art songs for voice and guitar that have interesting guitar parts. The first piece, *The House Was Quiet and the World Was Calm*, is based on arpeggiated chords over an open drone. The second, *Autumn Refrain*, is characterized by a bouncing rhythm and complex interplay between the voice and guitar. The third piece, *The Snow Man*, uses a medieval-influenced melody along with idiomatic guitar effects, including percussion, artificial harmonics and strumming the strings above the nut. The last, *Not Ideas About the Thing But the Thing Itself*, is also based on arpeggiated chords and featured a backup vocal part by David Starobin. Starobin's playing was superb. Mason's singing was excellent and his vocal style here (poetic, rather than operatic) was in keeping with the nature of the piece.

The other highlight was a pair of songs from *Sunday Song Set* by Stephen Sondheim, arranged for baritone and guitar by Michael Starobin. Both pieces were characterized by engaging guitar parts and thoughtful lyrics. It was an excellent and enjoyable ending to the program. David Starobin showed how to create a program that combined new and old, challenging and enjoyable, into a musically substantive and crowd-pleasing evening of music.

Recording Reviews

The Great Regondi
The Giulio Regondi Guild
David Starobin (guitar), Douglas Rogers (concertina), Julie Lustman (piano)
Bridge BCD 9039

David Starobin continues his foray into the world of nineteenth-century guitar composers, which began with his 1990 recording of music by Mauro Giuliani (*Giuliani Guitar Music*, Bridge BCD 9029). Since composer Giulio Regondi was both a guitarist and a concertinist, Starobin has formed the Giulio Regondi Guild to bring his works to the public. The inclusion of his works for the concertina and guitar on the same disc is welcome, as it provides a broader understanding of the composer and a better context for interpreting his guitar compositions.

The two works for Concertina—*Les Oiseaux, Op. 12* and *Serenade in A*—take up about a third of the recording. Although I do not find Regondi's concertina works as interesting from a compositional perspective as his guitar works, the concertina part nonetheless requires exceptional technical skill. Douglas Rogers proves that he is clearly up to the task. If one listens very carefully, it is even possible to hear the key clicks of the concertina on this recording, a reminder that guitarists are not the only ones who must battle instrument noise. The Andante con moto from the *Serenade in A* is noteworthy for the beauty of its melodic parts.

The Ten Etudes for guitar, which form the heart of this recording, were lost until their discovery in 1989 by Matanya Orphée. We owe a debt of gratitude to him for this discovery and to David Starobin for his performance of this piece. The Etudes are clearly the work of a composer with a superior sense of melody and harmony. They display none of the uninteresting scales and chord progressions that sometimes afflict Nineteenth-Century guitar works. Starobin makes use of a broad tonal palette to bring out the contrasting character both within and between Etudes. I particularly enjoyed his interpretation of the more lyrical Etudes—#4 in E, #7 in D, #8 in G and #9 in E.

The use of period instruments on this recording gives the music a grace and clarity that helps bring out their essence. Fans of Regondi will be pleased to learn that Starobin has also recorded Regondi's *Introduction et Caprice, Op. 23* on his recent disc *Romantic Guitar* (GHA 126.022), which also includes works of Napoleon Coste and Fernando Sor. The liner notes by Rogers and Starobin are informative and well-written.

Giuliani Guitar Music
David Starobin, guitar
Bridge BCD 9029

David Starobin is known primarily as a performer of contemporary music for the guitar and founder of a record label dedicated to the promotion of new music. So it might at first seem uncharacteristic that his latest recording is devoted to the guitar music of nineteenth century composer-guitarist Mauro Giuliani. On closer examination, it is not at all surprising. By choosing to perform Giuliani's music on the smaller nineteenth century guitar, Starobin makes it possible for us to hear Giuliani's works in a "new" way; that is, on the instrument for which they were originally composed. This approach is part of a larger trend toward performance on period instruments, which ranges from playing Dowland on lute and de Visée on baroque guitar, to Bach on harpsichord and Mozart on fortepiano. Since Starobin also eschews transcriptions, the use of a nineteenth century guitar avoids the "transcription" of Giuliani to the twentieth century guitar.

The instrument Starobin uses is a copy of a J.G. Staufer guitar (ca. 1829). Staufer was a leading guitar builder in the early nineteenth century and was responsible for two major improvements in guitar construction — raising the fingerboard above the soundboard for better tone and making the frets out of an alloy of brass, copper and silver. Happily, much is gained and very little sacrificed by playing Giuliani on a nineteenth century guitar. Starobin's instrument has a well-defined and well-balanced sound which is, in its own way, quite powerful. A concert pitch of A=430 (as opposed to standard pitch A=440) is used for this recording, to be consistent with nineteenth century performance practice. The smaller scale length avoids the unnatural stretching that guitarists must often overcome when playing Giuliani on a twentieth century guitar, resulting in a more musical performance. It is interesting to compare this recording to Starobin's recording of Fernando Sor's *Souvenir de Russie* (*A Song from the East*, Bridge BCD 9004), which Starobin plays on a very twentieth century Humphrey *Millenium* guitar.

A period instrument in and of itself is not enough to make for a musically satisfying performance. A feeling for the composer's intentions, an understanding of the performance style of the time and the technical ability to play an unfamiliar period instrument are also vital. Starobin succeeds along all of these dimensions. Starobin's programming approach, which involves alternating larger scale works such as *Grande Ouverture (op. 61)* and *Six Variations sur un Theme original (op. 20)* with a series of small Preludes, Rondos and Etudes, works well. With the exception of the *Grande Ouverture*, nearly all of the other pieces on this recording appear for the first time on compact disc. These include the previously mentioned *Variations*, excerpts from *Leçons Progressives (op. 51)*, *Rondeaux Progressives (op. 14)*, *Choix de mes Fleurs chéries (op. 46)* and *Variazioni sulla Cavatina favorita (op. 101)*. The liner notes, which were prepared by Starobin, are substantive and informative.

Discography

Newdance
Bridge 9084
Jaffe: *Spinoff*; Morel: *Reflexiones Latinas*; Carter: *Shard*; Lavista: *Natarayah*; Bland: *Rag Nouveau*; Sørensen: *Angelus Waltz*; J.A. Lennon: *Gigolo*; Mackey: *San Francisco Shuffle*; Wernick: *Da'ase*; Paraskevas: *Chase Dance*; Duarte: *Valse en Rondeau*; Babbitt: *Danci*; M. Starobin: *The Snoid Trucks Up Broadway*; Harvey: *Sufi Dance*; Nørgård: *Serenita*; Ruders: *Chaconne*; Lansky: *Crooked Courante*; Johanson: *Open Up Your Ears*.

Guitar Concertante
Bridge 9071
with David Starobin (guitar), Speculum Musicae/William Purvis (conductor), Don Palma (conductor), SMU Meadows Symphony/David Milnes (conductor)
Crumb: *Quest*; Ruders: *Psalmodies*; J.A. Lennon: *Zingari*.

Poul Ruders
Bridge 9057
Ruders: *Etude and Ricercare;* other non-guitar works.

The Great Regondi, Vol. 2
Bridge 9055
Regondi: *Introduction et Caprice (op. 23), Rêverie (Nocturne pour la guitarre, op.19)*.

Eight Compositions (by Elliott Carter)
Bridge 9044
Carter: *Changes*; other non-guitar works.

New Music with Guitar, Volume 5
Bridge 9042
J.A. Lennon: *Zingari* (with David Starobin, guitar; SMU Meadows Symphony/David Milnes, conductor); Davidovsky: *Synchronisms #10* (with David Starobin, guitar); Reynolds: *The Behavior of Mirrors* (with Todd Seelye, guitar); Flaherty: *Cross-Currents* (with Elgart-Yates Guitar Duo); Powell: *Setting* (with David Starobin, guitar); Babbitt: *Soli e Duettini* (with Anderson-Fader Duo).

The Great Regondi, Vol. 1
Bridge 9039
Regondi: *Ten Etudes*; other non-guitar works.

Giuliani: Guitar Music
Bridge 9029
Giuliani: *Grande Ouverture in A major, Leçons Progressives (op 51, nos. 3, 7 and 14), Six Variations sur un Theme original (op. 20), Préludes (op. 83, nos. 5 and 6), Rondeaux Progressives (op. 14, nos. 1 and 5), Choix de mes Fleurs chéries (op. 46, nos. 4, 5 and 9), Minuetto (op. 73, no. 9), Etudes (op. 100, no. 13), Variazioni sulla Cavatina favorita: "De calma oh ciel" (op. 101)*.

New Music with Guitar, Vol. 4
Bridge 9022
with David Starobin (guitar), Patrick Mason (vocal), Susan Palma (flute and piccolo), Tim Eddy (cello), Benjamin Hudson (violin), Oren Fader (guitar), Daniel Kennedy, (percussion), Tod Machover (conductor/data-glove)
M. Starobin: *Chase*; Searle: *Two Practical Cats*; Saxton: *Night Dance*; Kolb: *Umbrian Colors*); Roxbury: *Songs of Walt Whitman*; Machover: *Bug-Mudra*.

A Song from the East
Bridge 9004
with David Starobin (guitar), Kim Kashkashian (viola), Oren Fader (guitar), Benjamin Hudson (violin), David Taylor (trombone), Susan Palma (piccolo)
Nemerovsky: *Etude in A Minor*; Sokolovsky: *Etude in D major*; Sor: *Souvenir de Russie*; Sugár: *Hungarian Children's Songs*; Kurtág: *A Kis Csáva*; Ivanov-Kramskoi: *I Am Sitting on a Rock, Lullaby*; Jemnitz: *Trio*.

New Music with Guitar, Vols. 1, 2 & 3
Bridge 9009

with Patrick Mason (baritone), Susan Palma (alto flute), Peter Press (mandolin), Susan Jolles (harp)
Carter: *Changes*; Sondheim: *Sunday Song Set*; Babbitt: *Composition for Guitar*; Takemitsu: *Toward the Sea*; J.A. Lennon: *Another's Fandango*; Kolb: *Three Lullabies*; Bland: *A Fantasy-Homage to Victoria*; Henze: *Carillon, Récitatif, Masque*.

Romantic Guitar
GHA 126 022
Coste: *Caprice sur l'air espagnol "La Cachucha" (op. 13), La Romanesca*; Sor: *Menuet (op.11, no. 12), Etude (op. 6, no. 9), Septieme fantaisie et variations brillantes (op. 30), Larghetto (op. 35, no. 3), Andantino (op. 31, No. 13), Souvenirs, d'une siorée a Berlin (op. 56)*; Regondi: *Introduction et caprice (op. 23)*.

Websites: www.bridgerecords.com
georgecrumb.com/crumb.html

6

Harold Shaw: The Art of Artist Management
May 1997

Francis Harold Shaw was born in 1923 in Hebron, New York. In his youth he studied piano, violin and cello. After World War II, he became an associate at Hurok Concerts. From 1969 to 1996 he was the chairman and owner of Shaw Concerts. The firm's roster included such legendary artists as Vladimir Horowitz, Jessye Norman, Jacqueline du Pré and Dame Janet Baker. Shaw also guided and supported the careers of more classical guitarists than any artist manager in history. His clients included Julian Bream, John Williams, the Assad Brothers, Carlos Barbosa-Lima, Eduardo Fernández and Angel Romero.

Harold Shaw greeted me at the door to his apartment in New York City's historic Apthorp Building. The spacious living room, filled with art and mementos, was a fitting setting for a lesson on twentieth-century artist management.

THE SHAW CHRONICLES

Jim Tosone: How did you become an artist manager? It's not something you major in at college.

Harold Shaw: When I came out of the Air Force at the end of World War II, everybody was running back to school to get their degrees. I didn't want to do that. So I went to school at night and in the daytime worked at Samuel French, a company that published plays. Sadly, in all the time I was there I never read a submitted script that was really good enough for publication or production. I finally got tired of reading five bad plays a day and began to take note of other activities in the field. I became aware of a firm called National Concert Artists Corporation (NCAC), which had lecture, theater, and music divisions. That sounded much more interesting, so in 1949 I joined NCAC.

JT: NCAC and other large corporate artist management firms were a relatively new phenomenon when you joined.

HS: Yes. Surprisingly, corporate artist management firms had their origins in the early days of radio. At that time, there were two major radio corporations — the Columbia Broadcasting System (CBS) and the National Broadcasting Corporation (NBC). They were signing up people like Orson Welles to long-term contracts. Well, these radio personalities weren't always on the radio and the companies found they could raise additional revenue by having their celebrities do other things, like personal appearances. So CBS and NBC created personal appearance departments that arranged for their stars to be seen by the public. Then along came the Federal Communications Commission, which said, "Now wait a minute, boys. You're either a personal appearance company or you're a broadcasting corporation. Which will it be?" They both decided to stick to broadcasting and the heads of the two personal appearance departments at CBS and NBC were given the job of running those departments as independent companies. One became Columbia Artists Management and the other became the National Concert Artists Corporation (NCAC).

JT: Wasn't NCAC the representative for booking and scheduling artists represented by legendary impresario Sol Hurok?

HS: Right. I began there as a sales representative, getting bookings and dates for Mr. Hurok's artists. Essentially, I drove around the country talking with promoters. At first I traveled by Greyhound bus, but then graduated to a little English Ford. I would leave in mid–September, come back for Thanksgiving, go back out again in December, return for the holidays, leave again in January and come back after Easter. By the end of May, practically all the promoters had taken off for the summer. In September, I would start again. I have been to all fifty states time and time again, and can tell you the capacity of the auditoriums, their acoustical properties, and the nature of the town they are located in.

JT: How do you go about figuring out the character of a town?

HS: When I arrive, I go to the museum and look at the paintings and their collections. I speak with the drama department at the local college to find out whether they are rehearsing the most recent English farce or Shakespeare. I would arrive late afternoon and say to the promoter, "Will you and your wife please come and have dinner with me?" We would spend the evening talking and they would tell me about the level of their public, in terms of musical comprehension. From those things, I got an idea of what would fit in that community to make their concert series successful. A small percentage of the public was interested in a series featuring Schoenberg and Berg. Others wanted music that was more accessible. This approach to learning the cultural level of the community is not done very much anymore.

JT: What was the marketplace for classical music concerts like at that time?

HS: The colleges and universities were a major portion of the independent market, but their students and teaching staff were only a small percentage of the audience. The colleges were really using their concert series to service the surrounding community. In many cases, the reason they did this was because the town had a major manufacturing plant or corporation nearby that made substantial donations. The series was a way for the colleges to contribute back to the activity in the community. When the manufacturing plants started closing and business moved out, the colleges started eliminating their concert series, because the funding dried up. I am talking here mostly about the Northeast and Midwest. If you go out to Silicon Valley, the colleges are very interested in sponsoring concerts because the industries in the area are interested and able to provide support.

JT: Are all promoters pretty much the same?

HS: The people in charge of engaging artists vary incredibly in their interests and ability. Some are good promoters, good advertising people or good public relations people — but they know very little about music. A few are genuinely interested in music and extremely knowledgeable. Between those two extremes you have many gradations. There are also people who simply do not belong in the job. At colleges, people are sometimes appointed to run the concert series because they're on tenure, they're wearing out, and the president needs to find something for them to do. I remember one major university where the chairman of the concert committee said to me, "I didn't ask for this job, I don't want it, and I would like you to help me get this problem of next season off my desk in forty minutes, so I can go back to my chemistry department and do my work" [laughter].

JT: Yikes! What were the good ones like?

HS: The chairman of the committee at William Jewel College in Missouri was very knowledgeable. He would spend his summers in Europe talking to various people and he wound up engaging Pavarotti to perform there. If I'm correct, it was actually Pavarotti's American debut!

JT: In 1969 Hurok sold his firm to *Tomorrow's Entertainment*, which was owned by General Electric. What did he say to you when he did that?

HS: We had a thirty-second conversation. He said, "You know, I'm selling the firm. Do you want to be a part of the sale?" I said, "No." And he said, "Okay." Most of our business discussions were about that long [laughs]. So I moved out and started Shaw Concerts. I took with me only the artists who I had brought to the firm. Later some of the artists from the old Hurok roster, like Dame Janet Baker and John Shirley-Quirk, came over to me. I was particularly strong with artists from Great Britain and Western Europe. But I was very careful never to go into areas like the Soviet Union or East Europe while working for Mr. Hurok, since those were places he covered.

JT: You also were one of the major contributors to bringing classical music artists to Japan. How did you spot that opportunity?

HS: It was an indirect outgrowth of when I was engaged to be the performing arts director for the 1960 Seattle World's Fair. They built a lovely seventy-six acre cultural center. I had charge of an outdoor stadium, an arena, an opera house, a theater and a number of other places on the grounds. I had to be sure there was activity in every place on every day. This included having two acrobats riding a motorcycle back and forth from the top of the arena to the top of the space needle every day at noon. And a burlesque show with girls doing striptease on roller skates [laughter].

JT: Tough job. I'm not seeing the Japan connection.

HS: As part of that engagement, we brought over the Bunraku — the lovely puppets of Japan. And at that time, the Japanese were building a new concert hall called Bunka Kaikan. I could see the possibilities so I just went at it. I eventually took the Chicago Symphony, the Philadelphia Orchestra, Isaac Stern, Van Cliburn and a whole group of others to Japan. That got the interest going.

JT: Why did you decide to retire?

HS: I worked for fifty-one years and I'm seventy-four. I really wanted to have a year of fun, away from everything. This summer I'm going on a boat tour through Scandinavia on the North Cape cruise to see the northern lights, then on to St. Petersburg and see the Hermitage for two or three days. When I'm seventy-five, I'll settle down, focus on something and see if I can behave myself [laughter].

JT: I imagine you encountered your share of frustrations along with your triumphs.

HS: There were days when things got unbelievably frustrating, but that's a major part of this business. I remember once when [soprano] Jessye Norman was coming from Scandinavia. She was performing at a commemoration for the 100th anniversary of [soprano] Kirsten Flagstad's birth. And Jessye's limousine hit a moose! [laughter]. She was covered with blood and the car windows were all broken. Artist managers must be prepared to deal with those situations. Sol Hurok once had a Soviet dance company on tour in Canada when their truck turned over and all the costumes burned up.

Harold Shaw (left), mezzo-soprano Dame Janet Baker and her husband, Keith, New York City (courtesy of Harold Shaw).

JT: Shaw Concerts was the last of the major independent artist management companies. What happened to the staff when you retired and closed the firm?

HS: Within two weeks of when I made the announcement to the staff, everyone had a job. Some decided to open their own agencies, others went to firms like ICM.

Sol Man

JT: Sol Hurok is considered by many to be the greatest impresario of all time. What was he like to work for?

HS: Our relationship was unique because I was an associate, not an employee. I had my own artists who I brought to his roster. We'd talk about what I wanted to do, what he thought I should do, but I had a great deal of leeway.

JT: What did you learn from working with him?

HS: He was the kind of person that was incredible in a crisis. Calm, didn't say much. He would just sit quietly and finally say, "We do this." He

Harold Shaw and soprano Jessye Norman celebrating Thanksgiving at an Italian restaurant in Tokyo (courtesy of Harold Shaw).

was very capable, very shrewd and he'd come out covered with roses every single time. A good example: He had the Bolshoi Ballet on tour when the box office man in Baltimore took the ticket money and fled to South America. The performance was sold out, the people had the tickets they had paid for and they were expecting a performance. But if Hurok allowed the performance to go on, he wouldn't have the money to pay expenses. Well, he ended up talking with the mayor of Baltimore, the tickets were honored by the city and Mr. Hurok became honorary mayor of the day [laughs]. He also knew how to flatter. I'll never forget the time when a lovely little lady from Iowa who had been booking from us for years wanted to meet the famous "S. Hurok." So I said, "Okay, dear, you come and I'll introduce you to him." He had her so charmed you would've sworn they were old friends and he'd known her all his life. When he was on, he was on.

JT: During the 1950s, S. Hurok was the sole management firm for the cultural exchange of artists between the U.S. and the Soviet Union. He must've had some fascinating stories of dealing with the Soviet authorities.

HS: He was very discreet about that. The one time he said something to me was one morning when he was having breakfast at his desk. I said to him, "Tell me, how is the coffee in the Soviet Union?" He smiled and he said,

Harold Shaw and impresario Sol Hurok (left), Santa Barbara, California (courtesy of Harold Shaw).

"Better you should drink tea." So I said, "Okay, how is the tea?" He said, "It's better to drink water. But be sure you bring it from Paris — Evian" [laughter]. And he did, he would arrive with cases of it.

Guitar Man

JT: You have had more guitarists on your roster than any other artist manager. How did you become so closely involved with the guitar?

HS: One of the first people I was asked to take care of at NCAC was a troubadour named Richard Dyer Bennett. He dressed in white tie and tails, sang English and early American ballads, and accompanied himself on guitar. He played very well. Before that all I ever heard was the folk tradition of guitar, mostly in my college days when I was playing violin at square dances. Our guitarist did basic chord changes (I, IV, V, I, IV, V). It was through Richard Dyer Bennett that I first realized the guitar was a fascinating musical instrument.

JT: Then along came a man named Andrés Segovia....

HS: ... Who was playing absolutely exquisite guitar, a kind of guitar playing that was a revelation. Segovia was managed by Sol Hurok and it was my job as sales representative to arrange bookings and dates for Segovia. Unfortunately, it was very difficult to make the promoters understand what I was talking about. I would go to different cities — Kansas City, Topeka, Denver — and talk to promoters about their concert series. When I mentioned that we had a guitarist, Segovia, I got a very sharp answer which was essentially, "Look, fella, we've got guitar guys playing and singing around here all day, all night, every day of the week. We don't need anymore, thank you very much." That isn't precisely what people said, but that's what they were basically saying. Until they could actually hear Segovia play, they wouldn't be able to understand. Fortunately, Decca came out with a Segovia recording and when I played it for the promoters, it really opened up their ears. They said, "This is fascinating! This is beautiful music, well played. We will engage him. It'll be something unique, something different." You see, most promoters at that time took it as a rather elite novelty to present to their people — but it helped build Segovia's career.

JT: Unlike Segovia, who was managed by Hurok, Julian Bream was managed by you.

HS: Yes. I discovered Bream forty years ago in the Doubleday book shop that was downstairs in our office building. I would pore through the bins looking at various recordings. One day I saw a Westminster recording by a young Englishman playing the lute. I took it home and thought it was marvelous. The next day, I was poring through the bins again and, lo and behold, there was another Westminster record with this same guy Bream — this time playing guitar. That album had what I call the "Spanish chestnuts" for guitar — music of Torroba, Turina and Albéniz. Again, I thought he was just fabulous. So I chased him down through the recording company and got in touch with his agent in England. I then went over there, spoke with Bream, and he agreed to come here for a tour the following summer. He went on to perform for us for thirty-nine years. I arranged his first tour, his subsequent tours and his last tour in 1997. At least he says it's his last tour [laughs].

JT: And of course no guitar roster would be complete without John Williams.

HS: Interestingly, I first heard John Williams in London when he was around eleven or twelve years old. I thought he was very talented. Then I didn't see him then again for quite some time. When he was around twenty-one, we brought him over. John is the kind of performer who can walk on stage and the audience is immediately with him, from the moment his foot

Harold Shaw (left), and guitarist Julian Bream, New York City, November 1981 (Martin Reichental).

comes out on the platform. When John walks on stage, sometimes you even hear people yelling from the balcony, "We love you, John." I'm proud of the fact that we were not only the first ones to really move on the guitar, but through the years we presented more guitarists than anyone else. And we presented the best there was.

THE ART OF ARTIST MANAGEMENT

JT: How has being an artist manager changed over the years?

HS: In the early days, we were the employer. We would say to an artist, "I will pay you this much money per concert, pay your travel fares and your hotel bill." The artist listened to what we had to say, because we were the ones giving him the check. Then it changed. We became artist representatives, as opposed to managers. When we became representatives, we were the ones doing the listening and doing what the client wanted. Some artists today are receptive to discussing their careers, but many are not. In general, today's artist wants what he wants and really doesn't want to hear anything else. Fortunately, those artists who have major careers do listen and are very concerned about their receptivity in a given community.

JT: And you would take what you learned about the community and feed it back to your artists so they could tailor their repertoire?

HS: Absolutely. We used to say to the artists, "Give us three programs, one at a basic level, one at an intermediate level, and one that's a bit challenging." Artists today don't like to do that. They want to fix a program for the season with minor changes. They really don't adapt their programs anymore for the community they are going into. It requires persistence on the part of the manager to give the artist a comprehensive picture of the concert market, where they fit in, where you hope they'll be successful and how they're going to get there.

JT: What problems did you face because of the power shift from manager to artist?

HS: I remember one artist coming into my office and saying, "My fees have to triple for next year." And I said, "In the marketplace today, that's not a possibility for you. Why do you want your fees tripled?" After a long discussion, I found out that he and his wife had decided to buy a very expensive Oriental carpet [laughter]. His demand had nothing to do with what his draw would be at the box office, what the consequence of raising his fee to that extent would be commercially. There was no logic to it other than "We've seen this lovely Oriental rug, we want it and if we triple the fees we can have it." That kind of thinking is more in evidence than the public might believe. One other thing that artists seldom take into consideration is that many concerts are sold as part of a subscription series — so the basic audience is already there. The Palm Desert series in California is always sold out. People who get a new subscription probably get it because someone died or moved away. Now, many an artist will perform in such a community, come back and say, "We sold out!" [laughs]. That's a total lack of perspective. In part, the fault goes back to the conservatories. The musician who is going to be a professional seldom thinks that he's going to be running a business and even if he does, the conservatory doesn't give him the required skills. But it is a business. The artist has to understand that there is a thing called the marketplace and has to know where he fits into it.

JT: Are there special challenges with new and younger artists?

HS: The difficulty is in deciding whether you are going to risk seven years of income to develop the artist to a point that you will be getting back your investment. Most artists are convinced that the commission they pay you goes right into your savings account. Let me tell you, it doesn't. By the time you pay rent, phone bills, travel for sales people to go around the country, the artist does not carry his own weight until his fees get to a substantial level. If you bring a new artist onto your roster and introduce him to the concert world at a concert fee of $1,500 — let's see, twenty percent of $1,500 is $300. If he has ten concerts his first season, you get $3,000. There's no way in the world that you can represent an artist for $3,000 a year. It generally takes at least three years to get a promoter to engage a new artist. He will not engage a new artist the first year. The second year he'll watch the music scene to see if what you're saying is true, and maybe gets a little more receptive. The third year, he may bite. So that's three trips to Omaha, Nebraska. There's no way in the world that a new artist is covering that cost. The person who is paying for it is the major fee artist, whose larger commission you are using in part to assist the younger artists. Of course the established artist says, "I don't know why I should be supporting them, nobody supported me." That's not true, but he's apt to feel that he's paying you too much.

JT: How do you spot a potential major artist?

HS: I sometimes find that listening to an artist play is not half as helpful as listening to him speak. I get an awful lot from talking to artists and following the avenues their minds take. That kind of person has a relaxed confidence, an understanding of what they can and cannot do, and is very honest.

JT: A lot of your recommendations about artists came from established performers and established teachers whose opinions you valued.

HS: And sometimes from promoters. There's no standard way, just a number of different sources and a lot of shop talk. But you must realize that every teacher is only as famous as the number of famous pupils he has. So teachers are always ready to push the person that they believe has the best chance of succeeding.

JT: Who were some of the people whose assessments and recommendations you valued highly?

HS: The department heads of many major music schools, like Dorothy Delay [head of the Violin Department] at Juilliard, Joe Gingold [head of Violin Department] at the University of Indiana at Bloomington.

JT: What kinds of advice or insights do you give to young artists to help them navigate through their careers?

HS: Well, the one thing they are definitely not told early on is that if you are a success, it can be a very empty life. You'll have no community. Can you imagine what it is like to do a world tour? You're in Europe for five weeks, two or three days in each city. You come home for two weeks, then tour the United States for four or five weeks, come home for another two weeks, then off to Japan. You do this for ten, twenty years and you suddenly realize that the people you know are the people who show up for your concert every other year in Paris. And you see them for one minute while you sign an autograph. You may have a small *coterie* of four or five people that you see once every two or three years. For many artists that life eventually becomes very difficult. As they become more successful, they really realize they would like to be home a lot more. Performing artists sacrifice a lot. Their children don't know them like most children know their fathers.

JT: Does that present a dilemma to an artist manager whose commission depends on how much the artist works?

HS: Many managers who depend on commissions for their earnings want the performer to work as much as possible. But a good manager will help select the important things and make sure the artist has sufficient time for recuperation. If you push an artist, all you wind up with is a last-minute cancellation. There is no such thing as an artist always being at his peak and at his best. If you ask an artist if he will play a concerto on Tuesday and on Friday give a recital, he will probably say yes. The manager must know whether the artist can really do it. Some artists can read through an entire Sonata once and practically know it by the time they finish. John Ogdon, a marvelous pianist, could play anything on any day of the week. It was unbelievable. I remember saying to him, "Columbus, Ohio, has a cancellation on the Busoni concerto." That's fifty minutes of a very, very difficult piece. I said, "Can you do it? Rehearsal's tomorrow." And he said, "That's okay, I'll do it." And John would have it in his head in practically seconds.

JT: So you have to take the long view.

HS: It's funny, if you had asked me last September about Julian's American tour in April of '97, I could've told you every place he was going and every date he would be performing. Today I couldn't tell you where he had been, because it's in the past. Since we schedule several years in advance, the artist manager is always focused on the future. And once it is over, it's erased.

GOVERNMENT AND THE ARTS

JT: You've been the head of several national performing arts committees and have been associated with the National Endowment for the Arts (NEA). Are taxpayer subsidies for the arts necessary?

HS: I think federal subsidy of the arts is essential, but I don't agree totally with the structure of National Endowment. Ever since the NEA was formed, it has avoided like the plague putting any commercial manager on their board. Big mistake. England, Germany and other countries do it. We're so frightened of mixing the commercial with the nonprofit. The NEA has also gone for image, thinking that if you have a major artist on your advisory board, that is a big stamp of expertise as far as the public is concerned. But most artists have a very limited knowledge of the economic and administrative aspects of the music field. Artists know what their reception was like in a particular city, but they really don't know the makeup of that community, its cultural values and its economic capability. And if the National Endowment is about anything, it's about the economic capability of our cultural institutions.

JT: Is the NEA concerned about the artist manager having a conflict of interest? If so, why doesn't NEA exclude artists, since they have their own conflicts of interest?

HS: There's no reason why if a conflict of interest arose that the commercial manager couldn't recuse himself. But for the typical grant, the board would be able to take advantage of the artist manager's knowledge of the commercial and cultural aspects of a community. I think having [artist managers] Ronald Wilford or Herbert Barrett on the board would strengthen NEA. Individuals and institutions that apply for grants only tell NEA what it wants NEA to hear. I could give the NEA an additional, different perspective. Institutions also exaggerate their needs because they anticipate that they're only going to get "x" percent of what they ask for anyway — so the requests often have a total lack of reality. Politics plays a big part because you must get the appropriation bill passed. If you don't give a certain amount of money to the various cities and states — even those with little interest in cultural activities — you won't get the associated senator's or the congressman's vote.

JT: Do you think there's any validity to the point that a lot of the subsidy money goes to artists and/or institutions that are already established?

HS: I have always been annoyed that a certain portion of the money which is given to a particular community will probably end up engaging a superstar who doesn't need it. On the other hand, the person presenting the series will say, "If we didn't have the subsidy, we couldn't afford the superstar and we need the superstar to sell the whole concert series." So there are arguments on both sides. I feel that there should be some limit on the amount given to established artists and the subsidies should be used only for American artists.

The Secret of Success

JT: What should guitarists and other artists keep in mind as they navigate through their careers?

HS: There are two things. The first is to not limit yourself to the standard repertoire. Explore things beyond that. A lot of guitarists reach a level where they can play the standard repertoire well and feel they're done, but they're not stretching themselves musically. I think that's a big mistake. Second, a person who wants to be a major artist has to understand why he's in music. Many artists wind up doing it because it pleased mommy or got them attention. Those artists wind up having what I call zigzag careers. They will work very hard until they reach a certain pinnacle. Everybody loves them and the critics give them a great review. Then they slack off and their career goes right back down. Those artists really aren't interested in music. They'll never believe it, but the truth is that although they are *somewhat* interested in music, it's not really part of themselves, it's not a love affair that goes on forever.

 JT: So they'll never achieve the artistry of someone like Horowitz.

 HS: True. I will never forget a critic that I took for an interview with Horowitz. It was when Horowitz was going to Chicago for his first concert after coming out of retirement. The critic said to him, "Mr. Horowitz, how wonderful you're going to play again." And Horowitz was slightly offended, but didn't show it too much and said, "I *always* play." And the man said, "I mean you're going to play for the public." And Horowitz said, "Oh, I don't mind if they are there" [laughter]. You see, every day of his life, under no pressure, for no reason whatsoever, he came down and sat at his piano and played. Two hours, maybe three, depending on what he found that was interesting in the stacks of music he had all over. He wasn't rehearsing or forcing himself to do anything. Music was just an essential part of his life. If that's not you, I don't think you'll ever have a great career. You can have a career, but I don't think you'll have a great career.

 JT: That passion certainly came through in his concerts.

 HS: Well, he also did something I think would shock most artists. He wouldn't touch the program that he was going to play for two days before the concert. I remember saying to him, "You're not going to play anything on the program for two days?" And he'd said, "No. It will be risky, but it will be fresh." And boy, was it! [laughter].

A Word of Advice

 JT: What should an artist look for in an artist management firm?

 HS: First, is the firm well financed? Second, do they have people who will travel around the country and talk enthusiastically and knowledgeably about you? That's the way to get a promoter in Pella, Iowa, to decide to engage a new artist for his concert series. The personal contact between the agency and the presenter is essential for a new artist. It can't be done by letter or over the phone. Later, the presenter can send out a disc or a tape. But the truth is they may never listen to it and even if they do, they may say, "Well, with technology the way it is today, you have could have repaired this recording." It sounds great but they really don't know if it accurately represents the artist. Over time the presenter gets to know and trust the artist manager to understand his series. In the Hurok office many years ago, there was a lady who used to irk her competition incredibly. The sponsors would say to them, "Well, you know, we're very happy to see you, Mr. Competition, but Miss Illingworth has not been here yet and we'll let you know after she's come." What she told them was true turned out to be true. They relied on her and she brought them through season after successful season. That you cannot replace with any kind of push-button electronic system. Money and credibility, those are the essential things.

JT: So through all the changes in the business and in technology, it's still about relationships and personalized knowledge.

HS: I am sad to say that system is going downhill rapidly because the computerized methods of management today eliminate a great deal of the long-term relationship between the artist's management and the people who are presenting the concerts. It's getting to the point where if you want a soprano — push "1," a tenor — push "2." But maybe you don't know what you really need. Maybe it should say, "If your budget is $50,000 and you want a successful season filled with artists who are going to give something special to your community — push '276' now."

JT: What about agencies that ask new artists for retainers — $15,000 to $25,000 or more?

HS: I've never liked that. I think it's up to the agency to take the risk that they're going to build this into something that's worthwhile for both the artist and themselves. If an agency is willing to do that, that's a sign that they have some belief in what you can do.

WHITHER GUITAR?

JT: What will be the biggest challenge facing classical music in the twenty-first century?

HS: Music as an art form has a disadvantage in our current culture because it has one predominant sensory appeal — listening. When you lack a visual, except for something static like a person sitting playing guitar, it doesn't have the same impact as a strong visual-auditory combination. That's one reason why opera is the one growth area in classical music. In contrast, recitals are getting harder and harder to find.

JT: And the biggest challenge specifically facing the classical guitar?

HS: The sense of sound in our society has changed as well. It's been ruined by music being played too loud. If it isn't blaring, you don't listen. There's a whole group of instruments that we have lost our sense of hearing for. When was the last time you saw an ad in the *New York Times* for a harpsichord recital? Think of the concerts that we've lost. I don't know whether Wanda Landowski or George Malcolm could tour today.

JT: Are you suggesting the dreaded "A" word?

HS: Yes, amplification, that is the question for the classical guitar. Segovia certainly didn't want amplification. Years ago he could give a recital in Avery Fisher Hall or Carnegie Hall and the public would pull their hearing down and listen carefully. I don't think that today's audience is capable of that type of listening. Bream does not want to use amplification, while Williams uses a slight bit. But it means Julian plays in 1,100 to maximum 2,000-seat houses while John can play a 3,000-seat house. The promoter has to ask if he can afford to pay an artist to play a house with 800 or 1,200 seats. And even if he has a 2,000-seat hall, is that going to be too many seats for the number of people who are interested in coming and listening to the guitar? The guitar market is a very special market but it's going to have to deal with this financial squeeze play as we enter the new millennium.

7

John Williams: The Guitarist

March 1994

John Williams was born April 24, 1941, in Melbourne, Australia, and moved to London in 1952. He was trained assiduously from earliest childhood by his father and subsequently earned a scholarship to the Accademia Musicale Chigiana di Siena, where he studied over the course of five summers with Segovia. From 1956 to 1959, he studied piano and music theory at London's Royal College of Music. In 1958, Williams made his debut at Wigmore Hall in London, followed by debuts in Paris and Madrid. One year later, he released his first two recordings. He toured Russia in 1962 and the United States and Japan in 1963. Williams performed throughout the world in the 1960s and in the 1970s formed a historic duo with fellow guitarist Julian Bream, which resulted in several tours and three recordings. From 1960 to 1973, he also taught at the Royal College of Music. During this period, his recordings featured both the main guitar repertoire and contemporary music.

As he pursued his own musical vision, Williams challenged the demands and constraints placed on the classical performing artist. He began touring less and he traded traditional concert garb for more colorful and casual attire. In 1979, Williams formed the classical-rock group "Sky." His interest in musical styles covered the gamut from classical to folk, jazz, pop and non-western idioms. In the classical arena, Williams had guitar concertos written for him by composers Stephen Dodgson, Andre Previn, Richard Harvey and Steve Gray. He worked with composers from his native Australia — including Phillip Houghton, Peter Sculthorpe and Nigel Westlake — to produce guitar works that captured the spirit of their homeland. Williams' exploration of jazz led to collaborations with singer Cleo Lane and guitarist Joe Pass. His interest in non-western musical forms resulted in the first complete disc devoted to the guitar

John Williams (David Montgomery).

works of Japanese composer Toru Takemitsu. By crossing and blurring musical boundaries, Williams created a bigger and richer landscape for the classical guitar.

Many musicians and aficionados consider Williams to be the most technically proficient classical guitarist that ever lived. Over time, his musical expressiveness has grown even more sublime. As a result, Williams conveys to an audience the essence of a composer's intentions, unconstrained by the limitations of the classical guitar.

On a sunny March morning in 1994, John Williams greeted me at the door of his room in New York City's Essex House. He was dressed in his customary casual shirt and slacks. Since this was our first meeting, he asked me if I played classical guitar. When I replied that I was a serious amateur, his response was, "That's great. That's what we'd all like to be." Williams was exceedingly *generous with his time, answering questions for nearly two hours on the morning of his last of three concerts in New York. As he spoke while sipping his grapefruit juice, Williams would continually search for the precise word or phrase to express himself — much as he does when he performs.*

The Concert Stage

Jim Tosone: Your current guitar series in New York, which consists of three completely different concert programs performed in a ten-day period, is a rare event in the classical guitar world. How did the idea come about and what prompted you to undertake this series?

John Williams: I first did something similar about seventeen years ago in London at the Wigmore Hall. I did three concerts with the same idea of a baroque, a Spanish–South American, and a contemporary program — using the word contemporary to denote something that's reasonably contemporary, but not necessarily fixed to any particular style. On that occasion, I did the series on three successive days, which is what I also did a month ago at Wigmore Hall, and what I originally wanted to do here. But the 92nd Street Y theater was a bit nervous with three days in succession, I think quite rightly — who would want to go to a guitar concert every day for three days?

Anyway, it's something I wanted to do and I thought it would be nice to do in New York. I've been playing a lot of new pieces recently and I wanted to include them in the program. But I didn't want to be doing a one-program tour that only had new pieces, because I know there are a lot of people who like to hear the old favorites and the standard repertoire. So it struck me as a good idea, especially in a large city like New York, to do all three programs. Other cities on the tour are a mixture. In places like Toronto and Pasadena where I've done two concerts, I've kept the contemporary program and mixed the baroque and Spanish–South American programs into one. In the places where I'm playing only once, I've basically combined all three programs.

JT: Are there any areas, such as memorization or technical preparation, that require special consideration for a concert series, as opposed to a single concert?

JW: No, just more work [laughter]. It is actually a lot of work keeping three programs going even for a short time, because although you're doing standard repertoire, you have to have it in your head, not just your fingers. If you've got something approaching five hours of music to perform at a level where you're really on the ball all the way through, it's a lot to do. So it means a little more practice and careful pacing.

JT: For some of the new pieces in your contemporary program, you referred occasionally to the written music on stage. How do you prevent that from becoming an inhibitor to the performance?

JW: That's a very good question. With some pieces—for example, *Into the Dreaming* by Peter Sculthorpe—I had the music for only two weeks, because he had only just completed revisions to it. So obviously I needed the music for that. In the case of the Philip Houghton piece *Stélé*, I had played it before, but not often enough to have learned it by heart. If I were to play it often enough, I would gradually learn it and play it by memory. The third piece I did with the music is a piece—*Nunc* by Petrassi—that no matter how well I know it, I would always use the music, because having the music there is not an inhibitor. The dynamics in *Nunc* are so integral to the meaning and the style of the music that they must be observed as closely as possible to get it right. The piece depends on its dynamics, pauses and crescendos to be musically articulate. It's very difficult for someone like myself, who plays a range of music, to remember a piece like *Nunc*. I've heard it played several times by people without music and it's been totally unlike the dynamics that Petrassi has written in the score.

IN THE STUDIO

JT: Your contemporary program in the concert series included works by two Australian composers. A recording devoted to Australian guitar works would be a nice companion to your *Spirit of the Guitar: Music of the Americas* recording. Are you planning a recording devoted to Australian composers?

JW: You couldn't have asked a better question, because the day before coming on this tour, I completed that record. It's got all of Peter Sculthorpe's music. The two solo pieces that I played on this tour—*From Kakadu* and *Into the Dreaming*—and a piece called *Nourlangie*, which I played last year at Carnegie Hall with the Australian Chamber Orchestra. It also has a piece by the Australian composer Nigel Westlake that is a kind of concerto or suite based on music that Nigel wrote for the IMAX film *Antarctica*. It's a fantastic score. But the comparison with *Spirit of the Guitar: Music of the Americas* is not quite a true one, because *Spirit of the Guitar* was a deliberately lightweight selection of pieces celebrating different moods and colors of the guitar. This Australian album is much more substantial.

JT: Your CD of pieces by Takemitsu is pretty much a definitive recording, although *All in Twilight* is conspicuous by its absence. Do you have any plans to record it?

JW: Well, Takemitsu's one of the great composers and anything he writes is wonderful. The reason I didn't do *All in Twilight* was simply because it was, when I was making the recording, a very recent composition for Julian Bream. And although it was published, I felt that out of friendship and loyalty with Julian it was not right to record, at that stage, a piece written for him. There's a bit of gentle etiquette that comes into it.

JT: About your earlier recordings: the advent of the compact disc has resulted in a reissuing of previously released works by artists. Some are mid-priced, some are "two-for-one," and others are remastered, reorganized sets like Segovia's and Bream's. What are your feelings about the reissues of your works to date?

JW: Oh that's a helluva question [laughter]. Well, there are the very first records that I made when I was seventeen that have been reissued a number of times. I don't mind those being out because Decca, who has done them most recently, puts on the records when they were made. But I object when companies reissue without indicating that. As for the rest, there's no one answer. I think reissues and compilations, as long as they're mid-priced or less, are good in principle. When possible, if the compilation involves pieces drawn from different records, I like to help do that. On the ones I've done, I've had all the original bits of tape and have done the remixing, the re-editing and the ordering of the pieces. Another type of reissue is compilations of larger works, like putting a collection of concertos onto a double CD. The record companies in each country know how to do that best, since they know their market. There are many works in my case that are not so far on CD, like some of the earlier Stephen Dodgson and Patrick Gower works. Presumably, the companies don't think there's enough of an audience. A lot of the problem is with the megastores, who would rather have bulk of a few titles than a great range of things.

There's one other category of compilations, where they recouple different things by adding additional pieces to an original recording to fill up enough time on a CD. That's fair enough. But sometimes they needlessly recouple or recombine one's old records for spurious commercial reasons to reduce the royalty rate Compilations and reissues in most contracts get half the royalty rate. They give all sorts of reasons for doing it, but a lot of artists are unhappy. You have to take the overall picture. It's a business. The days of the old classical record firm building up and keeping the catalogue full of repertoire — they're gone.

JT: What are your thoughts about the acoustic aspects of compact discs?

JW: I have mixed feelings, but it's a *fait accompli*. Overall, it is an advance and they're developing and improving it all the time. I have slight reservations about the way it was done. For the last two or three years of vinyl production, because they were trying to sell the public on CDs, the quality control of vinyl was absolutely appalling. But now the industry knows fully well that the early CD recordings were not what they were cracked up to be. It was sold as the ultimate perfection, but up until a couple of years ago, it was very seriously flawed musically.

I'll give one perfect example. About six years ago, there was a record I made with the Inti Illimani (a Chilean group) and Paco Peña called *Fragments of a Dream*. It was recorded analog. We mixed it in London, and because vinyl was still being sold there, it was made in vinyl as well as CD. We made simultaneous masters. In other words, when you're reducing the twenty-four track original recording to a two track master, which is what you end up buying, we did the reduction to digital master and analog master simultaneously. After recording a piece called *Danza*, I went out to get a cup of coffee and came back in to hear the middle section, where this wonderful sampana (panpipes) is playing. And I said to the engineer doing the mixing, "What have you done? We had it right just a few minutes ago!" He said, "I'm just playing back the digital master to check it." Well, the digital two track master was totally unlike the twenty-four track original *or* the analog two track master. The digital master changed, for example, the panpipes — which are set in the middle of that mix — by literally moving them forward four or five feet in perspective. These are all very precise things when you're doing a mix that you spend a lot of time getting right. It's not just the relative volumes, it's the position so you can feel the relationship among the instruments. The digital master had completely scrambled that, so much so that I thought we'd lost our original mix.

The thing we're talking about with digital is not just whether violins sound screechy and metallic. We're dealing with a much subtler thing than that, which has to do with the technology of processing digital sound. It's full of problems. And I suppose the reason that musicians, and even the general public, reacted against it is because the nature of digital distortion — by distortion I mean lack of truthfulness — is of a kind that the ear is not accustomed to. But its potential for development, both in audio and video, is terrific.

Performance on Video

JT: Since you mentioned video, *The Seville Concert/The Film Profile of John Williams* is your first video release. What elements make a successful documentary video and what elements make a successful performance video?

JW: In terms of a music documentary, the prime thing is whether the content is interesting. But whether it's a documentary or a performance

Julian Bream (shown here playing the lute), with whom John Williams joined forces in the 1970s for a series of recordings and recitals (Sophie Baker).

video, as in *The Seville Concert*, I think it is mandatory that the camera work and the direction are very good. I don't mean that it's got good shots of the fingers and hands. The point of having the video is not to see someone do vibrato. The changes of instrument and the changes of phrase are part of a larger musical picture, and it's finding the visual language to follow that picture through that's important. Musicians tend to forget this. A musician who does not welcome the visual aspect as an equal partner in the performance would be better to stick with just sound. It was a challenge doing *The Seville Concert*. You can't do as many retakes and edits as you'd like because of the time schedule and the equipment. But I must say, *The Seville Concert* was beautifully edited and I was absolutely thrilled with it.

THE ART OF THE TRANSCRIPTION

JT: In your baroque concert, you played a transcription of a Vivaldi Concerto for solo guitar. How did you choose that particular concerto among the hundreds that Vivaldi wrote?

JW: I think Wanda Landowska used to play it and certainly Rafael Puyana, from whom I learned an enormous amount about music. So it's a piece I've always liked, and I've liked in the version that Bach transcribed for harpsichord. It seemed like an ideal piece for the guitar in looking at the harmonies, the melody in the bass line, as well as the chords and the nature of the melody in the slow movement. I used quite a lot of Bach's harpsichord version. There are one or two places where the Bach harmonies are particularly nice on the guitar. His descending bass line at the end in the slow movement, just before the repeat of the arpeggiated chords, is a typical harmonic progression of Bach's. It's in the style of the period and it sounds magical on guitar. You've got a dissonance while the bass is walking down step by step which is very beautiful. And there are one or two other figures in the other movements where the arpeggiated harmony sounds very guitaristic.

JT: The Vivaldi is a transcription from orchestra to a solo instrument. In contrast, the title track from your recording *Iberia* is an orchestration of Albéniz's suite for solo piano. In some ways the orchestration reminds me of Ravel's orchestration of *Pictures at an Exhibition*, in that the use of different timbres and colors brings a new perspective to the piece. What was involved in creating your version of *Iberia*?

JW: *Iberia* seemed an obvious source for orchestral arrangement. It's very interesting that when you look at the individual pieces in *Iberia* closely, arranging them for guitar and orchestra is not so simple. I don't only mean the orchestration, but selecting what parts the guitar will play. You might

John Williams (Julian Nieman).

think you just take, as in a concerto, the main tunes and put an accompaniment around it. Well, you can put a certain tune on the guitar because it technically possible, but musically it doesn't work. For example, *El Albaicín* from *Iberia* has quite a long orchestral buildup in the middle. The cellos have a lot of the tune and the scale of that music needs an orchestral tutti at that point. In effect, the guitar is not playing for large chunks of the piece. So it shouldn't be thought of as a concerto. It's a setting for guitar and orchestra. The flamenco single line is clearly the guitar's voice speaking and it serves as the counterpart to the orchestral sound. Steve Gray, the arranger, and I spent a long time going over *Iberia* bar by bar to figure out which pieces would work and how.

JT: Do you have any plans to publish your transcriptions or arrangements?

JW: I have published a few in the past, but I place a limited value on publishing transcriptions. In pieces where there is a lot of work done to remodel the piece for guitar, I think it's worth doing. There are some borderline things that I've published, like the Praetorius dances, which are really not arranged at all. They're very simple, but they're not in their original form. Many people can't afford to buy the original volume of 600 dances, so they were worth publishing for that reason. *Córdoba* is a favorite piece of mine, so I did that. It didn't need a lot of work, but there are different ways of doing it, and many people wanted it.

But there are a lot of things—like Scarlatti and Bach—that I don't believe need publishing. I don't think guitar editions should be published solely for their fingering. One of the first things you should learn on any instrument is how to finger. It should be up to the person who's playing, not the person who's done the edition. If you want to play a note on the second string, play it on the second string. There's no great musical reason why you should play it on the first or third string. Guitarists generally read badly and in an unmusical way in part because they tend to read fingering. I suppose there would be a case for doing the Vivaldi Concerto we were talking about. I learned it as I was arranging it, so I just sort of remembered it. But I will write it out when I get around to it.

The Twentieth Century and the Future

JT: Your work with the ensemble groups Sky and Attica stem from your interest in creating contemporary music that draws upon different musical styles, including classical, jazz, folk and rock. Do you listen to other artists who are making similar efforts—for example Elvis Costello's song cycle *The Juliet Letters*, which he composed and recorded with the Brodsky Quartet?

JW: Strange you should mention *The Juliet Letters*, because I had a chance to look at the video of that just before coming here. It was beautifully done and really interesting. I think we're in very exciting early days, in that there are so many possibilities for film and video production of music.

JT: In your current concert series, what were you trying to communicate through your selection of pieces and composers for your Twentieth Century program?

JW: Well, my main point was to play music that I like. In my contemporary program there's a great contrast of styles, including some pieces that some people may think are not actually contemporary. For example, *Sakura Variations* by Yocoh or *Elogia de la danza* by Brouwer. But I absolutely do not subscribe to the view that contemporary has to mean experimental and *avant-garde*. Contemporary means it's happening now. I think that the experimental and the so-called *avant-garde* are a part of contemporary music life, but are not the soul of it.

JT: According to the program notes, your Twentieth Century program was made possible in part through support from AT&T. What are your thoughts on how to best get new and innovative music presented?

JW: Well, the 92nd Street Y theater was full, so it was no different from the other concerts in the series. But what happened in New York was the same as happened in London. The Baroque and the Spanish programs sold out first. People wanted to come to those programs, but couldn't, so they instead bought tickets to the contemporary program. I could tell immediately who those people were. But I have never felt a duty to play contemporary music because "it should be done for the good of music or for the good of the guitar." The music I play, whether it's contemporary or otherwise, is simply music that I like. I really enjoy playing the Petrassi *Nunc*, which in many ways is, for the general public, the least approachable piece. New music has to live by performers wanting to play it and people wanting to listen to it. Sponsorship is great, whether it's public or private, as long as no influence is brought to bear on the programming. But buying a ticket is also sponsorship.

JT: Recently, one of New York's two full-time classical radio stations went off the air, along with the weekly program *The Classic Guitar*. The station adopted a light classical format several years back and was unable to retain serious listeners of classical music or attract a large enough general audience. How can guitarists expand the audience for the classical guitar while at the same time provide a forum for challenging and innovative music?

JW: I think you've chosen a good example. But there is no simple answer. I don't think we can look at it purely from the guitarist's point of view or even from music's point of view. It's a social and cultural phenomenon that cannot be looked at in isolation. Asking how do we have more good classical music for the guitar and how do we get more of the public to listen to it is asking the wrong question. The real question is how does a person get enjoyment out of music? As soon as you select classical guitar music and assume that there is something intrinsically good about there being more of it for a hypothetical audience that you want to improve, you're putting up a whole lot of assumptions about what should be done — which I'm afraid I can't do. I can't say it's better that Britten or Takemitsu wrote this wonderful piece for guitar and we as serious guitarists are playing it, and we want more people to listen to it. I can't honestly say that is more significant than the jazz group around the corner at the club or the Chieftains at a folk music festival. We as classical players should try and learn from that and be part of it. I like playing Takemitsu at home and I love it even more if someone else shares that enjoyment with me when I play it on the concert platform. I also love playing Barrios, and if someone passes me an arrangement of *The Man I Love*, I'll enjoy playing that too. A lot of opportunities for doing interesting musical things are continually arising. It's not a question of looking for something significant to do. There are hundreds of alternatives all the time and you select the things that get you enthusiastic.

To come back to your example about the radio station: in England, Radio Three, which is the BBC's serious music station, has over the last few years lost listeners. But Classic FM, which the equivalent of the radio station you mentioned, is a new station that plays lighter classics. They've straightaway got three or four million listeners and are a tremendous success. So you see, it's different from what you described. That's why these questions can't be looked at as purely musical ones. It's social and cultural and it varies in different countries.

JT: So what are the key social and cultural trends that are occurring?

JW: I think there's only one. And it's all embracing and inevitable. It is that the assumed superiority of the European classic music tradition is being questioned, and rightly so. The European classical tradition is only one of many wonderful musical cultures in the world. For our culture to accept that idea is quite a dramatic change because there has been a belief that yes, jazz is wonderful, South American music is very vibrant, Indian music is full of improvising fantasy — but when all is said and done, Brahms, Beethoven, and Mozart are it. That assumption has got to go. It's ironic for us in the guitar world because much of our recent history has been to try and become a part of that European classical tradition. But this is such an exciting age for anyone that's interested in the world, culturally, to be associated with the guitar — because of its links to so many different cultures. The guitar is a fundamental instrument in jazz and it has strong links to all other plucked-string instruments, like the sitar. And it originally was a popular instrument, a social instrument, which can embrace a variety of styles. It has magic in its sound, probably the most magical sound of all instruments. For guitarists to be able to be a part of all those different cultures is a unique opportunity that other musicians don't have as much. It's an ongoing process of discovery and enjoyment. And that's why we love the instrument.

Concert Reviews

John Williams, guitar
Kaufmann Concert Hall, New York City
Baroque Concert
March 10, 1994

The wood-paneled recital hall at the Kaufmann Concert Hall was filled to capacity for the first of the eagerly awaited series of three concerts by John Williams. His trademark purple turtleneck and pants set a tone of informality that was to be a characteristic of each of the concerts. The program began with six Sonatas by Domenico Scarlatti. Williams' performance of the Sonata in E major (K. 380) was characterized by cross-string trills in opening measures, a light rhythmic bounce and changes in tonal color between sections. In contrast, the Sonata in D minor (K. 213) featured broad shifts in color *within* phrases. As Williams tuned his sixth string from D back up to E after the second piece, he commented good-naturedly that his tuning changes were designed to give latecomers a chance to get to their seats. The Sonata in A major (K. 448) followed, with a strict and brisk tempo capturing the spirit of the harpsichord original. The set of six ended with the Sonata in A minor (K. 175). Here Williams brought out the contrast between the inherent drama of the minor passages and the sunniness of the major passages. Common to all six Sonatas was a clear definition of phrase and line. The performance sounded as fresh as Williams' recording of these pieces nearly two decades ago (John Williams, *Scarlatti: Six Sonatas*, CBS MT34198). The applause was loud and sustained.

The last piece before the intermission was the Bach Chaconne (from the Partita in D minor for Solo Violin, BWV 1004). The Chaccone is a complete contrast to the Scarlatti Sonatas in terms of texture, weight and complexity. Williams' transcription differs markedly from Segovia's, in that Williams adds only a minimal number of notes — primarily for harmonic support. The rapid scale passages in mm. 65–88, which challenge even the best guitarists, were clean and musical. This was due in part to the economy of motion in his left and right hands, along with their precise synchronization. In the extended arpeggio section, the inner voice was always clear. The D major section began almost hymn-like and built to a triumphant conclusion before returning to the darkness of the final D minor section. This was a performance of perfect balance and cohesion.

After the intermission, it was back to Bach in the form of Lute Suite No. 4 in E major (BWV 1006a). Although the Prelude and Gavotte are the best known movements from this work, Williams seemed to have a particular affection for the second movement, Loure, which received a very sensitive reading. A small slip in the Gavotte was noticeable only because imperfection is such an infrequent visitor to a Williams performance. There was absolute clarity of voicing in the rapid passages of the concluding Gigue. Next was *Tombeau sur la mort de M. Cajetan* by Sylvius Leopold Weiss, a contemporary of J.S. Bach. Williams described Weiss as "extraordinary at writing for the lute in the expressive style [of the Tombeau]." The program ended with a transcription for solo guitar of the Vivaldi Concerto in D major (op.3, no. 9). Although the chordal sections of the second movement seemed somewhat awkward, the transcription of the rest of the movement and of the outer movements worked very well.

In response to the heartfelt applause at the end of the concert, Williams returned for two encores. The first was a *Bach Sarabande* (from *Partita No. 1 in B Minor for Solo Violin*, BWV 1002). The second was *Two Dances from Terpsichore* by Michael Praetorius, originally published in 1612 as part of a collection of several hundred dances. Williams played these pieces with the same care and attention he gave to the more substantive works. This concert reinforced that Williams is a distinguished performer whose interpretations are always graceful and expressive.

John Williams, guitar
Kaufmann Concert Hall, New York City
Twentieth Century Concert
March 15, 1994

The rare three-concert series format made it possible for Williams to devote one program exclusively to Twentieth Century music, including the New York premiere of three new works. The program began with *Darwiniana*, written for Williams last year by Czech composer-guitarist Štepán Rak. The arpeggio section in the opening was reminiscent of Villa-Lobos, both melodically and harmonically. In contrast, the middle section was characterized by rapid passages soaring into the upper registers before returning to a recapitulation of the quieter opening. A rousing climax then followed. Williams' performance of *Darwiniana* was distinguished by a sound that was both full and clearly defined.

Australian composer Phillip Houghton's *Stélé* is a four-movement work with a slow-fast-slow-fast structure. *Stélé* was inspired by the art, mythology and landscape of Greece. The first movement describes a headstone or monument erected on the coastline in memory of those lost at sea. Williams' performance of this movement was somewhat constrained, perhaps due to the fact that he has played the piece infrequently and he was reading from score. His playing opened up in the second movement, *Dervish*, which was characterized by rapid scale passages in both the upper and lower registers.

Bronze Apollo, the third movement, signaled a return to the arpeggiated chords of the first movement ending on dying harmonics. The last movement, *Web*, used a rhythmic motive of four 16th notes followed by quarter note, along with a low A pedal. Williams' interpretation brought a pleasing sense of unity to these diverse movements.

Rodrigo's *Invocation et Danse* is subtitled *Homage to M. de Falla*. The piece is very much about tonal color and Williams succeeded in bringing this dimension of the work to the forefront. He also imparted a lively rhythmic pulse to the dance section, which contrasted nicely with the mysterious opening and close. It was only fitting to pair Rodrigo's Homage to Falla with Manuel de Falla's own composition *Hommenje (pour le tombeau de Debussy)*. The *Hommenje* is a small gem for the guitar, employing myriad guitar techniques in a manner that is thoroughly integral to the music. Unlike many guitarists, who perform the piece as if it's a funeral march, Williams played it more like a habanera, with a tempo that had a comfortable sense of motion.

The first half of the program ended with Australian composer Peter Sculthorpe's *From Kakadu*. The work was inspired by the terrain of Kakadu National Park in northern Australia. The opening Grave has a modal sound while the dance-like *Comodo* is characterized by repeating motives with distinct starts and stops. The third section, *Misterioso*, opens in the lower registers before moving to a section consisting of counterpoint in contrary motion. The closing *Cantando* has a singing line and ends on a haunting harmonic chord. Sculthorpe and Houghton demonstrate that Australia is finding its voice in the classical music world. In large part due to the efforts of Williams, the rest of the world is beginning to listen.

The second half of the program began with *Nunc* by Goffredo Petrassi. Williams described it "one of the great modern works for the guitar." The piece is organized loosely in five sections — the key ones being an opening that states the main material, a cadenza with percussion, a recapitulation and a coda with harmonics. The use of dynamics in *Nunc* is key to its expressiveness and in this regard Williams made sure to accurately bring forth Petrassi's intentions. *Usher Waltz* (op. 29), composed by Nikita Koshkin and inspired by the Edgar Allan Poe story, has enjoyed increasing popularity since it was first published. Williams gave the piece a wild, virtuosic performance that was greeted by enthusiastic applause.

Next was Peter Sculthorpe's *Into the Dreaming*, a piece for which Williams received the final score only two weeks before the concert. Perhaps because it was my first hearing of the piece, or perhaps because it was placed in the program between Koshkin and Brouwer, I found it to be lacking a distinctive character, although certainly pleasant. The program ended with

Leo Brouwer's *Elogia de la danza*, *Jongo* by Paulo Bellinati and an encore of Brouwer's *Danza Characteristica*. *Jongo* had an intense rhythmic motion and jazz-like harmonics, which received a flawless performance from Williams to end this imaginative program.

John Williams, guitar
Kaufmann Concert Hall, New York City
Spanish–South American Concert
March 19, 1994

A capacity crowd greeted Williams with warm applause for his third and final concert in New York. The program got off to a rousing start with the rapid arpeggios of Albéniz's *Torre bermeja*. By employing a strong pulse while remaining rhythmically fluid, Williams' interpretation made this standard seem fresh and alive. "Now that we're all here," Williams said, acknowledging the late arrivals admitted to the concert hall after the first piece, "I'd like to play *Mallorca*, a piece depicting a mysterious, beautiful island with a Moorish influence." Williams' interpretation had a rich, warm sound. For the most part, his rubato was effective, although a couple of hesitations stretched the lines a bit too much. Williams' Smallman guitar, like the Fleta he played earlier in his career, is very piano-like in its rich sound and its even balance between bass and treble. This makes the Smallman particularly suitable for piano transcriptions, such as works of Albéniz, Falla and Granados.

Córdoba is one of Williams' favorite pieces. As he quipped to the audience, "*Córdoba* has a quiet beginning, so if you have to cough — cough now." The opening chords of the piece shimmered as they left the guitar. Other pieces in the first half included Albéniz's *Asturias* and *Sevilla*, and Falla's *Dance of Corregador* and *Miller's Dance*— the last concluding with rousing, wild strumming. The first half ended with *La Maja de Goya* by Granados, a piece inspired by a famous Spanish painting. Williams was at his most expressive in this piece. My only reservation about the Spanish program was the fact that the homogeneous harmonic and melodic language of this school of composition imparts a certain sameness to the pieces that becomes evident when they're played *en masse*.

The second half of the program was devoted entirely to the music of South American composer-guitarist Agustín Barrios. Several of the pieces performed (*Aconquija*, *La última canción* and *Cueca*) appear on Williams' recording *Spirit of the Guitar: Music of the Americas* (CBS MK 44898). Williams played the opening to *La Catedral* as one long cohesive overarching idea. The articulation in the last section, which was characterized by the slightest pause before the pickup note of each phrase, propelled the piece toward the end. *La última canción*, originally titled *Amour de Dios*, was the last piece Barrios ever composed. Williams' playing of the tremolo section was noteworthy in that the music seemed totally natural and unencumbered. However, *Julia Florida* was less successful, primarily because the musical ideas were not substantial enough to sustain the piece. Other Barrios pieces in the second half included *Mazurka appassionata*, with its nineteenth century influence, *Cueca, Alconquija, Vals no. 3* and the popular *Un sueño en la Floresta*.

Sustained applause, a standing ovation and a shout of "We love you, Johnny" were a fitting tribute to this program, to the other two programs in the series, and to the long and distinguished career of this remarkable guitarist. His encores included a sensitive reading of Barrios' *Canción di Navidad* followed by *Preludio*, the latter being an ironic ending to a truly memorable concert series.

Recording Reviews

The Mantis & the Moon: Guitar Duets from Around the World
John Williams, guitar
Timothy Kain, guitar
Sony Classical SK 62007

Welcome to world music, Williams style. *The Mantis & the Moon* is a collection of eighteen pieces by twelve composers from six lands. The musical journey begins in the guitar's birthplace — Spain — and continues on to Australia, Ireland and the Americas, before it ends with brief stopovers in Japan and Russia. Despite the diverse origins of the works, they are — in terms of their rhythms, harmonies and melodies — rooted firmly in Western classical music.

This marks the first time since the legendary Bream-Williams collaborations of the 1970s that Williams has teamed up on disc with a fellow guitarist, this time Timothy Kain. While the Bream-Williams duo was a study in contrasting musical styles, the Williams-Kain duo sounds more like a twenty-fingered John Williams playing on twelve strings.

The first three works on *The Mantis & the Moon*, by Manuel de Falla and Enrique Granados, can be found as well on the Bream-Williams recordings *Together* (BMG Classics 61450-2, recorded 1971) and *Together Again* (BMG Classics 61452-2, recorded 1974). In general, the Bream-Williams performances have a more relaxed Romantic feel, while the Williams-Kain interpretations are more rhythmically straight. There is a warmer and more spacious sound to the latter recording, due to advances in recording techniques and technology since the Bream-Williams recordings. The performance of Dance from *La vida breve* by Falla manages to balance strong accents and articulation with flowing forward motion. In Granados' Intermezzo from *Goyescas*, the duo creates an insistent opening, a lyrical middle section and a tranquil ending. Danza española No. 6 by Granados, comprising three short sections, is characterized by frenetically controlled playing in the outer parts.

Nigel Westlake, who contributed *Antarctica* to Williams' CD *From Australia* (Sony SK 53361), wrote *Songs from the Forest* for Williams and Kain. Fellow Australian Phillip Houghton penned Three Duets. The first of the duets is the title track, a rhythmically difficult work that brings Rodrigo's *Invocation y Danse* and Koshkin's *Usher Waltz* to mind. *Lament* is a somber work that makes wide use of the guitar's tonal palette, while the closing *Alchemy* has a playful, jazzy feel. The performances on these four pieces are so precise that it is hard to believe there are two guitarists.

The three Irish pieces are by Turlough O'Carolan. Of particular note is Carolan's Concerto, a brief work that is perfect in the construction of its melody and harmony. Anyone who enjoys Carolan's music should listen to Chieftains' harpist Derek Bell on his recording *Carolan's Favourite* (Shanachie 79020).

The five works from the Americas include a potpourri of composers ranging from Leo Brouwer to Frederic Hand. Japan and Russia are represented by two of their most famous composers, Toru Takemitsu and Dmitry Shostakovich. Their pieces are both arrangements of music they composed for film scores (*Bad Boy* and *The Gad Fly*, respectively). Both work well on guitar. The Takemitsu piece has the same gentle spirit as his other guitar works, while the Shostakovich work shows us his more accessible side.

Once again, Williams has come up with a recording of both style and substance.

Harvey, Gray: Guitar Concertos
John Williams, guitar
London Symphony Orchestra/Paul Danile, conductor
Sony Classical SK 68337

Built from a set of compatible themes drawn from old song and dance forms, Richard Harvey's *Concerto Antico* for guitar and small orchestra creates a mood of an earlier, simpler time. The scoring for small orchestra helps distinguish the guitar, by providing light harmonic and rhythmic support while the guitar is playing. Of particular note is the substantial third movement, with the warm, pastoral feeling evoked by the solo woodwinds and strings. The piece has a cohesive architecture, although the fifth movement feels somewhat out of place, with a more Spanish flavor than the formal Italian quality of the first four movements. Overall, this is a delightful work that deserves to become an integral part of the guitar concerto literature.

In contrast, Steve Gray's Guitar Concerto draws its inspiration from more contemporary sources — film noir scores and jazz primarily — and is scored for large orchestra. Gray, who arranged excerpts from Albéniz's *Iberia* for guitar and orchestra (John Williams, *Iberia*, Sony SK 48 480), has again successfully met the challenge of balancing them. Here he does it by having the guitar interact mainly with the strings, and less so with the winds and brass. This piece may be less accessible than *Concerto Antico*, but its relative complexity sustains interest on repeated listening.

Critiquing Williams' performance on these two works is somewhat like describing the weather in Southern California, since his musical interpretation and technical realization are at their customarily high level. Williams should be commended for bringing these works to the public.

Sony should be applauded on both this and *The Mantis & the Moon* CDs for the visually interesting artwork and photographs, as well as for the substantive liner notes.

From Australia
John Williams, guitar
London Symphony Orchestra/Paul Daniel, conductor
Australian Chamber Orchestra/Richard Hickox, conductor
Sony Classical SK 53 361

In 1989, John Williams recorded *Spirit of the Guitar: Music of the Americas*. Six years later, Williams' newest recording focuses on his homeland. *From Australia* is made up of four works — three by Peter Sculthorpe and one by Nigel Westlake. Sculthorpe is one of Australia's best known composers, having written for a variety of instruments, including piano, cello, percussion, string quartet and orchestra. He began writing for the guitar thanks to the persuasiveness of John Williams.

Sculthorpe's *Nourlangie* is a twenty minute work for guitar, strings and percussion that takes its name from a giant rock in Australia's Kakadu National Park. The influence of Japanese and Indonesian music on Sculthorpe can be clearly heard in this work. Some elements are reminiscent of Takemitsu; there is lots of space in the music and a focus on simply beautiful sounds. The piece alternates between two motifs. The first is a simple melody presented on the guitar that showcases the charm of the guitar's open strings. The second, based on dance song, is rhythmically active and reinforced by the percussion. This motif evolves into an extended, cheerful, more relaxed melody. From the opening notes, *Nourlangie* transports us to a different sonic world. There is a transparency to Williams' sound that conveys the feeling of spaciousness in the music. As a native Australian, he clearly shares and understands the feelings Sculthorpe was trying to impart. The Australian Chamber Orchestra is also to be commended for its shimmering, crystalline performance.

Sculthorpe's *From Kakadu* was also inspired by the terrain of Kakadu National Park. The opening Grave is played with consummate precision; however, I would have liked more rhythmic bounce in Williams' interpretation of the dance-like *Comodo*. In the closing *Cantando*, Williams' playing floats toward the ending.

Sculthorpe's *Into the Dreaming* consists of three sections and a short coda. The long pedal notes on open strings mimic the didjeridu, an aboriginal wind instrument. Characteristically, the piece has a distant, haunting feel to it. When I first heard Williams perform *Into the Dreaming* in his 1994 New York concert, I found it to be a pleasant work, but lacking in distinctive character. The excellent performance on this disc aside, my opinion remains unchanged on repeated listening.

Nigel Westlake also is very much influenced by his native homeland, as illustrated by his earlier compositions, *Omphalo Centric Lecture for Percussion* and *Refractions at Summer Cloud Bay*. *Antarctica, Suite for Guitar and Orchestra* is based on a score Westlake originally wrote for the IMAX film *Antarctica*. The score was meant to depict the grandeur, beauty, desolation and harshness of the images on the screen. *Antarctica* is in four movements—*The Last Place on Earth*, *Wooden Ships*, *Penguin Ballet* and *The Ice Core/Finale*. *The Last Place on Earth* has elements that remind me of Holst's *The Planets*. The orchestra dominates the dramatic opening, which leads to the entrance of the solo guitar. Williams uses a variety of tonal colors to portray the image of the ice cap under the midnight sun. A lovely single note melody on guitar, coupled with Coplandesque orchestration, characterizes *Wooden Ships*. *Penguin Ballet* is similar in nature to *Wooden Ships*, with its beguiling melody passing back and forth between guitar and orchestra. In each of these movements, Williams shows how exquisite a sound can be created from simple material. These two movements give way to the dark and unsettled *The Ice Core/Finale*, again with echoes of *The Planets*. Here I specifically like the way Williams interspersed staccato and legato effects to bring out the contrasting moods in this section.

The liner notes by Williams, Sculthorpe and Westlake are very good.

Iberia
John Williams, guitar
London Symphony Orchestra/Paul Daniel, conductor
Sony Classical SK 48 480

Few events in the classical guitar world are as eagerly awaited as a new recording from John Williams. *Iberia*, his most recent release on Sony Classical, is a worthy successor to his triumphant 1991 recording of the works of Toru Takemitsu. *Iberia* opens with Williams' transcription of *Valses Poéticos* by Enrique Granados. This piece — originally written for piano — consists of an introduction, seven waltzes and a coda. Williams first made an incomplete transcription of this piece more than twenty-five years ago (*John Williams Plays Spanish Music*, Columbia Masterworks). At that time, he did not transcribe Waltzes 2, 5, 6 and 7, which were described on the liner notes of that recording as being "uncongenial for the guitar." Williams' new arrangement of the complete work clearly refutes this characterization. His performance is completely unconstrained by the limitations of the guitar and displays a warmth and fullness indicative of his growth as a musician over the years.

Often lost among Rodrigo's larger scale works, *En los Trigales (In the wheatfields)* is one of the small gems of the guitar literature. The mysterious opening theme and harmonies, the alternating scale and chordal passages, and the quiet harmonics combine to achieve a perfect balance in the space of less than four minutes. Williams infuses the opening and closing sections of the piece with a rhythmic forward motion that nicely balances the pensive middle section. This performance of *En los Trigales* is a welcome addition to the CD catalog, which currently includes Roberto Aussel's recording on GHA. The other Rodrigo composition on this disc is *Invocation et Danse (Hommage à Manuel de Falla)*. In this piece, Rodrigo quotes from de Falla's *Homenaje a Debussy* and the ballet *El Amour Brujo*. Williams navigates the technically difficult scale, arpeggio and tremolo sections in the piece with his usual aplomb. He makes effective use of tonal colors throughout — dark and distant one moment, bright and powerful the next. It is interesting to note the differences in phrasing, articulation, dynamics and tempo between Williams' recording and Manuel Barrueco's 1987 recording (Barrueco's tempo is faster). Happily, both performances are very satisfying.

Miguel Llobet's transcription of the Catalan folk song *El Noi de la Mare* is perhaps best known to guitar audiences as a favorite encore piece of Andrés Segovia. Although many artists have recorded a few of the transcriptions Llobet made of Catalan folk songs, Williams treats us to a performance of nine of them. In addition to *El Testament d' Amelia, Cançó del Lladre, El Mestre*, and *La Nit de Nadal*, Williams also plays the less frequently heard *La Filadora, L'Hereu Riera, Lo Fill del Rei* and *La Pastoreta*. The ordering of the pieces balances nicely the lively songs and the more reflective ones. Williams' subtle use of rubato is particularly effective in highlighting the folk origins of these pieces.

The grand finale to this disc is a transcription for guitar and orchestra of three pieces from *Iberia*, Isaac Albéniz's towering masterpiece for solo piano. *Iberia* is a suite consisting of twelve pieces collected into four books. Williams has selected three pieces that relate to the province of Andalusia — *El Albaicín*, after the old gypsy quarter near Granada; *Triana*, a part of Sevilla; and *Rondeña*, from the town of Ronda. This twenty-two minute arrangement begins with a repeating opening theme played on the guitar and answered by chordal responses from the brass and strings. Many sections of the arrangement recall the concertos of Rodrigo. Steve Gray, the arranger, has worked carefully to provide a good division of the parts between the guitar and the orchestra. He has also done an excellent job of assigning instruments to parts in a way that provides an evocative tonal palette. My only criticism of this recording of *Iberia* is that guitar is sometimes lost in the orchestral mix.

Takemitsu: To the Edge of Dream
John Williams, guitar
Sebastian Bell, flute
Gareth Hulse, oboe d'amore
London Sinfonietta/Esa-Pekka Salonen, conductor
Sony Classical SK 46720

A recording devoted to the guitar music of composer Toru Takemitsu has been long overdue. This recording by John Williams is likely to remain the definitive recording of these works for some time to come. It is fitting that Takemitsu and Williams should find each other. Both share an interest in musical styles ranging from classical to folk, jazz and pop. These influences are most overtly observed in Williams' performances of four of the *12 Songs for Guitar* that were transcribed for solo guitar by Takemitsu — Lennon-McCartney's *Here, There and Everywhere*, Convese's *What a Friend*, Kosma's *Amours perdues* and Gershwin's *Summertime*. In each of these pieces, Williams' employs the phrasing appropriate to the style, and does so in a way which seems entirely natural.

There has been much discussion recently about the need for the guitar to expand beyond its solo repertoire into ensemble music. As this recording demonstrates, Takemitsu's original compositions have been an important contribution to this trend. *To the Edge of Dream for Guitar and Orchestra, Toward the Sea for Alto Flute and Guitar* and *Vers, l'arc-en-ciel, Palma for Oboe d'amore, Guitar and Orchestra* all provide the guitar with a substantive role while maintaining the requisite balance and cohesiveness. These works represent a more mature phase of Takemitsu's ensemble works for fretted string instruments, which began in the '60s with *Ring* in 1961 (terz guitar and lute), *Sacrifice* in 1962 (lute), *Valeria* in 1965 (guitar) and *Stanza I* in 1969 (guitar). These earlier ensemble works can be heard on the Deutche Grammophon 20th Century Classics recording *Takemitsu* (DG 423 253-2).

The only original composition for solo guitar on the recording is *Folios*. Written in 1974, it was the first piece that Takemitsu wrote for solo guitar. *Folios* makes full use of the broad tonal palette that is characteristic of the guitar. In this regard, Williams' musical and technical prowess is ideally suited for realizing the composer's intentions. Notably missing from the Williams recording is Takemitsu's other major work for solo guitar, *All in Twilight — Four Pieces for Guitar*. It would have been nice to have a recording of Williams performing this work — there was certainly room for it on the disc. Fortunately, an excellent performance of this piece by David Tanenbaum is available on his recording *Acoustic Counterpoint* (New Albion NA 032 CD).

The compositions on this recording are very characteristic of Takemitsu, combining the melodic and harmonic elements of the Modern French period with the textures and timbres of the Orient. As usual, the performance by Williams is both musically and technically near perfect. Programmatically, the alternation of the ensemble and solo works provides a nice balance.

Discography

Giuliani, Schubert
Sony Classical SK 63385
with Australian Chamber Orchestra
Giuliani: *Concerto for Guitar no. 1 in A Major (op. 30)*; Schubert: *Sonata for Arpeggione in A Minor (D. 821)*.

The Guitarist
Sony Classical SK 60586
with William Goodchild (conductor)
Theodorakis: *Three Epitafios*; Domeniconi: *Konyunbaba*; Satie: *Gymnopedies no. 3, Gnossiennes nos. 1 and 2*; Anon.: *Lamento di Tristano, Ductia, Saltarello*; Williams: *Aeolian Suite for Guitar and Small Orchestra*; Houghton: *Stélé*.

Brouwer: The Black Decameron
Sony Classical SK 63173
with London Sinfonietta (Steven Mercurio, conductor)
Brouwer: *Hika "In Memoriam Toru Takemitsu," Concerto de Toronto, Elogio de la Danza, El Decamerón Negro*.

172   Classical Guitarists

John Williams Plays the Movies
Sony Classical SK 63000
with Christopher Gunning (conductor), Steve Gray (conductor), Bruno Fontaine (conductor), John T. Williams (conductor), Nick Ingman (conductor) and Pollyanna Gunning (recorder), Mitch Dalton (electric guitar), Nicole Tibbels (soprano), Guy Barker (flugelhorn), Brendan Power (harmonica), Kenneth Sillito (violin), Andy Findon (pan flute, whistle)
Seal: *Kiss from a Rose*; Adams: *Everything I Do*; North: *Unchained Melody*; Presley: *Love Is All Around*; Rota: *The Godfather*; Mancini: *Moon River*; Arlen: *Wizard of Oz*; Morricone: *The Mission, Once Upon a Time in America, Once Upon a Time in the West*; Myers: *Cavatina*; Hupfeld: *As Time Goes By*; Legrand: *Parapluies de Cherbourg*; Jones: *It Had to Be You*; Telson: *Calling You*; Joplin: *The Entertainer*; Bacalov: *Il Postino*; J.T. Williams: *Schindler's List*.

The Mantis & the Moon: Guitar Duets from Around the World
Sony Classical SK 62007
with Timothy Kain (guitar)
de Falla: *La vida breve (Spanish Dance)*; Granados: *Goyescas (Intermezzo), Danza española (no. 6)*; Soler: *Sonata in A Major (R. 84)*; Westlake: *Songs from the Forest*; Houghton: *Three Duets (The Mantis and the Moon, Lament, Alchemy)*; Carolan: *Carolan's Concerto, Fanny Power, Planxty Madam Maxwell*; Brouwer: *Micropiezas*; Madlem: *Monte Carlo*; Verdery: *Capitola*; Hand: *Prayer*; Bellinati: *Jongo*; Takemitsu: *Bad Boy*; Shostakovich: *Gadfly (op. 97, Guitars)*.

Harvey, Gray: Guitar Concertos
Sony Classical SK 68337
with London Symphony Orchestra (Paul Danile, conductor)
Harvey: *Concerto Antico for Guitar and Small Orchestra*; Gray: *Guitar Concerto*.

From The Jungles of Paraguay
Sony Classical SK 64396
Barrios: *Medallon antiguo, Choro da saudade, Aire de zamba, Aconquija, Prelude in G minor (op. 5, no. 1), Sueño en la floresta, Villancico de navidad, Mazurka apasionata, Las abejas, Vals nos. 3 and 4, Prelude in C minor, Cueca, Maxixa, La catedral, Julia Florida, Una limosna por el amor de Dios*.

From Australia
Sony Classical SK 53 361
with London Symphony Orchestra (Paul Daniel, conductor) and Australian Chamber Orchestra (Richard Hickox, conductor)
Sculthorpe: *Nourlangie, From Kakadu, Into the Dreaming*; Westlake: *Antarctica*.

The Seville Concert
Sony Classical SK 53 359
with Seville Symphony Orchestra (Jose Buenagu, conductor)
Albéniz: *Suite española (op. 47, Sevilla, Asturias)*; Bach: *Suite no. 4 for Lute in E Major (BWV 1006a, Prelude)*; Scarlatti: *Sonata in D Minor (K. 213)*; Vivaldi: *Concerto for*

Lute, Two Violins and Basso Continuo in D Major (RV. 93); Yocoh: *Sakura Variations*; Koshkin: *Usher Waltz (op. 29)*; Barrios: *Sueño en la floresta*; Rodrigo: *Concierto de Aranjuez (Adagio)*.

Iberia
Sony Classical SK 48 480
with London Symphony Orchestra (Paul Daniel, conductor)
Granados: *Valses Poéticos*; Rodrigo: *Invocation et Danse, En los Trigales*; Llobet: *Nine Catalan Folksongs*; Albéniz: *Suite Iberia (El Albaicín, Triana, Rondeña)*.

Takemitsu: To the Edge of Dream
Sony Classical SK 46720
with London Sinfonietta (Esa-Pekka Salonen, conductor) and Sebastian Bell (flute), Gareth Hulse (oboe d'amore)
Takemitsu: *To the Edge of Dream, Folios, Toward the Sea, Vers, L'arc-en-ciel, Palma, From 12 Songs for Guitar* (Converse: *What a Friend*; Lennon-McCartney: *Here, There and Everywhere*; Kosma: *Amours perdues*; Gershwin: *Summertime*).

Echoes of Spain
Sony SK 36 679
Albéniz: *Granada, Sevilla, Córdoba, Cádiz, Asturias, Tango, Zambra granadina, Torre bermeja, Mallorca*.

Vivaldi Concertos
Sony Classical SK 46556
with Franz Liszt Academy Chamber Orchestra (Janos Rolla, conductor) and Agnes Szakaly (cimbalom), Benjamin Verdery (guitar), Janos Rolla (violin), Maria Frank (cello), Zsuzsa Pertis (harpsichord), Norbert Blume (viola d'amore)
Vivaldi: *Concerto in D Major (RV. 230), Concerto in A Minor (RV. 356), Concerto in G Major (RV. 532), Trio Sonata for Violin, Lute and Basso Continuo in C Major (RV. 82), Concerto for Viola d'Amore and Lute in D Minor (RV. 540), Concerto in A Major (RV. 345), Concerto for Lute and 2 Violins in D Major (RV. 93)*.

The Baroque Album
Sony Classical SK 44518
Scarlatti: *Sonata in E Major (K. 380), Sonata in D Minor (K. 213), Sonata in F# Minor (K. 448), Sonata in A Minor (K. 175), Sonata in C Major (K. 159)*; Bach: *Chaconne*; Couperin: *Les Barricades mistérieuses, Les moissonneurs*; Roncalli: *Passacaglia*; Weiss: *Tombeau sur la mort de M. Cajetan, Fantaisie, Passacaglia*; Telemann: *Bourée alla Polacca*.

Bach for Guitar and Organ
Sony Classical SBK 62973
with Peter Hurford (organ)
Bach: *Suite in E major (BWV 1006a), Chaconne, Wachet auf ruft uns die Stimme, Prelude, Fugue and Allegro in E Flat Major (BWV 998), Prelude and Fugue no. 8 in E Flat Minor (BWV 877), Suite in C Major (BWV 1009, Bouree), Sonata in C Minor*

(BWV 1017, Adagio), Trio Sonata in G Major (BWV 530), Italian Concerto (BWV 971).

Bach: Lute Suites
Sony Classical SBK 62972
Bach: *Suite in E Minor (BWV 996), Suite in C Minor (BWV 997), Suite in G Minor (BWV 995), Prelude in C Minor (BWV 999), Fugue in G Minor (BWV 1000).*

Paganini, Scarlatti, Villa-Lobos, Giuliani
Sony Classical SBK 62 425
Paganini: *Capriccio (op. 1, no. 24), Grand Sonata in A Major*; Scarlatti: *Sonatas (K. 380, K. 208, K. 175, K. 322, K. 213, K. 159)*; Villa-Lobos: *Five Preludes*; Giuliani: *Harmonious Blacksmith.*

Rodrigo: Concierto
Sony Classical SBK 48168
with Philadelphia Orchestra (Eugene Ormandy, conductor), English Chamber Orchestra (Sir Charles Groves, conductor), Colin Tilney (harpsichord)
Rodrigo: *Concierto de Aranjuez, Fantasía para un gentilhombre*; Giuliani: *Concerto for Guitar and String Orchestra in A (op. 30)*; Vivaldi: *Concerto for Guitar and String Orchestra (RV. 93).*

Latin American Guitar Music
Sony Classical SBK 47669
Barrios: *La catedral, Madrigal (Gavota), Minuet, Mazurka apasionata, Estudio, Preludio, Sueño en la floresta, Valse no. 3, Cueca, Aire de zamba, Aconquija, Maxixa, Limosna por el amor de Dios, Villancico de Navidad*; Ponce: *Folia de España.*

Spanish Guitar Music
Sony Classical SBK 46347
Albéniz: *Asturias, Tango, Córdoba, Sevilla*; Sanz: *Canarios*; Rodrigo: *Fandango*; Torróba: *Nocturno, Madroños*; Sagreras: *El Colibrí*; M. Albéniz: *Sonata in D*; de Falla: *Corregidor's Dance, Fisherman's Song, The Miller's Dance, Homanaje*; Trad.: *La Nit de Nadal, El Noy de la Mare, El Testamen de Amelia*; Granados: *La Maja de Goya, Spanish Dance no. 5*; Tárrega: *Recuerdos de la Alhambra*; Villa-Lobos: *Prelude no. 4 in E Minor*; Mudarra: *Fantasia*; Turina: *Fandanguillo (op. 36).*

Spirit of the Guitar—Music of the Americas
CBS MK 48898
York: *Sunburst, Lullaby*; Barrios: *Aconquija, La Ultima Canción, Cueca*; Piazzolla: *Verano porteño*; Ponce: *Scherzino mexicano*; Lauro: *Natalia, El niño, Maria Luisa*; Brouwer: *Bercuese, Danza caracteristica*; Byrd: *Three Blues (Spanish Guitar Blues, Blues for Felix, Swing 59)*; Villa-Lobos: *Chôros no. 1*; Sagreras: *El Colibri*; Crespo: *Norteña.*

Rodrigo: Concierto de Aranjuez
CBS MDK 45648

John Williams

with Philharmonia Orchestra (Louis Fremaux, conductor)
Albéniz: *Granada, Asturias, Sevilla, Majorca, Córdoba*; Rodrigo: *Concierto de Aranjuez, Fantasía para un gentilhombre.*

Guitar Concertos
CBS MB2K 45610
with English Chamber Orchestra (Sir Charles Groves, conductor and Daniel Barenboim, conductor)
Giuliani: *Concerto in A Major*; Vivaldi: *Concerto in D Major, Concerto in A Major*; Rodrigo: *Concierto de Aranjuez, Fantasía para un gentilhombre*; Villa-Lobos: *Concerto for Guitar and Small Orchestra*; Castelnuovo-Tedesco: *Concerto no. 1 in D Major (op. 99).*

Spanish Guitar Favorites
CBS MK 44794
Granados: *Spanish Dance no. 5, Valses poéticos, La maja de Goya*; de Falla: *Homenaje, Dance of the Corregidor, Fisherman's Song, Miller's Dance*; Albéniz: *Sevilla, Asturias, Córdoba*; Tárrega: *Recuerdos de la Alhambra*; Turina: *Fandanguillo, Soleares, Rafaga*; Trad.: *El testamen de Amelia, El noy de la mare*; Sagreras: *El Colibri*; Rodrigo: *Fandango*; M. Albéniz: *Sonata in D Major*; Llobet: *La nit de nadal.*

The Great Guitar Concertos
CBS M2K 44791
with English Chamber Orchestra (Sir Charles Groves, conductor and Daniel Barenboim, conductor), Philharmonia Orchestra (Louis Fremaux, conductor), London Symphony Orchestra (Andre Previn, conductor), Christine Pendrill (English horn)
Vivaldi: *Concerto for Guitar and String Orchestra in D Major, Concerto for Guitar and String Orchestra in A Major*; Rodrigo: *Concierto de Aranjuez, Fantasía para un gentilhombre*; Castelnuovo-Tedesco: *Concerto no. 1 in D major (op. 99)*; Giuliani: *Concerto for Guitar and String Orchestra (op. 30)*; Villa-Lobos: *Concerto for Guitar and Small Orchestra*; Ponce: *Concierto del Sur.*

Echoes of London
CBS MK 42119
McTell: *Streets of London*; Byrd: *La Volta*; Purcell: *Air on a Ground Bass*; Clare: *Holland Park*; Handel: *Harmonious Blacksmith, Courante, Sarabande/Air*; Elgar: *Salut D'Amour*; Wilson: *A Room in Bloomsbury*; Coward: *London Pride*; Coates: *London by Night*; Gregg: *Maybe It's Because I'm a Londoner*; Sherwin: *A Nightingale Sang in Berkeley Square*; Gershwin: *Damsel in Distress: A Foggy Day.*

Bach: Lute Suites
CBS MK 42204
Bach: *Suite in E Minor (BWV 996), Suite in A C Minor (BWV 997), Suite in E Major (BWV 1006a), Suite in A Minor (BWV 995).*

Bach, Handel, Marcello: Concertos
CBS MK 39560
with Academy of St. Martin in the Fields (Kenneth Sillito, conductor)
Marcello: *Oboe Concerto*; Bach: *Violin Concerto, Aria (Andante from Solo Violin Sonata)*; Handel: *Organ Concerto*.

The Guitar Is the Song
CBS MK 37825
with Chris Taylor (flute, recorder, tin whistle), Chris Lawrence (double bass), Gary Kettel (percussion), Chris Karen (percussion), Brian Gascoigne (marimba and celeste), Paul Hart (fiddle), Marilyn Sansom (cello), John Leach (cimbalom), Claudia Figueroa (cuatro and guitar), Mauricio Venegas (charango), Paul Westwood (guitarron), Chris Gradwell (clarinets), Richard Morgan (oboe), Niel Levesley (bassoon), James Brown (horn), Les Thatcher (mandolin), Pat Halling (violin), Eric Bowie (violin), Kenneth Essex (viola), Brian Hawkins (viola), Peter Halling (cello), Mike Brittain (double bass)
Trad.: *Wraggle-Taggle Gypsies, Hajrá Kati, Csák Egy Kislány Van A Világon, Queen of Hearts, Petronella, St. Patrick's Day, Búacallán, Buíde, Scarborough Fair, Carnaval, Seis por derecho, Over the Sea to Skye, Mashilaé, Music Box Tune, Waly Waly, Shenandoah*; Dyer-Bennett/Byron: *So We'll Go No More A-Roving*; Cardillo/Cordiferro: *Catri Catri*; Bovio/de Curtis: *Tu Ca' Nun Chiagne*.

Portrait of John Williams
CBS MK 37791
Lauro: *Seis por derecho, El negrito*; Clare: *Castilla*; Tárrega: *Recuerdos de la Alhambra*; Bach: *Prelude*; Vivaldi: *Concerto in D major*; Lennon-McCartney: *Fool on the Hill*; Barrios: *Vals (op.8, no. 4)*; Brouwer: *Guajira, Danza Caracteristica*; Myers: *Cavatina*; Yocoh: *Sakura*.

Rodrigo: Concerto de Aranjuez
CBS MYK 36717
with English Chamber Orchestra (Sir Charles Groves, conductor)
Rodrigo: *Concierto de Aranjuez, Fantasía para un gentilhombre*.

John Williams & Friends
CBS MK 35108
Telemann: *Bouree alla polacca*; Purcell: *Trio Sonata no. 11*; Bach: *Gigue, Bouree, Jesu Joy of Man's Desiring*; Mozart: *Adagio (K. 356), Turkish Rondo (K. 331)*; Vivaldi: *Concerto for Two Guitars*; Daquin: *Le Coucou*.

Duos by Paganini and Giuliani
CBS MK 34508
with Itzhak Perlman (violin)
Paganini: *Centone di Sonate (op. 64, no. 1), Sonata no. 6 in E Minor (op. 3), Sonata Concertata in A Major, Cantabile for Violin and Guitar*; Giuliani: *Sonata for Violin and Guitar*.

Rodrigo, Villa-Lobos: Guitar Concertos
CBS MK 33208
with English Chamber Orchestra (Daniel Barenboim, conductor)
Rodrigo: *Concierto de Aranjuez*; Villa-Lobos: *Concerto for Guitar and Small Orchestra*.

Together Again
RCA Victor Gold Seal 09026-61452-2
with Julian Bream (guitar)
Carulli: *Serenade in A (op. 96)*; Granados: *Danza española (op. 37, no. 6), Danza española (op. 37, no. 11)*; Albéniz: *Bajo la palmera (op. 232, no. 3), Evocacion (from Iberia)*; Giuliani: *Variazioni Concertanti (op. 130)*; Johnson: *Pavan and Galliard*; Telemann: *Partie polonaise*; Debussy: *Golliwogg's Cakewalk, Rêverie, Clair de lune*.

Together
RCA Victor Gold Seal 09026-61450-2
with Julian Bream (guitar)
Lawes: *Suite for Two Guitars*; Carulli: *Duo in G (op. 34)*; Sor: *L'encouragement (op. 34)*; Albéniz: *Córdoba (op. 232, no. 4)*; Granados: *Intermezzo (from Goyescas), Danzas española (op. 37, no. 2, Oriental)*; de Falla: *La vida breve (Spanish Dance no. 1)*; Ravel: *Pavane pour une Infante défunte*; Fauré: *Dolly (op. 56)*.

Spanish Guitar Favorites
London 421165-2
Albéniz: *Torre bermeja*; Ponce: *Three Mexican Songs*; Villa-Lobos: *Etude no. 1 in E Minor*; Crespo: *Norteña*; Duarte: *Variations on a Catalan Folksong*; Sor: *Variations for Guitar on a Theme of Mozart*; Segovia: *Oracion, Estudio*; Madriguera: *Humorada*; Tansman: *Barcarolle*; Granados: *La maja de Goya*; Lauro: *Valse Criollo*.

Guitar Recital
London 452 173-2
Bach: *Suite nos. 1 and 3*; Scarlatti: *Sonata in E Minor*; A Scarlatti: *Gavotte*; Albéniz: *La Torre Bermeja*; Ponce: *Three Mexican Popular Songs*; Villa-Lobos: *Etude no. 1*; Crespo: *Norteña*; Duarte: *Variations on a Catalan Folk Song*; Sor: *Variations on a Theme of Mozart*; Segovia: *Oración, Estudio*; Madriguera: *Humorada*; Tansman: *Barcarolle*; Granados: *La maja de Goya*; Lauro: *Vals criollo*.

Website: www.johnwilliamsguitar.com

Appendix: Creating a Core Collection of Classical Guitar Recordings

A major Internet record store lists thousands of classical guitar CDs by more than 650 artists. The discographies in the preceding chapters alone contain nearly 100 CDs. Where to begin?

To get you started, I have put together a "Core Collection" of classical guitar recordings — thirteen CDs selected from the artists featured in this book.

This Core Collection spans musical history from the Renaissance to the twentieth century. It features the guitar in solo, ensemble and orchestra settings. And it includes works transcribed for the guitar from other instruments, as well as works written expressly for the guitar. In short, the Core Collection captures in a small number of CDs those attributes of the guitar that make it so special.

The Core Collection

Renaissance

Bream — *The Woods So Wild* (Julian Bream Edition, Vol. 4, RCA 09026-61587)

Baroque

Fisk — *Vivaldi Concerti* (MusicMasters 67097)
Isbin — *J.S. Bach: Complete Lute Suites* (EMI/Virgin Classics 59503)
Williams — *The Baroque Album* (Sony Classical SK 44518)

Classical/Romantic/Post-Romantic

Bream — *Romantic Guitar* (Julian Bream Edition, Vol. 11, RCA 09026-61594)
Fisk — *Paganini: 24 Caprices* (MusicMasters 67092)
Starobin — *Giuliani: Guitar Music* (Bridge 9029)

Nationalist

Fisk — *Mountain Songs* (MusicMasters 7038)
Isbin — *Road to the Sun/Estrada do Sol: Latin Romances* (EMI/Virgin Classics 59591)
Tanenbaum — *Piazzolla: El Porteño* (New Albion NA 065)

Twentieth Century

Starobin — *New Music with Guitar, Vols. 1, 2 & 3* (Bridge 9009)
Tanenbaum — *Acoustic Counterpoint* (New Albion NA 032)
Williams — *Takemitsu: To the Edge of Dream* (Sony Classical SK 46720)

From the Renaissance era (1450–1600), I chose Julian Bream's recording *The Woods So Wild*. Although this is a lute — not a guitar — recording, it provides an opportunity to understand the sound and style that guitarists try to convey when playing lute music on the guitar. Bream was in many ways the Segovia of the lute, in that he played a major role in reviving it as an active concert instrument. *The Woods So Wild* features Fantasias by da Milano, and works by Dowland, Holborne and Cutting. Although lute purists might object to Bream's use of fingernails and hybrid guitar-lute playing techniques, this was the inevitable result of the guitar being his primary instrument. Regardless, it is a delightful recording that provides a satisfying musical experience over repeated listenings. If it were still in print, I would have also included David Tanenbaum's recording *Lute Masterworks* (Innova Digital IDA 1001). This CD features works of da Milano and Dowland, along with a Bach Lute Suite, all transcribed for and played on the guitar. If you are lucky enough to locate this buried treasure, scoop it up.

The three recordings I selected for the Baroque era (1600–1750) showcase its many dimensions. Eliot Fisk's heartfelt *Vivaldi Concerti* features works originally written for lute or mandolin. It is a model showcase for the guitar in ensemble settings. Sharon Isbin's *J.S. Bach: Complete Lute Suites* provides both a scholarly and engaging performance of works that have become an important part of the guitar repertoire. In general, the ability to transcribe Bach's works for solo string instruments and keyboard to guitar was an important element in the guitar's acceptance as a serious concert instrument in the twentieth century. John Williams' *Baroque Album* features his transcriptions of works by other noteworthy Baroque composers, including harpsichord works by Scarlatti and Couperin, lute works by Silvius Leopold Weiss, and Bach's majestic Chaconne.

From the Classical period (1770-1830) and Romantic/Post-Romantic period (1830-1910), I selected three recordings with very different characters. David Starobin's enchanting performance of works by composer-guitar virtuoso Mauro Giuliani, played on a reproduction of a nineteenth-century guitar, gives a glimpse into how this music might have sounded to Giuliani's audiences. [See Chapter 5 for a detailed review.] Modern day virtuoso Eliot Fisk's dazzling transcriptions of Nicolò Paganini's *24 Caprices* stretch the boundaries of what is considered possible on the guitar, while providing a new perspective on these classic violin pieces. [See Chapter 2 for a detailed review.] Julian Bream's wide-ranging *Romantic Guitar* features transcriptions of works by Schubert, Mendelssohn, Ravel and Albéniz, along with works written for the guitar by Paganini, de Falla and Tarrega. Most of the great composers of the Classical/Romantic era did not write for the guitar, but Bream's recording gives us the next best thing.

The Nationalist category is less a historical period and more a movement that existed at the same time as the Post-Romantic period. My selections for the Nationalist category include works by composers from the United States, Argentina, Brazil and Spain. Eliot Fisk teamed up with flutist Paula Robison on the charming *Mountain Songs*, which features works by Robert Beaser and early American composers Edward McDowell, Stephen Foster and Charles Ives. David Tanenbaum's sublime recording of Argentine composer Astor Piazolla's works shows how Piazzolla took the traditional tango and, through his inventive compositions and arrangements, created sensuous art music. [See Chapter 4 for a detailed review.] Sharon Isbin's *Road to the Sun/Estrada do Sol* is a collection of Latin romances for the guitar. This recording features several important works for the guitar, including Rodrigo's *Invocatión y Danza*, Barrios' *La Catedral* and Brouwer's *El Decamerón Negro*.

The breadth of Twentieth Century (1910–present) musical styles, combined with the commitment of all of these performers to creating new repertoire for the guitar, made the selections for this period particularly difficult. David Starobin's *New Music with Guitar, Vols. 1, 2 & 3* is a collection of selected works from the first three volumes in his New Music series. Works on this recording by major composers such as Carter, Sondheim, Babbitt, Takemitsu and Henze are inventive in conception and breathtaking in performance.

David Tanenbaum's *Acoustic Counterpoint* is a snapshot of new guitar music during the 1980s. Works range from the formalism of Tippet's *The Blue Guitar* and Davies' Sonata to the minimalism of Reich's *Electric Counterpoint*, here transcribed for acoustic guitar. Sierra's *Triptico* for guitar and string quartet showcases Tanenbaum in an ensemble setting. John Williams' *Takemitsu: To the Edge of Dream* was the first recording dedicated to the guitar music of Toru Takemitsu. It includes the color-rich *Folios* for solo guitar, works for the guitar with orchestra and with alto flute, as well as Takemitsu's transcriptions for the guitar of works by composers such as Lennon-McCartney and George Gershwin. This is a recording of great beauty. [See Chapter 7 for a detailed review.]

A number of worthy classical guitarists, who for various reasons of chance and circumstance are not profiled in this book, have recordings that could certainly be part of a Core Collection. Those artists include the Assad Brothers, Manuel Barrueco, the Los Angeles Guitar Quartet, Pepe Romero, David Russell — and, of course, Andrés Segovia.

One day, this Core Collection will expand to include a new period — the twenty-first century. There is no doubt that recordings by the performers showcased in this book will be on that list as well. It is something to which we can all look forward.

Glossary

[Note: These definitions have been tailored to reflect the context in which they are used in the preceding interviews and reviews.]

arpeggio a chord whose notes are sounded successively, rather than simultaneously.

cadenza in a concerto, an improvised or written-out ornamental passage for the soloist.

canon imitation of a musical passage at fixed intervals of time and possibly of pitch.

chromatic the scale made up of all twelve pitches (semitones) contained in an octave.

consort in Renaissance England, a small instrumental ensemble.

contrapuntal in counterpoint, the combination of two or more independent but related melodic lines.

course in regard to the guitar, lute and vihuela: a paired set of strings played as one, tuned in unison or octaves, to enhance tone color, volume or both.

diatonic a scale made up of the seven pitches contained in an octave, where the intervals between pitches conform to the major or pure minor scales.

dolcemente sweetly.

enharmonic tones that are identical in pitch but are written differently based on the key in which they occur.

equal temperment a slight modification to the acoustically pure intervals of just intonation. This results in most intervals being very slightly out of tune, but makes transpositions or modulations to other keys possible without them sounding noticeably out of tune.

flexion the act of bending a joint or limb. In guitar playing, generally used when referring to the techniques for plucking the strings with the fingers of the right hand.

fortissimo played very loudly.

glissando on stringed instruments, a sliding of a left-hand finger up or down the string to move from one pitch to another.

harmonic a tone produced on a stringed instrument by lightly touching an open or stopped vibrating string at a given fraction of its length, to create a higher pitched note with a bell-like sound.

just intonation the tuning of the intervals between notes to be acoustically pure by making them simple ratios of integers. The limitation of just intonation is that transpositions or modulations to other keys may sound out of tune.

legato played smoothly and connected.

luthier one who builds or repairs stringed instruments.

minimalism a school of contemporary music characterized by extreme simplification of rhythms and patterns, extended chordal or melodic repetitions, and often the creation of a pulsing, hypnotic effect.

modal in medieval music, the use of scales in which the interval relationships between the notes are based on church modes, such as those used in Gregorian chants.

modulation a passing from one key or tonality to another by means of a regular melodic or chord progression.

motive (or motif) a short, significant phrase in a composition.

ostinato a short melody or phrase that is continually repeated, usually at the same pitch.

pedagogy the art or profession of teaching.

Glossary

pianissimo played very softly.

pizzicato played by plucking rather than bowing the strings.

pedal-point an unchanging note in one voice, played while harmonies change in the other voices.

plectrum (also pick) a piece of tortoise shell or plastic used to pluck a stringed instrument.

ponticello (or sul ponticello) on the guitar, plucking the strings close to the bridge to produce a nasal, brittle effect.

postmodern music that reacts against earlier modernist music by reintroducing traditional or classical elements of style, such as tonality.

rasgueado (or rasgado) a strumming of the guitar strings, in contrast to plucking them.

recapitulation a restatement of the thematic material of a composition.

rest-stroke (apoyando) after plucking a string with a right-hand finger, the finger comes to rest on an adjacent string. In contrast to free-stroke (tirando), where the finger passes over the adjacent string.

rubato rhythmic flexibility within a phrase or measure; a relaxation of strict time.

scordatura unconventional tuning of stringed instruments, like lutes and violins, to make possible otherwise difficult pitch combinations or to reinforce certain pitches by making them available on open strings.

serial (or twelve-tone or atonal) music compositions that use the twelve semitones of an octave as the basis for its construction

sforzando accented (usually a single pitch or chord).

slur two or more notes played smoothly, with no articulation of the successive notes. On a plucked stringed instrument, this can be done by plucking the first note with the right hand and using the left-hand fingers to hammer the remaining notes.

sonata form a form consisting of three sections: exposition, development, and recapitulation, often followed by a coda.

staccato played crisply and disconnected.

syncopation a temporary transformation of the prevailing meter, for example from a duple to a triple rhythm.

tambour in reference to the guitar, drumming on its body with the fingers or palm as a musical effect.

tasto (or sul tasto) on the guitar, plucking the strings near the fingerboard to produce a warm, fuzzy sound.

transcription the adaptation of a musical work from one instrument to another; e.g., from the lute to the guitar.

transposition the technique of raising or lower the pitch of a composition or section by changing the key.

tremolo (or tremolando) the quick and continuous repetition of a single pitch.

trill the rapid alternation of two notes either a whole- or a half-step apart.

tutti in a concerto, a passage for the ensemble, as opposed to the soloist.

vibrato in string playing, to slightly vary the pitch of a note by rocking the left hand from the wrist as the note is played.

voice leading in contrapuntal music, the principles governing the progression of the different voice parts.

References

Apel, Willi. *Harvard Dictionary of Music (2nd ed.)*. Cambridge: The Belknap Press of Harvard University Press, 1974.

Randel, Don Michael (editor). *The New Harvard Dictionary of Music*. Cambridge: The Belknap Press of Harvard University Press, 1996.

Shearer, Aaron. *Learning the Classic Guitar (Part 1)*. Pacific, MO: Mel Bay Publications, Inc., 1990.

Soukhanov, Anne H. (editor). *The American Heritage Dictionary of the English Language (3rd Ed.)*. Boston: Houghton Mifflin Company, 1992.

Index

Italic page numbers indicate illustrations or captions.

Academy Award 64
Acoustic Guitar 18
Adams, John 22, 72
Aguado, Dionysio 6
Albéniz, Isaac 6, 52, 57, 140, 156–158, 164, 167, 170, 181
Alice Tully Hall 10, 20, 28
Almeida, Laurindo 19
amplification, guitar 7, 13, 26–28, 67–68, 106, 123, 126, 148
Angeles, Victoria de los 34, 48, 50
Appalachia 18, 29, 121–122
Arnold, Malcolm 74
artist management 37, 93, 133–148
Aspen Music Festival 9, 45, 47, 51–*52*
Assad, Sergio 107
Assad Brothers 118, 133, 182
Augustine, Albert 4
Augustine, Rose 50, *117*
Augustine Foundation 118 120
Augustine Guitar Series 98, 118, 125
Australia 149, 152, 165, 167–168
Austria 34, 36

Babbitt, Milton 110, 114, 123, 181
Bach, Johann Sebastian 34, 43, 72; compositions 7, 16, 102, 158: 'cello, 55, 104; keyboard 9, 15, 129, 156; lute 16, 19, 161–162, 179–181; violin, 41, 55, 106, 161–162, 181
Baker, Dame Janet 133, 136, *137*
Barbosa-Lima, Carlos 19, 31, 133
Baroque Period 4–5, 42, 55, 75, 98, 179–181

Barrios, Agustín 6, 160, 164–165, 181
Barrueco, Manuel 81, 90, 118, 169, 182
Beaser, Robert 34, 44, *45; Mountain Songs,* 44, 56, 181
Beethoven, Ludwig van 6, 20, 34, 42, 53, 59, 61, 87, 160
Bennett, Richard Dyer 139
Bennett, Richard Rodney 40, 64–80; and Bream, Julian 66–70, 73–76; *Concerto* for guitar and orchestra 64, 67–68, 74–75; film scores 64, 66, 79; *Five Impromptus* 64, 66–68, 71, 74–75, 77–79; and Leisner, David 68, *69; Sonata* for solo guitar 64, 68, *69,* 74–75, 77–80
Berg, Alban 65, 135
Berio, Luciano 34, 44, 48–49, 52, 97, 99; *Chemin* for guitar and orchestra 45–46; *Sequenza XI* 39, 45–46, 54, 60–61, 100–102
Berkeley, Lennox 64–65, 106
Block, Rory 22
bluegrass 13
Bonell, Carlos 30
Boulez, Pierre 64–65, 72, 116
Brahms, Johannes 6, 42, 53, 57, 59, 87, 160
Bream, Julian 7, 30, 41, 50–51, 55, 74, 94, 118, 148, *155,* 165, 179–181; and Bennett, Richard Rodney 66–70, 73–76, 78; and Shaw, Harold 133, 140, *141;* and Williams John, 149, 165–166
Bridge Records 110, 118–119
Britten, Benjamin 6, 74, 78, 160; *Nocturnal* 30, 54, 69, 79, 124

187

Index

Brouwer, Leo 30, 81, 90–91, 104, 106, 118, 159, 163–164, 166, 181

cadenza 12, 29, 53
career, music 18–20, 37, 40, 89, 92–93, 118, 141–147
Carnegie Hall 21
Carter, Elliott 6, 97, 110, *115*, 119, 181; *Changes* 114–116, 125–126
Castelnuovo-Tedesco, Mario 7, 49, 58
Chester String Quartet 85, 102–103
China 11, 81, 96
Classical Period 4–6, 41, 180–181
Cliburn, Van 136
Columbia Artists Management 18, 134
commissions, composition 12, 19, 51, 69, 73, 116
competitions, guitar 9, 18, 20; Toronto International 9, 76, 81
conservatories, music 20, 34, 36, 88–90
Copland, Aaron 14
Corbetta, Francesco 5, 42
Corigliano, John 14; *Troubadours* 12–14, 17, 29
Coryell, Larry 19
Crumb, George 110, 119–125; *Mundus Canis* 114, 120, *121*, 122–123, 126; *Quest* 111, 114, 120–124

da Milano, Francesco 5, 180
Dartington Summer School 66, 74
Debussy, Claude 57, 69, 91, 120, 163, 169
Diaz, Alirio 34, 36, 51
Dowland, John 5, 55, 129, 180
Duarte, John 76, 118; *Appalachian Suite* 18; *English Suite* 17, 31
Dun, Tan 12, 27; *Marco Polo* 11; *Yi²* 11
du Pré, Jacqueline 133

education, music 88–89
electronics 14, 87–88, 106, 117
Ellis, Herb 22
England 4–5, 7, 18, 30, 41, 64, 73, 144
ensemble playing 91–92, 111
Europe 11, 34, 39, 88, 97

Falla, Manuel de 163–166, 169, 181
Fernández, Eduardo 60, 118, 133
festivals, music 11, 21, 37
fingerboard (fretboard) 5, 49, 78, 96
fingering, left- and right-hand 6, 10, 16, 18, 70, 78, 111, 158
Fisk, Eliot 7, 34–63, 100, 118, 179–181; *Best of Eliot Fisk* 55; and composers 44–46; concert reviews 56–57; discography 61–63; *Guitar Fantasies* 53; *Paganini: 24 Caprices* 58–59, 180–181; recording reviews 57–61; *Rochberg: Caprice Variations* 53, 59; *Segovia* 53, 55, 57; *Sequenza!* 54, 60; and transcriptions, 41–44
flamenco 12, 47–48, 56, 60, 100–101, 105
flute 34, 37, *38*, 44, 100, 104, 124
Foss, Lukas *15*, 110; *American Landscapes* 12–15, 29
France 4, 11, 13, 29, 39, 52, 64, 115
Franck, César 57–58
Fuller, Albert 51
funding, arts: community 39, 97, 135, 159; government 39, 88, 97

Germany 11, 34, 36, 39, 52, 97, 144
Gershwin, George 19, 182; *Three Preludes* 31
Ghiglia, Oscar 9, 34, 36, 51, *52*
Ginastera, Alberto 79, 106
Giuliani, Mauro 6, 41, 128–130, 180–181
Grammy Award 9, 110, 119
Granados, Enrique 6, 164–166, 169
Graves, Denise 22
Gray, Steve 149, 158, 166–167, 170
Great Britain *see* England
Guitar Review 17, 49, 82, 107, *117*, 127
Guitar Summit 22
Guitarjam 21
guitars: four-, five and six-course 4–5, 129; Humphrey *Millenium* 5, 9, 49, 57, 95–96, 102, 112; latina and morisca 4; nineteenth century 112, 129–130, 181; six-, seven-, eight- and ten-string 4–5; SoloEtte 22
Guitarstream 9

Handel, George Frideric 43
harpsichord 5, 9, 16, 34, 42–43, 51, 98, 156, 161, 181
Harrison, Lou 84, 87; *Harp Suite* 83, 104–105; *Serenade for Guitar and Percussion*, 83, 105
Harvey, Richard 149, 166–167
Haydn, (Franz) Joseph 34, 42
Hedges, Michael 22
Henze, Hans Werner 6, 41, 74, 81, 94, 97, 181; *An Eine Aölsharfe* 92; *Drei Tentos* 44, 53

Index

Hochschule für Musik 36
Horowitz, Vladimir 133, 146
Houghton, Phillip 149, 152, 162–163, 166
Hurok, Sol 133–140, 147

impresario *see* artist management
improvisation, music 19, 89
Internet 8, 179
Inti Illimani 154
intonation, just 4, 83–84
Isbin, Sharon 9–33; *American Landscapes* 17, 22, 29–30; *Classical Guitar Answer Book* (aka *Acoustic Guitar Answer Book*) 9; *Complete Lute Suites* 16, 19, 179–180; and composers 9–15, 19; concert reviews 28–29; discography 31–33; *Journey to the Amazon* 9; and Kernis, Aaron Jay 22–27; *Love Songs and Lullabies* 18; *Nightshade Rounds* 16–17, 30–31; recording reviews 29–31; *Road to the Sun* 16, 180–181
Italy 4–5, 36–37, 52
Ives, Charles 40, 181

Japan 136, 165–166
jazz 10, 19, 24, 26–29, 40, 47–49, 64–66, 72–73, 79, 82, 89, 149, 158, 160, 167
Juilliard School of Music Guitar Department 9, 20–21
Juilliard String Quartet 34, 48

Kain, Timothy 165–166
Keillor, Garrison 19
Kernis, Aaron Jay 12, 22–27, 46, 72, 85, 86, 94, 103; *Double Concerto for Violin & Guitar* 9–10, 22–29; *100 Greatest Dance Hits* 22, 24, 26, 85, 102–103; *Partita for solo guitar* 22, 95, 99
Kirkpatrick, Ralph 34, 51, 53
Koshkin, Nikita 163
Kraft, Norbert 30
Kremer, Gidon 34, 48
Kuralt, Charles 19

Lane, Cleo 72, 149
Latin and South America 7, 18–19, 55
Leisner, David 68, 69, 76–80
Le Roy, Adrian 5
Lin, Chao-Liang 10
Lincoln Center 67
lute 4–5, 7–8, 12, 16, 74, 112, 129, 140, 162, 171, 179–180; *see also* Bach, Johann Sebastian
Lutyens, Elisabeth 65

Maayani, Ami 12, 19
McCartney, Paul 64
MacCombie, Bruce 30
Mackey, Steve 85, 94
Mahler, Gustav 59–60, 102, 114, 120
Man, Wu 12
Mangone, Agustín Barrios *see* Barrios, Agustín
Manhattan School of Music 76, 81, 110, 118, 125–126
Mason, Patrick 111, 127–128
master classes 7, 88–89, 118
Maw, Nicholas 34; *Music of Memory* 44, 49, 54
Mello, Thiago de 18
Mendelssohn, Felix 6, 44, 54, 61, 181
Mentzer, Susanne 22
Merkin Concert Hall 161–164
methods, instructional 5–6
Middle Ages 3–4
Milán, Luys 5
Minimalism 6, 41, 71–72, 75, 82, 85
Modernism (Post-modernism) 6, 41, 60, 71, 75, 85–86, 90
Mozart, Wolfgang Amadeus 6, 34, 42, 53, 129, 160
Mudarra, Alonso 5

Narváez, Luys 5, 58
Nationalist Period 180–181
NCAC (National Concerts Artists Corporation) 133–134, 139
NEA (National Endowment for the Arts) 96–97, 144–146
New England Conservatory of Music 34–35, 37, 76
New York Chamber Symphony 10
92nd St. Y Tisch Center 22, 46, 99, 102, 151
non-Western music 83, 85, 104, 149, 160
Norman, Jessye 133, 136, *138*

Orchestre National de France 11
Ordway Music Theatre 21, 23
Orphée, Matanya 129

Paganini, Niccolò 34, 40, 42, 48, 53–54, 61; *24 Caprices* 41, 58–60, 180–181

Pass, Joe 48, 149
Peabody Conservatory of Music 64, 81, 110–111, 120
Peking Opera orchestra 11
Peña, Paco 47–48, 154
percussion 10–11, 18, 26, 28–29, 48, 69, 83, 86, 104–105, 111, 114–115, *121*, 122, 128
Petrassi, Goffredo: *Nunc* 41, 152, 159, 163
Piazzolla, Astor 94, 99, 106, 180–181
pipa 12
Ponce, Manuel 7, 49, 55
Prairie Home Companion 19
premieres 10, 12–13, 46, 67–68, 99
promoters 135, 143
Pulitzer Prize (music) 12, 22, 120

recordings: audio 7, 8, 16, 18–20, 24, 53–55, 93, 114, 118–119, 123, 153, 179–182; video 152, 154, 156, 158, 168
Regondi, Giulio 128; *Introduction et Caprice* 129; *Ten Etudes* 112, 127, 129
rehearsal 10, 19, 26
Reich, Steven: *Electric Counterpoint* 30, 85, 90, 106, 182
Renaissance Period 4–5, 55, 179–180
Ricci, Ruggiero 50, 53, 58
Riley, Terry 81–82, *83*, 94–95; *Ascensión* 82–83; *Barabas* 99; *In C* 41, 85
Robison, Paula 34, 37, *38*, 181
Rochberg, George 34, *54; American Bouquet* 44; *Caprice Variations* 59; *Muse of Fire* 38
Rodrigo, Joaquín 6–7, 15, 169; *Invocation se Danse* 31, 56–57, 163, 169, 181
Romantic-Post Romantic Period 4, 6, 41, 124, 180–181
Romero, Angel 133
Romero, Pepe 49, 182
Rouse, Christopher 12
Royal College of Music 7, 64–65, 73, 149
Ruders, Poul 114; *Psalmodies* 111, 116
Russia (Soviet Union) 96, 138–139, 165–166

St. Paul Chamber Orchestra 10, 13, 29
Salerno-Sonnenberg, Nadja 9–10, 22–23, 28
Salzburg Mozarteum 34
San Francisco Conservatory of Music 81, 89, 93

Sanz, Gaspar 5
Scarlatti, Domenico 5, 34, 42–43, 51, 54, 98, 158, 161, 181
Schoenberg, Arnold 65, 114, 135
Schubert, Franz 42, 59, 181
Schumann, Robert 42, 58
Schwantner, Joseph: *From Afar* 12–13, 29
score, reading on stage 126, 152
Sculthorpe, Peter 149, 152, 163, 167–168
Segovia, Andrés 4, 7–8, 15–16, 31, 36, 47–51, 58, 93–94, 110, 112, 140, 180, 182; as composer 53, 126; and composers 31, 49, 55–57, 118; in performance 3, 7, 58, 169; as teacher 9, 34, 50–51, 149; as transcriber 42–43, 53, 55, 57
Serialism (twelve-tone) 6, 65, 68, 71, 74–75, 79
Shanghai Quartet 34
Shaw, Harold 133–148
Shearer, Aaron 81, 110, 118
Shostakovich, Dmitry 166
Sierra, Roberto 81, 99, 182
Slatkin, Leonard 13
Smith, Neil 31
Sor, Fernando 6, 41, 81, 125–127, 129
Soundboard 13
Spain 4, 34, 47, 52, 181
Speculum Musicae 111
Starobin, David 76, 110–132, 180–181; and composers 114–118; concert reviews 125–128; and Crumb, George 110–111, 114, 119–125; discography 130–132; *Giuliani Guitar Music* 129–130, 180–181; *The Great Regondi* 128–129; *Newdance* 119, 125; recording reviews 128–130
Starobin, Michael 114, 116–117, 127
Stern, Isaac 136

Takemitsu, Toru 6, 26, 91, 97–99, 150, 152, 160, 166, 169, 180–182
Tanenbaum, David 22–23, 81–109, 180; *Acoustic Counterpoint* 93–94, 171, 180, 182; and composers 94; concert reviews 98–103; *Concert Series* 81; discography 107–109; *The Essential Studies* 81; *Great American Guitar Solo* 94, 105; *Harrison: The Perilous Chapel* 104; and Harrison, Lou 83–85, 87, 94, 105; and Kernis, Aaron Jay 81, 85–86, 94–95, 102–103; *Lou Harrison Guitar*

Book 104; *Piazzolla: El Porteño* 106, 180–181; recording reviews 104–107; and Riley, Terry 81–83, 94–95, 99
Tanenbaum, Elias 22, 81, 87–88, 99
Tansman, Alexander 7, 49, 58
Tárrega, Francisco 6, 43, 93, 181
technique: left-hand 15, 27, 46, 48, 56–58, 91; right-hand 6, 12, 15, 17, 29, 89, 100, 102
Telemann, Georg Phillip 43
tempo 71, 79, 121
Tippett, Michael 74, 182
tone 4, 7, 11, 31, 57, 104, 123
Tonight Show (Johnny Carson) 24
Torke, Michael 72, 85
Torres, Antonio de 4
Torroba, Federico Moreno 7, 140
Tower, Joan: *Clocks* 30–31
transcriptions (arrangements), guitar 19, 34, 41–43, 49, 57–59, 89, 105, 129, 156–158
Tureck, Rosalyn 9, 15–16, 17, 21
Turina, Joaquín 7, 56, 140
Twentieth Century Period 6, 30, 54, 90, 151, 158–159, 162–164, 179–181

Verdery, Benjamin 35, 104, 118
vihuela 4–5, 7, 112
Villa-Lobos, Heitor 7, 41, 49
violin 5, 9, 22–28, 40, 42, 46, 55, 58–59, 70, 100, 133, 180–181

Visée, Robert de 5, 42, 129
Vivaldi, Antonio 156, 158, 162, 179–180

Walton, William 6, 67, 74; *Five Bagatelles* 30, 107
Webern, Anton von 59–60, 65
Websites 33, 63, 80, 109, 132, 177
Weiss, Sylvius Leopold 5, 43, 55, 98, 162, 181
Westlake, Nigel 149, 152, 166–168
Wigmore Hall 68, 151
Williams, John 7, 41, 50–51, 58, 70, 74, 87, 148, 149–177, 179, 181; concert reviews 161–165; discography 171–177; *Fragments of a Dream* 154; *From Australia* 152, 167–168; *Harvey, Gray: Guitar Concertos* 166–167; *Iberia* 156, 166–169; *The Mantis and the Moon* 165–166; recording reviews 165–171; *The Seville Concert/The Film Profile of John Williams* 154, 156; and Shaw, Harold 133, 140–141; *Spirit of the Guitar* 107, 152, 164, 167; *Takemitsu: To the Edge of Dream* 170–171, 180, 182
Williams, Len 149
Wincenc, Carol 20
Wolf, Jan 30
Wolff, Hugh 23, 29

Yale School of Music 34–35, 44, 51

www.ingramcontent.com/pod-product-compliance
Ingram Content Group UK Ltd.
Pitfield, Milton Keynes, MK11 3LW, UK
UKHW042011140426
5217IPUK00015B/1110